The Political Potential of Upper Silesian Ethnoregionalist Movement

International Studies in Sociology and Social Anthropology

Series Editor

Alberto Martinelli (*University of Milan*)

Editorial Board

Vincenzo Cicchelli (*Ceped, Université Paris Descartes/IRD*)
Vittorio Cotesta (*Università degli Studi Roma Tre*)
Benjamin Gregg (*University of Texas at Austin*)
Leo Penta (*Katholische Hochschule für Sozialwesen Berlin*)
Elisa Reis (*Universidade Federal do Rio de Janeiro*)
Madalina Vartejanu-Joubert (*Institut National des Langues et Civilisations Orientales, Paris*)

VOLUME 138

The titles published in this series are listed at *brill.com/issa*

The Political Potential of Upper Silesian Ethnoregionalist Movement

A Study in Ethnic Identity and Political Behaviours of Upper Silesians

By

Anna Muś

BRILL

LEIDEN | BOSTON

Cover illustration: The view from Wolności Square at 3-Maja Street in Katowice, Poland. Silesian Autonomy March 2015. Photo courtesy of Krzysztof Wąsala, DronEye.pl.

The Library of Congress Cataloging-in-Publication Data is available online at https://catalog.loc.gov
LC record available at https://lccn.loc.gov/2021036432

Typeface for the Latin, Greek, and Cyrillic scripts: "Brill". See and download: brill.com/brill-typeface.

ISSN 0074-8684
ISBN 978-90-04-46143-7 (hardback)
ISBN 978-90-04-46645-6 (e-book)

Copyright 2022 by Anna Muś. Published by Koninklijke Brill NV, Leiden, The Netherlands.
Koninklijke Brill NV incorporates the imprints Brill, Brill Nijhoff, Brill Hotei, Brill Schöningh, Brill Fink, Brill mentis, Vandenhoeck & Ruprecht, Böhlau Verlag and V&R Unipress.
Koninklijke Brill NV reserves the right to protect this publication against unauthorized use. Requests for re-use and/or translations must be addressed to Koninklijke Brill NV via brill.com or copyright.com.

This book is printed on acid-free paper and produced in a sustainable manner.

Contents

Acknowledgements   IX
List of Tables   X
List of Abbreviations   XII

Introduction   1

1   **Region, Ethnicity and Politics**   4
   1.1   The Lipset-Rokkan Theory   4
   1.2   Centre-Periphery Opposition   8
   1.3   Political Behaviours   10
   1.4   Region and Regionalism   11
   1.5   Ethnic Conflict and Ethnic Mobilisation   15
   1.6   New Social Movements   20
   1.7   Regionalist and Ethnoregionalist Parties   22
   1.8   Issue and Value Voting – Theory   26
   1.9   Communities and Nationalism   27
   1.10   Ethnic Identity and Ideology   29
   1.11   Communities and International Law   32
   1.12   Communities and Polish Law   40
   1.13   Region, Ethnicity and Politics – Conclusions   43

2   **Political Situation in Upper Silesia**   45
   2.1   Upper Silesia – Definition, Names, Borders   45
   2.2   Upper Silesia – Subregions   47
   2.3   Upper Silesia – Historical Remarks   54
   2.4   Inter-War Period in the Silesian Autonomous Voivodeship   57
   2.5   Silesian Harm (or Upper Silesian Harm)   60
   2.6   Upper Silesia as a Periphery   62
   2.7   Upper Silesians   66
   2.8   Upper Silesians in Scholarly Literature   70
   2.9   (Upper) Silesian Movement   72
   2.10   History of the Movement   77
   2.11   European Context   81
   2.12   Political Situation in Upper Silesia – Conclusions   85

VI

3 Methodology 87
- 3.1 Aim and Object 87
- 3.2 Research Questions and Hypothesis 87
- 3.3 Terminology and Indicators 89
- 3.4 Methods, Techniques and Tools 90
- 3.5 Sampling 92
- 3.6 Procedure 93

4 Political Organisations in Upper Silesia 95
- 4.1 Rada Górnośląska 95
  - 4.1.1 *Fundacja "Silesia"* 96
  - 4.1.2 *Pro Loquela Silesiana* 97
  - 4.1.3 *Ruch Autonomii Śląska* 100
  - 4.1.4 *Stowarzyszenie Osób Narodowości Śląskiej* 103
  - 4.1.5 *Ślōnskŏ Ferajna* 104
  - 4.1.6 *Związek Górnośląski* 106
  - 4.1.7 *Niemiecka Wspólnota "Pojednanie i Przyszłość"* 108
- 4.2 Organisations from outside the Upper Silesian Council 109
  - 4.2.1 *Demokratyczna Unia Regionalistów Śląskich* 109
  - 4.2.2 *Nasz Wspólny Śląski Dom* 110
  - 4.2.3 *Towarzystwo Społeczno-Kulturalne Niemców Województwa Śląskiego* 111
  - 4.2.4 *Związek Ludności Narodowości Śląskiej* 112
- 4.3 Śląska Partia Regionalna 114
- 4.4 Ślonzoki Razem 115
- 4.5 Electoral Committees 117
  - 4.5.1 *Autonomia dla Ziemi Śląskiej* 117
  - 4.5.2 *Mniejszość na Śląsku* 117
  - 4.5.3 *Zjednoczeni dla Śląska* 119
  - 4.5.4 *Ślonzoki Razem* 120
- 4.6 Electoral Results in the Region 120
- 4.7 Electoral Campaigns in the Region 128
- 4.8 Initiatives 129
  - 4.8.1 *Autonomy March* 130
  - 4.8.2 *The Day of Commemoration of the Upper Silesian Tragedy* 131
  - 4.8.3 *National Census 2011 – Campaign* 132
  - 4.8.4 *Regional Education and Teaching Silesian Language* 132
  - 4.8.5 *Recognition of Silesians as a Minority and Silesian as a Regional Language* 133

CONTENTS VII

4.9 Protests 134
    4.9.1 *Protest against Further Centralisation of Public Television* 134
    4.9.2 *Protest against Rejection of the Citizens' Legislative Initiative* 134
    4.9.3 *Protest against Naming the Square in Katowice after Maria and Lech Kaczyński* 134
4.10 Political Organisations in Upper Silesia – Conclusions 136

5 Programmes and Postulates of Upper Silesian Organisations 139
    5.1 Introduction 139
    5.2 Ethnicity 140
        5.2.1 *Auto-identification* 140
        5.2.2 *Silesianism* 142
        5.2.3 *Heritage* 149
        5.2.4 *Collective Memory* 151
        5.2.5 *Categorisation* 159
    5.3 Political Programmes and Postulates 160
        5.3.1 *Recognition of the Ethnic Group* 160
        5.3.2 *Regional Education* 164
        5.3.3 *Teaching and Promotion of the Silesian Language* 167
        5.3.4 *Decentralisation and Autonomy* 170
        5.3.5 *Functions and the Role of the Organisation* 176
        5.3.6 *Plans for the Future* 181
    5.4 Programmes and Postulates of Upper Silesian Organisations – Conclusions 186

6 Political Behaviours and Political Potential 189
    6.1 Introduction 189
    6.2 General Information about the Respondents 189
    6.3 Ethnicity – Elements of Silesian Identity 191
        6.3.1 *Auto-identification* 191
        6.3.2 *Territorial and Familial Ties* 192
        6.3.3 *Categorisation and the Role of the Region* 193
        6.3.4 *Stereotypes and Migration* 195
        6.3.5 *Diversity and Separateness* 197
        6.3.6 *Language and Traditions* 199
    6.4 Political Postulates – Popularity 201
        6.4.1 *Recognition and Education* 201
        6.4.2 *Legal Status and Borders of the Śląskie Voivodeship* 203
        6.4.3 *Priorities for Newly Registered Silesian Parties* 205

VIII

6.5 Political Behaviours – Popularity of Studied Organisations 205
  6.5.1 *Voting Behaviours* 205
  6.5.2 *Participation in Electoral Campaigns, Membership and Participation in Events* 216
  6.5.3 *Political Behaviours Index* 218
6.6 Relation between Silesian Identity and Political Behaviours 220
6.7 Political Behaviours and Political Potential – Conclusions 225

Concluding Remarks 228

Annex 235
References 236
Index 261

Acknowledgements

I would like to offer special thanks to my colleague from the University of Silesia in Katowice – Dr hab. Małgorzata Myśliwiec, Prof. UŚ. Her expertise in the subject, vast knowledge and constant support guided me throughout the project and during the process of writing this book. I am grateful for her help and inspiration.

The advice given by another colleague from my Alma Mater, Dr Agata Zygmunt, proved to be valuable, especially at the end of the project. I would like to thank her for her critical remarks, insight and discussions during the project.

I would like to express my gratitude to the respondents in the survey and the participants in the focus group interviews. Above all, I greatly appreciate the involvement, help and cooperation of members of organisations that took part in the study. They gave me their time, provided me with materials for the study and were happy to engage in discussion.

Lastly, I am grateful to my family and friends for hours of debates on the various issues covered in this book.

Tables

1   Elections to Sejmik of Śląskie voivodship 2002. Results RAŚ   121

2   Elections to Sejmik of Śląskie voivodship 2006. Results RAŚ   122

3   Elections to Sejmik of Śląskie voivodship 2010. Results RAŚ   123

4   Elections to Sejmik of Śląskie voivodship 2014. Results RAŚ   123

5   Elections to Sejmik of Śląskie voivodship 2014. Results MnŚ   124

6   Elections to Sejmik of Śląskie voivodship 2018. Śląska Partia Regionalna   124

7   Elections to Sejmik of Śląskie voivodship 2018. Ślonzoki Razem   125

8   Elections to Sejmik of Śląskie voivodship 2018. En bloc   126

9   Elections to Senate 2019. District 74   127

10   Parliamentary Elections   137

11   Elections to Sejmik of Śląskie voivodship   138

12   Declared auto-identification   191

13   Attitude toward stereotypes about the group   195

14   Views on separateness of the Silesian culture   198

15   Who do you speak Silesian with?   200

16   Teaching Silesian language at schools   203

17   Legal status of the Silesian voivodship in the future   204

18   Possible changes to the borders of the Śląskie voivodship   205

19   Priorities for the newly registered Silesian parties (Śląska Partia Regionalna and Ślonzoki Razem)   206

20   Attitude toward voting on ethnoregionalist party   206

21   Voting in the upcoming elections in 2018 and 2019   208

22   Elections to Sejmik of Ślaskie Voivodeship 2018. En bloc   208

23   Votes, IRM, IEM and the share of Silesians (all presented in %)   210

24   Survey. Election of the mayor (Prezydent) of the city of Katowice. September 2018   213

25   Results. Election of the mayor (Prezydent) of the city of Katowice. October 2018   213

26   Voting behaviour and ethnicity   215

27   Supporting electoral campaigns in the past   217

28   Membership in ethnoregionalist organisations   218

29   Basic statistics   219

30   Distribution   220

31   Differentiation. Categorisation as a separate nation and PBI – ranks   221

32   Differentiation. Categorisation as a separate nation and PBI – test   221

33   Differentiation. Being born in Silesia and the PBI – ranks   222

34   Differentiation. Being born in Silesia and the PBI – test   222

TABLES XI

35 Differentiation. Mother comes from Silesia and PBI – ranks 222
36 Differentiation. Mother comes from Silesia and PBI – test 222
37 Correlation. *Silesia is important for me* and the PBI – test 223
38 Correlation. *Silesia is my Heimat* and PBI – test 224
39 Correlation. Silesian traditions and the PBI – test 224
40 Correlation. Auto-identification and PBI – test 225

Abbreviations

DURŚ	Demokratyczna Unia Regionalistów Śląskich (Democratic Union of Silesian Regionalists)
Dz. U.	Dziennik Ustaw or Dziennik Ustaw Rzeczypospolitej Polskiej (Journal of Laws of the Republic of Poland)
ETS	European Treaty Series (now CETS – Council of Europe Treaty Series)
FŚ	Fundacja "Silesia" ("Silesia" Foundation)
IKAS	Initiative der kulturelle Autonomie Schlesiens (Inititive for the Cultural Autonomy of Silesia)
MnŚ	Mniejszość na Śląsku (Minority in Silesia)
NWŚD	Stowarzyszenie "Nasz Wspólny Śląski Dom" (Association "Our Common Silesian Home")
OJ	Official Journal of European Union
PiS	Prawo i Sprawiedliwość (Law and Justice)
PLS	Pro Loquela Silesiana Towarzystwo Kultywowania i Promocji Śląskiej Mowy (Pro Loquela Silesiana Society for Cultivating and Promoting Silesian Speech)
PO	Platforma Obywatelska (Civic Platform)
RAŚ	Ruch Autonomii Śląska (Silesian Autonomy Movement)
SPS	Stowarzyszenie "Przymierze Śląskie" ("Silesian Alliance" Association)
SONŚ	Stowarzyszenie Osób Narodowości Śląskiej (Association of Persons of Silesian Nationality)
ŚF	Ślōnskŏ Ferajna (Silesian Band)
ŚPR	Śląska Partia Regionalna (Silesian Regional Party)
ŚR	Ślonzoki Razem (Silesians Together)
TSKN	Towarzystwo Społeczno-Kulturalne Niemców Województwa Śląskiego (Social and Cultural Society of Germans of the Śląskie Voivodeship)
UNTS	United Nations Treaty Series
ZdŚ	Zjednoczeni dla Śląska (United for Silesia)
ZG	Związek Górnośląski (Upper Silesian Union)
ZLNŚ	Związek Ludności Narodowości Śląskiej (Union of People of Silesian Nationality)
ZŚ	Związek Ślązaków (Union of Silesians)

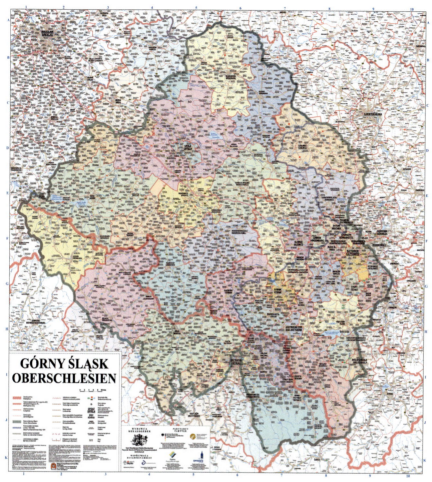

MAP 1   Map of Upper Silesian, 2011
WITH KIND PERMISSION BY THE PUBLISHER DOM WSPÓŁPRACY POLSKO-
NIEMIECKIEJ/HAUS DER DEUTSCH-POLNISCHEN ZUSAMMENARBEIT

Introduction

Over the last two decades, we can observe growing discontent in Upper Silesia as a region and, at the same time, the politicisation of Silesian ethnicity. All this is happening in a region with its own history of autonomy, culturally diversified heritage and multi-ethnic society. Similarities and differences between the inhabitants of this region are divided along unusual borders and characterised in complicated ways.

The Upper Silesian ethnoregionalist movement in the region is composed of many different organisations with diverse ideologies and scopes of activity, but many of them can be regarded as ethnoregionalist. This movement has been undergoing rapid change over the last 30 years. Today it is taking on new forms, e.g., political parties, which are able to represent the interests of the inhabitants of the region, including ethnic Silesians. This period, marked by the formation of new political organisations, seems to be the best moment for posing questions about the influence of ethnicity and regional identity on the political behaviours of people. Moreover, it appears to be a good time for introspection into the past of the Upper Silesian ethnoregionalist movement and to draw some predictions about its future.

The phenomena surrounding the Upper Silesian ethnoregionalist movement are recognisable for readers in Poland and abroad. The movement is also usually evaluated on the grounds of one's own national identity, emotions and the shallow opinions present in public debate. This situation leads to misunderstandings and even opposition towards the existence of such a movement. One of the goals of this work is to provide a clarification and description of the movement itself and the role it plays in the region. For the author, it seems that for many years, facts in the debate about the region were hard to come by, while subjective opinions and slogans were in abundance.

There are only a few regional parties in Poland, and regions do not have any strong representation in the decision-making process at the state level. Moreover, Polish society is rather ethnically and nationally homogeneous, which strengthens doubts as to whether differences based on dominant and non-dominant culture even exist. However, there is at least one territory where some political activities based on opposition towards central politics and the domination of Polish culture are undertaken, namely, Upper Silesia.

The Upper Silesia region is part of the historical region of Silesia, which lies in the South-Western part of the Republic of Poland, North-Eastern part of the Czech Republic and, according to some scholars, a small part of it is also located in the Eastern part of the German Federal Republic. Today, the Upper

© ANNA MUŚ, 2022 | DOI:10.1163/9789004466456_002

Silesia region is split between two states and three administrative units. Two of them lie in Poland: *województwo śląskie* (Śląskie Voivodeship)[1] and *województwo opolskie* (Opolskie Voivodeship).

In Upper Silesia, there exists a movement in the form of an ethnoregionalist mobilisation led by organisations gathered in the *Rada Górnośląska* [RG] (Upper Silesian Council). Today, though, it seems that the *Ruch Autonomii Śląska* [RAŚ] (Silesian Autonomy Movement) and the newly registered *Śląska Partia Regionalna* [ŚPR] (Silesian Regional Party) have taken on the main role. RAŚ became famous during an attempt to register the *Związek Ludności Narodowości Śląskiej* [ZLNŚ] (Union of People of Silesian Nationality) and, with time, evolved into a quasi-political organisation. From 2010 to 2018, RAŚ had representatives in the Sejmik of Śląskie Voivodeship and, in 2014, it prepared (in cooperation with other organisations) a legislative initiative aimed at amending the *Ustawa o mniejszościach narodowych i etnicznych i języku regionalnym* (*National and Ethnic Minorities and Regional Language Act*).[2] Its political program is based on promoting regional interest (or at least what members of the organisation perceive as such), to some extent in opposition to central politics. In 2015, during the parliamentary elections, the organisation took part in the Electoral Committee of Voters, *Zjednoczeni dla Śląska* [ZdŚ] (United for Silesia), which did not win any mandate, presumably because the popularity of the ideas and concepts promoted by RAŚ is dynamic and changeable. Still, Upper Silesia seems to be the best territory to examine the centre-periphery hypothesis, especially because it was already referred to as 'an exception' to the social and political patterns of behaviour of its population (Wódz 2010, 41). The region and its residents were the focal points of studies by such scholars as Marian Gerlich, Tomasz Kamusella, Małgorzata Myśliwiec, Tomasz Nawrocki, Leszek Nijakowski, Marek Szczepański, Anna Śliz, Jacek and Kazimiera Wódz.

This study is based on empirical data gathered during the research. It also examines the existing literature (mostly in English and Polish, but also in French and German), including compact publications, collections, articles and other publications. Moreover, international law texts: treaties, judgements, soft-law and Polish statutory law and judgements have been used. Statistical data and electoral results are included as subsidiary sources. Press releases, websites, manifestos and political programmes have also been used as sources for the study.

---

1 The English translation is based on the terminology used in the NUTS classification. See: GUS (Główny Urząd Statystyczny). n.d. "The NUTS Classification in Poland".

2 All Polish legal acts and their names in this book have been translated by me unless indicated otherwise.

The first chapter consists of a theoretical analysis of the problem of ethnic identity and political behaviours. Terms such as: 'ethnic conflict', 'ethnic mobilisation' and 'ethnoregionalist party' are elaborated therein. Furthermore, it includes the definition of what is political for the purpose of the study and, consequently, what kind of behaviours are studied. The second chapter consists of information about the past and present of the Upper Silesia region. The political, legal and social situation of the region is elaborated. Also, the Silesian movement is defined for the purpose of the study, and its history and context are presented. The third chapter consists of a presentation of the methodology chosen for the study. Research questions, hypothesis, methods, tools, sampling and research procedure are elaborated in this chapter. The fourth chapter consists of a description of organisations within the Silesian movement: associations, foundations, parties and electoral committees. Elections, campaigns, protests and initiatives relating to the organisations within ethnoregionalist movement are studied there as well. In the fifth chapter, the political programmes of the studied organisations are presented. Most importantly, the ways in which ethnic and regional identity influences them and the role of centre-periphery opposition on the political goals are studied therein. This chapter is based primarily on the results of a qualitative study using focus group interviews. In the sixth chapter, the political behaviours of the Upper Silesian population are analysed, particularly in the context of the role of ethnic and regional identity. In this chapter, the political potential of the Upper Silesian ethnoregionalist movement is studied with regard to its popularity and role on the political scene in Poland. This chapter is based mostly on the results of a quantitative study using a questionnaire.

The study is focused on the organisations that can be categorised as ethnoregionalist. The influence of ethnic identity on other political organisations and parties is not included in the study. Furthermore, Silesian organisations that do not present any kind of political programme or goals are excluded. The scope of the study encompasses the region of Upper Silesia in Poland from 1989 until December 2019.

CHAPTER 1

Region, Ethnicity and Politics

1.1 The Lipset-Rokkan Theory

The well-known theory of Seymour Lipset and Stein Rokkan of party systems and voters' alignment from 1967 was based on a comparative study of the political systems of Western states. The studied systems developed from two main revolutions, and each of them led to the emergence of two cleavages: the national and the industrial revolution, respectively, in the XIX and at the beginning of the XX century. These revolutions came at the breakthrough of universal suffrage, shaping the lines of political competition and, consequently, party systems. Furthermore, they argued that, on the whole, the social structure of Western states did not change much throughout the XX century and lead to the development of stable party systems of states, called the 'freezing hypothesis'. But a universal idea of the Lipset-Rokkan theory is that parties are organised around social cleavages and formulate different political programs according to the interests of opposite groups (bottom-up development of parties and party systems).

In the Lipset-Rokkan model, four dimensions are recognised:
- the centre-periphery opposition, which emerged in the process of nation-building;
- the State-Church opposition, which emerged in the process of state-building;
- the land-industrial opposition, which emerged during industrialisation;
- the workers-owners opposition, which emerged during industrialisation and the rise of capitalism.

Cleavages have their foundations in the social realm. However, they are politicised as they turn into issues of large-scale conflict and become tied first to the political interests of significant groups of people and then to political parties. This means that we can perceive the conceptualisation of political cleavage as a type of political division based on major social divisions (Zuckerman 1975, 234). The cleavage should be empirically definable (it departs from existing social division), it must have a normative element (members of such a structured group should have common interests), and it must manifest behaviourally (the division should influence voting behaviour) (Bartolini & Mair 1990). In almost all instances, their occurrence indicates the presence, at a minimum, of extensive (in terms of membership size) and persistent political divisions, which have their roots in social divisions. Political cleavage analysis generally

© ANNA MUŚ, 2022 | DOI:10.1163/9789004466456_003

presumes that individuals perceive their political interests and engage in political behaviour jointly with individuals understood to occupy similar positions in opposition to those occupying other positions in the social structure. As the consequence of stable social divisions, parties are developed in the bottom-up process to represent the opposite interests of groups of voters. They create strategies to meet the demands of a specific group of voters and rely on gaining the electoral support of their target group. Still, it is argued in modern scholarly literature that other cleavages and, consequently, other oppositions can also emerge, especially during times of change in the political system (regime) (Sitter 2002). Furthermore, it was also observed that since the 1980s, the number of voters strongly identifying with a party is diminishing, and voting behaviours are instead based on individualised, volatile and even temporary decisions. Still, as far as this may be true for class (worker-owners) cleavage, previous studies show that it is less so for centre-periphery cleavage (especially when it also involves ethnic division) (von Schoultz 2017).

What is obvious is that Central European states did not go through the same kind of evolution as Western states. The development of their political systems was stopped by the Second World War and the socialist regimes dictated to them by the Soviet Union. The new democracies, which emerged after 1989, in some cases, copied the party systems from before 1939 (Czechoslovakia), while in others, a new system was created (Poland). Moreover, they faced different circumstances and conflicts than Western States when their socio-political structure was developed. Still, the Lipset-Rokkan theory has already been used in studies of Central Europe by, e.g., James Toole (2007), with encouraging results.

The differences outlined above are the reason why, in Polish literature, the possibility of a direct application of the Lipset-Rokkan theory is contested. Authors sometimes modify it for their own purposes. One proposition of modification was presented by Radosław Markowski, who suggested that researchers should take into consideration three elements in the process of identifying cleavages:
- identification of two groups with opposite interests;
- recreation of ways in which the resources are available to the actors in the conflict;
- analyses of the ways of engagement of different groups in the conflict (2009).

However, this modification does not take into consideration two issues. Firstly, cleavages should be based on long-lasting social divisions. Secondly, the way in which they are politicised is crucial for the evolution from social division to cleavage.

Another author – Tomasz Zarycki – developed a theory in which the classic centre-periphery territorial axis is transformed into 'colonial' domination of the Soviet Union over so-called 'satellite states'. His ideas are clearly inspired by Immanuel Wallenstein's works. In the case of the larger part of Poland, the colonial status of dependency from Russia had already begun in the XVIII century during the Partition. In his theory, Poland itself is a periphery of a stronger and more powerful centre. However, he noticed that the centre-periphery conflict is also present in the Polish internal context in regions with strong identities and separate cultures, like Kashubia (English: Cassubia, Polish: Kaszuby, German: Kaschubien and in the Kashubian language: Kaszëbë) and Upper Silesia (Zarycki 2007).

On the other hand, the Lipset-Rokkan theory still provides us with a complex but flexible frame of study, which may be used to analyse certain patterns also found in the Polish centre-periphery axis of cleavages. It has already been argued in the scholarly literature that after the fall of communist regimes, new governments faced a mobilisation of the peripheries, which consolidated and concentrated resources around their historical centres in order to challenge the role of the modern centres consisting of the states' capitals (Surażska 1995). In some cases, this process led to a quest for sovereignty and the fall of multi-ethnic states, while in others, it led to the rise of autonomy claims and challenges to the unitarian system of state administration.

As to the ethnic dimension, Herbert Kitschelt argued that conflict is more likely to emerge when cultural divisions are disrupted by economic or political change. Moreover, individuals tend to define their interests not only in terms of individual market chances but also in terms of the group position, viewed as privileged or underprivileged (Kitschelt 1995). He saw ethnic differences as one of the possible features that could lead to the creation of cleavages. His arguments were based on the observation of political systems emerging in the new democratic states of the Post-Soviet zone.

In research from the last quarter of the century, it was shown that social status does not implicate voting behaviour as strongly as it did in the past. At the same time, the personalisation of voting and campaigns can be observed. Voting behaviour is based, to some extent, on short-term issues and events and on chosen topics. Still, important socio-cultural divisions (like ethnicity) have the potential to impact voting behaviour and voters' alignment (Dalton & Kligeman 2010, 43–46).

The territorial axis of the Lipset-Rokkan theory is based on local (regional) opposition to the encroachments of dominant national elites and their administrations. These are typical reactions of peripheral regions and minorities put under pressure by centralisation (of a political and cultural nature). This is a form of conflict over values and identities, but also resources (especially power). Movements representing them may remain in their provincial strongholds or create alliances in the centre. According to the theory, existing cleavages transform into parties in the process of organisation, mobilisation and creation of alliances. Lipset and Rokkan outlined the conditions of creation of relevant territorial countercultures (non-dominant cultures):

– heavy concentration of the counterculture within one clear-cut territory;
– few ties towards the national centre and more ties toward external ones;
– minimal economic dependence on the political metropolis (centre) (1967).

The relation between territorial identity and politics was further studied by Rokkan and Urwin (1982). In scholarly literature, it is argued that the process of nation- and state-building is aimed at dismantling historical loyalties and identities, including regional ones. This happened when the loyalties based on a monarchical, hierarchical system, along with loyalty on a local level (the after-effects of feudal or feudal-like systems of social and political organisation), were replaced by the sovereignty of the nation (people residing over delimited territory) as early as the late XVIII century but mostly in the XIX century. This is how the principle of interterritoriality emerged, claiming that a state should exercise full (and, most desirably, the only) power over all of its territory (Stiepanović 2018, 14). In this way, the state and nation centre started to expand its powers and authority, dominating not only political discourse but also systems of symbols, narrations of history, institutions and law – a process sometimes called diffusion. In some works, it is argued that the process of diffusion stops when it meets another political centre. Thus, the existence of regional political centres is an anomaly grounded in the inability of the centre to expand further. On the other hand, there is also a stance that suggests the centre should only be seen as a politically privileged location within the state and, in most cases, other centres in different locations can be identified (for example, economic centres). Consequently, the process of diffusion of the political centre is likely to meet the opposition (or rather competition) of another centre in another region. This competition can usually be characterised as competition over resources, but, in time, it is likely to evolve in the process of political mobilisation into a competition over symbols (identity). Still, it is not an anomaly, but rather a likely result of diffusion (Stiepanović 2018, 15–17).

In scholarly literature on post-communist party systems, it was argued that the process of political mobilisation differs in those systems from Western European systems, thus making it less stable. The main differences in the 1990s and at the beginning of the XXI century were the lack of organisations of civic society, which weakened voters' party identification and the minor role of the Church and worker unions. Arguably, since 2010, at least in Poland, the situation has been changing, and the cleavages are becoming more stable. Also, by the time the Lipset-Rokkan theory was published, the predominant model of party organisation was the mass party. Since the 1960s, parties evolved into professional cartel-party models and catch-all party models. In the post-communist states, both these latter models of party organisation can be observed.

Lipset and Rokkan also recognised that since the 1960s, at least, not only political parties but also other actors began shaping politics. They made references to the new social movements, especially student movements for human rights, that wanted to create an alternative to the traditional party-system policy-making process.

1.2 Centre-Periphery Opposition

The centre-periphery axis is used by many authors, but it seems clear that the concept takes on different meanings. On the one hand, the centre may be defined as a political decision-making centre, usually constituting the capital, which is also the centre of the dominant culture in the state, as opposed to the periphery, which is culturally heterogeneous, differs from the centre and takes little part in the political decision-making process. On the other hand, the centre may mean an economically important and developed city in opposition to rural areas (Langholm 1971, 275). In this study, the author uses the first understanding of the term. This approach makes it possible to distinguish between the centre of the decision-making process, with considerable access to economic and political resources, and the periphery, where there is considerably less access to the process of decision-making and where other resources may be harder to access as well.

The centre-periphery opposition can have cultural roots. It is visible when the dominant and non-dominant culture can be recognised and, especially, when the non-dominant culture (or cultures) is territorially concentrated. The dominant culture in a given society is understood as a group that is capable of dictating its patterns of behaviour, norms and culture to other groups and of successfully presenting itself as the entity representing the whole of society. Conversely, the non-dominant culture (counterculture) is the culture of the minority, which presents a certain separateness and is perceived by members of the minority group as discriminated (Mucha 1999, 20). In the relationship between dominant and non-dominant cultures, there is always an antagonistic aspect, as well as asymmetrical dynamics. The dominant culture tries to impose values and a hierarchy, while the non-dominant culture resists.

In the field of the theory of literature, the term 'minor literature' was introduced by Deleuze and Guattari (2003). They defined it using three aspects:
- deterritorialisation – literature is written in the language of the majority, but by the members of a marginalised minority;
- political quality – it is always political, and what was private became public because the mere existence of such literature is an act of political defiance;
- collective value – this literature, even though written by individuals, is always a collective voice and represents the cultural values of a separate minority.

The same may be said about minor cultures in general. They may even stem from the culture of the majority but differ from it. They are the cultures of marginalised minorities. Their representations are always acts of defiance, even if living in a chosen culture is essentially a private matter. In this way, what is private becomes public and political, even if it was not intended as such. Minor cultures are connected to groups and their collective values, which represent them in cultural terms. Consequently, they may be seen as forms of non-dominant cultures in the state.

The centre-periphery opposition in politics emerged during the process of nation-building. It became apparent that some units (regions) are too diverse and separate and aim to preserve their own cultures, while the ever-expanding state institutions aim to unify them with the dominant culture. These processes led to the creation of movements and parties, mostly at the beginning of the XX century, and they have remained strong, with new organisations emerging even today. These parties have been given a common name: parties of territorial defence (*partis de défense territoriale*). In this category, it is possible to recognise federalist, autonomist, regionalist, ethnoregionalist, ethnic and national parties (Seiler 2005, 24). The movements are also referred to as the 'contra-mobilisation of peripheries' (Seiler 2005, 36). The term is based on the particular identity of a region but emerges in similar forms throughout Europe and undermines the legitimacy of the process of state-centralisation. The emergence of such parties is one of the indicators that regional or ethnic differences (or both simultaneously) have become politicised, and the defence of a particular identity is no longer a private matter of the members of a community but has become a political matter affecting the whole of society.

1.3 Political Behaviours

'Politics' is defined in many different ways. Some defy it as leadership and power over resources (Weber 1926; Lasswell 1936). Another group of definitions states that politics is a social activity aiming at the creation, preservation and betterment of the general rules and conditions of life within a society (Heywood 2010, 4). In this work, the latter understanding of what politics is and, consequently, what is political, will be used. For this reason, further along in the study, the term *political* will encompass every action (individual or collective) aimed at the creation, preservation and betterment of the general rules and conditions of living in a society. Political activity becomes necessary when a conflict of interests of socio-political groups occurs and makes it impossible to regulate the behaviour of the members of a given society.

It is possible for individuals and collectives to become a political subject when they are conscious of their interests and able to articulate and implement them through influence over a social and political system (Gulczyński 2010, 36). As a result, many groups and individuals aim at becoming a subject, preferably one equal to others, while still preserving their own identity. Political influence is an intentional action aimed at influencing political processes. It can be achieved through participation in political but also social structures, which try to influence political structures by legal and illegal means (Gulczyński 2010, 60). The term 'political participation' is very similar to the term 'political behaviour'. The former can be defined as the voluntary engagement of citizens in actions aimed at achieving results in the sphere of politics (Faulks 1999). This encompasses such activities as taking part in campaigns, membership in political parties, social movements and individual contact with politicians. The term political behaviour is used further on in the study.

Any kind of political behaviour has its functions. On the one hand, according to the theory of rational choice, this occurs when an individual wishes to influence the social system in order to benefit from it (Haywood 2010, 301). On the other hand, political behaviour has other functions, such as solidarity with a group (the sociological theory of membership in groups) or the expression of one's views (Hamlin & Jennings 2011).

The research is based on a study of the political behaviours of persons with the right to vote. Here, political behaviour is understood as any form of individual or collective participation in political processes and in any activity that results in political consequences. The categories of political behaviour chosen for the study include:
- voting behaviour,
- participation in political campaigns,

REGION, ETHNICITY AND POLITICS

- belonging to an organisation that has political goals,
- participation in political protests,
- participation in initiatives that have direct political goals.

Voting behaviour is understood as the way in which a person voted or would vote. It is relevant only if votes were given (or were to be given) to a committee chosen for the purpose of this study. Participation in a political campaign means being a candidate or member of campaign staff and any other activity connected with campaigning. It is relevant only if it constitutes support for a committee chosen for the purpose of this study. Belonging to an organisation (regardless of its legal form) that has political goals is relevant only as long as the organisation is connected to the ethnoregionalist movement studied here. Participation in political protests (demonstrations, marches, strikes) is relevant only as long as the organisers are connected to the ethnoregionalist movement, and the aims of the protests involved ethnoregionalist ideology. Participation in initiatives (signing petitions, citizens' legislative initiatives, meetings and celebrations) that have direct political goals is relevant only as long as the organisers are connected to the ethnic movement studied here, and the aims of the initiatives involve ethnoregionalist ideology.

1.4   Region and Regionalism

There are few definitions of 'region' provided by researchers today, but many authors seem to believe that they recognise a region when they see one. Some researchers choose to refer to regions as 'cultural regions' or 'economic regions' or use other classifications (Applegate 2004, 129), but I refrain from that in order to keep the argumentation coherent and avoid making the term even more confusing. Moreover, regions differ from each other: they have a diverse history, political potential and social background, which makes the creation of a coherent definition even harder (Jones & Sully 2010, 4). These are the reasons why the concept is rather blurred and lacks a heuristic study. Still, there are four notions that are helpful in developing the definition of a region: space, population, time and recognition.

A region as a part of the Earth with specific geographical features exists independently, but region as a concept is a social fact (Montello 2008, 314). It is created in the process of categorising a space, an action performed by humans in order to rationalise the world around us. This idea cannot be detached from the space to which it refers (Hroch 2009, 2). An area, with its dimensions, landscape and delimitations, is a substrate of the social concept of the region and is rather homogeneous and compact (Montello 2003, 175). These features ensure that the interactions between its inhabitants take place at multiple levels. The concept of region is rooted in the everyday experience of its population; it is their area of existence and a place where they realise their needs (Möckl 1978, 17). Region is something familiar and functional at the same time. It is not intimate and limited as a locality but still remains comprehensible for an individual – a person can understand it and recognise it as his/her own. Region is usually conceptualised as a certain landscape or type of landscape (e.g., Süd-Tirol). The borders of a region are vague, with no certain boundaries and some flexibility. They are usually drawn arbitrarily: what is within the region and what is not depends on subjective assumptions. There are only a few cases in which the borders of regions are already agreed (e.g., Flanders).

A regional population consists of individuals not only having multiple connections to the region itself and to each other through space but who also share a general awareness of creating a community based on the common interest of the inhabitants. Therefore, this is further referred to as a 'regional community'. As Denis de Rougemont wrote: a region is an "*espaces de participation civique*" (1977, 219). It is important that a regional community has the ability to create its own area actively. The existence of regional political interest is vital for understanding the concept of the region. Differences in culture, development or economics among regions imply the need to create a 'regional common cause' – a political interest that will benefit the region and its inhabitants. The main goal of regional actors is defining their regions' relations with the state and, in some cases, with European institutions. An example of the growing role of regional interest in politics is the emergence of regional offices in Brussels as international representations of sub-national units (Huysseune & Jans 2008, 1). The regional community is a political one, based on the common interest and possibility of common decision-making.

The concept of the region is also strongly connected to time – a region is seen not only how it is today but also as it was historically. The regional identification of individuals differs among regions, and some regions are defined by the ethnic group inhabiting them. Ethnic and cultural unity, specific language and unique features can construct a strong regional identity, sometimes linked to the regional nationalism of stateless nations (Riedel 2006, 32–34). But this feature is not necessary for the existence of the concept of the region as such. It can be inhabited by many different ethnic groups and still be one regional community: a regional community does not have to be ethnically unified; it does not even need a cultural majority – it is purely a political entity. What makes regional identity possible is contemporary narration – it is created through a social process, during which communities emerge (Applegate 2004). Both of the actions seem to be linked – the emerging identification needs a history, and narration needs a community that cultivates it. Regions that correspond to former historical units usually have a collective memory (Hroch 2009). The region, understood as a territorial unit, is reinforced as an entity by the emotional connection of individuals: the feeling of belonging (Penrose 2002, 282).

Recognition is a social fact and is one of the features specific to a region. The region is seen as such by its population, as well as outsiders. It can derive from a historical background or from the current policy of regional actors. It is also closely related to regional consciousness. This is why the region is a region only as long as the inhabitants and outsiders see it as such. Additionally, certain levels of the subjectivity of such entities can be observed, which has made them a central point of political debate, economic policy-making and even legal concern (Storper 1995, 258). Today, many regions have become visible units with a certain 'kind of subjectivity'.

The relation between contemporary administrative units and regions is complex. In some cases, their borders overlap with slight differences. There are also cases when a region and an administrative unit are connected symbolically instead (Jones & Sully 2010, 7). Still, researchers tend to see regions as administrative units (e.g., Keating & Wilson 2014, 841). The existence of a political unit leads to changes in the recognition of the region and strengthens the regional community. Politically strong regions, such as Catalonia, develop from administrative units and their authority. But in regions like Silesia, where a similar administrative unit exists (Śląskie Voivodeship), it is only symbolically situated in the Silesia region. Although political (administrative) units usually have legal subjectivity, the scopes of their competences are diverse. International organisations, such as the European Union or the Council of Europe, also perceive regions as administrative units. Examples of such a policy are manifested, e.g., in the choice of entities represented in the Committee of Regions (EU) and in the Congress of Local and Regional Authorities (CoE). Moreover, regional policy is also reserved for the administrative units of Member States. An indication of such an assumption can be found in the common classification of territorial units for statistical purposes (NUTS), which is based on states' territorial policies.

To conclude: region is an entity determined by the social process of categorisation, perceived as such in relation to space and time, consisting of a vaguely delimited space and a fairly stable population. The idea of region is constructed. It is based on the assumption of territorial continuity and internal homogeneity (Ther 2003, XIV). Region is usually situated between the local and state level. Its spatial features ensure that individuals perceive it as their own and comprehend it. Every region has its own identity, emerging from the constant interaction between the population and the environment (Storm 2003,

247). The regional community is aware of itself and the existence of regional political interest. Some sort of regional identity can be observed, specifically in the form of 'collective memory' and individual identification, though its narration can be in the diverse stages of emergence. Regional identity does not endeavour to be the sole identity and can coexist with other levels of identification without any disturbances.

Regionalism and its ideology have been present in Europe since the xx century. As Peter Lynch stated: "this idea had also been explored before this by committed regionalists such as Bretons Maurice Duhamel (Duhamel 1928) and Yann Fouéré, with his idea of a Europe of a hundred flags (Fouéré 1968) as well as in Flanders by Maurits Van Haegendoren (1971)" (2007). The most famous works are those of Yann Fouéré, *L'Europe aux Cents Drapeaux* from 1968 (reprinted 1980), and another regionalist, Guy Héraud, who published *L'Europe des ethnies* in 1963 (reprinted 1990) and *Les principies du fédéralisme et la fédération européenne* in 1970. Denis de Rougemont created *Lettre ouverte aux Européens*, one of the manifestos of regionalism, in 1970. In the 1980s, German scholars become more interested in the topic. In that decade, works such as *Handbuch der westeuropäischen Regionalbewegungen* (1980) by Jochena Blaschke and *Die Nation ist tot. Es lebe die Region* (1984) by Hans Mommsen were created.

Today, problems of sub-state regionalism have not ceased to attract the interest of scholars. Many of them stress the difference between 'old' and 'new' regionalism. The 'old' regionalism is the process that took place from 1945 to around 1980 when regional policies were designed in the centre and were based on the redistribution of resources in the system of a welfare state. These policies were focused on the harmonisation of economic growth and help for underdeveloped regions. The 'new' regionalism is a process of change of the status of regions from objects to subjects of politics. The new regional policy started to be developed in those regions that had become aware of their interests and began to lobby in the centre (state institutions) and international organisations (Ollson 2009, 116).

Cezary Trosiak uses the terms of objective and subjective regionalism (suggested by Henryk Skorowski 1999). The objective aspect of regionalism is connected to the existence of a regional identity, which encompasses the social, cultural and historical particularity of a region. It includes the regional community and its ties of solidarity. A subjective aspect of regionalism is seen in the engagement of individuals in the region and its community. It encompasses activities aimed at protecting its identity, tradition and history, and engagement of the community in activities and political actions aimed at changing the relationship between the centre and the region (Trosiak 2016, 69).

Scholars have developed many definitions of regionalism throughout the years. One of them states that "[r]egionalism (...) is a movement (social, political, cultural etc.) which aims at promoting the region" (Szul 2012, 31). This short definition seems to be concise enough. But unfortunately, it does not address the main theoretical problem. The key question in many theories of regionalism is whether it is a state-led project – the top-down perspective – or rather a process developed by non-state actors (regional actors) – the bottom-up perspective (Söderbaum 2003, 9). In this book, the answer to this question is not a simple one. Regionalism will be seen as a process of change in the status of a regional community, which has changed from being the object of a regional policy to the subject and actor of a decision-making process in regional policy. And, at least the process of creating regional identity, building a community based on ties of solidarity and developing a representation of regional interests is seen here as a bottom-up process.

1.5 Ethnic Conflict and Ethnic Mobilisation

Ted Robert Gurr classified ethnic conflict as identity-based conflict in which tension between governments and challengers representing cultural, ethnic, religious or national identity groups leads to social anxiety (2000, 3). Another definition was presented by Karl Cordell and Stefan Wolff: "[g]enerally speaking, the term conflict describes a situation in which two or more actors pursue incompatible, yet from their individual perspectives entirely just goals. Ethnic conflicts are one particular form of such conflict: in which the goals of at least one conflict party are defined in (exclusively) ethnic terms, and in which the primary fault line of confrontation is one of ethnic distinctions" (2010, 1).

How do ethnic conflicts occur? The mechanism is described by Stefan Wolff: "(...) differences in what people appreciate as legitimate eventually lead to claims about relative group worth: if you cannot acknowledge the value of my symbols, your culture must be inferior. In turn, then, being seen and treated as inferior – in the job market, in the allocation of public housing, in admission to university, etc. – leads the discriminated group to question the entire political system that allows such discrimination to occur and to develop an alternative, in their view more legitimate, system. The more one group challenges the status quo and the less another is prepared to allow changes in it, the more likely is it that conflict will rapidly escalate into violence" (2006, 67). Also, he suggests that ethnicity can be used as a mechanism for organisational and mobilisation purposes in conflict groups, which are often ready to fight for resources that are sometimes only indirectly linked to their ethnic identity (Wolff 2006).

At first glance, one could say that the two statements are contradictory, but this is not necessarily the case. The description suggests that ethnic conflicts usually occur when ethnicity becomes socially relevant, which means that the existence of (at least) two groups within a conflict is based on the *a priori* differentiation influencing the everyday life of any individual within both groups, even if it is strongly perceived by members of only one of the groups. This leads to questions about the legitimacy of the existing social and political system, and later, it may turn into a call for change, which, if it is not accommodated to some extent, may evolve into violence. The stage when political demands and interests are based on ethnicity or explained in ethnic terms will be called 'politicisation of ethnicity' and a call for adequate ethnopolitics. If ethnopolitics is developed in an accommodating way, at least to some extent, the ethnic conflict may not necessarily turn into violence, although of course, there are other factors influencing this evolution (Wolff 2006, 69–71).

Furthermore, Wolff connects the emergence and radicalisation of ethnic conflict with security dilemmas, which occur in situations when "an increase in one person's, group's, or state's security is at the same time perceived as a threat, or decrease in security, by another actor. The ethnic security dilemma thus involves elements of physical security (literal survival of group members), political security (freedom from oppressive regimes that exclude group members from meaningful participation in the political process), economic and social security (freedom from economically and socially exclusive regimes that deny equal opportunities of economic and social advancement to group members), cultural security (freedom from forced assimilation), and environmental security (freedom from environmental destruction and resource scarcity)" (2006, 76–77). In modern democracies, physical, political, economic and social or environmental security is only very rarely linked to ethnicity, though still, it may happen. But cultural security is on the opposite side of this spectrum and is usually linked to ethnicity by its very definition: "(...) the security which is sought is one of being able to live with dietary, clothing, linguistic, intellectual and moral traditions, but also of being able to innovate, to invent, not to be attacked or threatened in one's integrity. This also includes the possibility of establishing oneself as a subject of one's experience on both an individual and a collective level (...) Cultural security is all the more difficult to ensure in view of the fact that it must take into consideration problems as they are experienced, either as social constructions or, on the contrary, as they are overlooked, which is also a social construction" (Wieviorka 2018, 21). The description suggests that cultural security should be considered at the community (collective) and personal (individual) levels. Moreover, it should not only be considered in a factual way but also as a collective and individual construct. This leads to the statement that cultural security should be studied from the factual perspective and from the perspective of perception, both individual and collective.

In the radicalisation of ethnic conflicts, so-called 'grievances' also play a role, recognised, for example, by Birnir et al. (2015; 2016). This model of ethnic conflict is based on three concepts: mobilisational capacity, incentives and opportunities (Saxton 2005). It draws mostly on social movements literature. Mobilisational capacity can be defined as the capacity of group leaders to mobilise the group for collective action, while opportunities are seen as elements external to the movement itself, like political systems, decision-making-process structures, the presence of political allies and others. Grievances are seen as a function of repression and collective disadvantages. Usually, they are based on two factors: loss of autonomy and impairment of security (cultural, economic, political or other). What is important is that the role of grievances is based on objective and collectively perceived criteria. The 'active grievance' is seen as one voiced by social and political actors claiming to represent the ethnic group (even if they do not do so officially).

Here, any kind of political conflict based on ethnicity (demands linked to ethnicity) is seen as ethnic conflict. This means that not only those that escalate into violence will be perceived as such. It is the role of ethnopolitics and politics in general to de-escalate the conflict. This means that policy should be focused not on eradicating conflicts but rather on creating a political and social environment that would be able to grant rights and representation to minorities within the democratic order of the state.

In Polish scholarly literature, an example of ethnic diversity studies in the category of conflict can be found in the work of Janusz Mucha (2005). His analysis of multi-ethnic societies is based on the conflict model of society. In this model, the majority presses for cultural assimilation by socialisation and by coercion in different forms, while minority groups resist this pressure. This leads to a dynamic model of society, where opposite interests are in constant struggle, leading to conflict, but also (after time passes) consensus and harmonisation. Conflict is present not only in open rebellion but also in the forms of debate, defiance and lobbying. Ethnic conflict is defined as one of the conflicts of interest over resources and, as such, is seen as a natural part of the existence of a social system. But it can also be classified as a conflict over values. This debate is present among today's scholars: is ethnic conflict simply a conflict over resources or (in a postmodernist spirit) is it a conflict over values and symbols? For the purpose of this study, both features of ethnic conflict are recognised and seen as coexisting and related.

David Lake and Donald Rothchild suggested the following possible origins of ethnic conflicts:
- inter-group differences,
- fall of repressive regimes (after the Cold War),
- fear for the future,
- competition for resources.

They also suggested possible solutions for its management: "[e]ffective management seeks to reassure minority groups of both their physical security and, because it is often a harbinger for future threats, their cultural security. Demonstrations of respect, power-sharing, elections engineered to produce group interdependency, and the establishment of regional autonomy and federalism are important confidence-building measures (...)" (Lake & Rothchild 1996, 24). In general, they suggested that in societies where ethnicity is an important basis for identity, group competition often forms along ethnic lines and the state, which is usually dominated by a set of rules chosen by the majority ethnic (national) group, becomes part of the conflict in the process (Lake & Rothchild 1996, 45).

Political mobilisation can be defined as the process whereby political actors encourage people to participate in some form of political action. In its concrete manifestations, this process can take on many different shapes. Political mobilisers typically persuade people to vote, petition, protest, rally, or join a political party, trade union or a politically active civic organisation.

Ethnopolitical groups are identity groups whose ethnicity has political consequences, resulting in either differential treatment of group members or political action on behalf of group interests (Gurr 2000, 5). Ethnic identity leads to political action when ethnicity has collective consequences for the group in relation to other groups and states. To the extent to which ethnicity is a major determinant of people's security, status or access to political power, it becomes a means and a tool in political mobilisation, and ethnic divisions gain relevance. This happens when differences based on ethnicity are greater than the ones based on class or other determinants. Most ethnopolitical movements since 1945 have emerged in response to changes in identity groups' political environments, which have prompted some of their leaders to find more effective ways to promote or defend the interests that they define in collective terms. In the Post-Soviet zone, this change took place in the 1990s, when the process of politicisation of ethnic cleavages had an encouraging political environment in which to thrive.

Ethnopolitical mobilisation (further on, the term 'ethnic mobilisation' is used to describe the process) is more likely to develop within those groups that have the strongest, most cohesive identities, the greatest grievances prompting the need to organise, the most elaborate networks and leadership capabilities giving them the capacity to mobilise and a set of external political factors furnishing the opportunities to mobilise against the state (Gurr 1993, 314). Ethnic politics is not exclusively a struggle to rectify the grievances of minority groups, as the minority-mobilisation school assumes, but it is more generally and fundamentally about the distribution of state power along ethnic lines (Wimmer & Cederman 2009, 320). Political officeholders tend to gain legitimacy by favouring co-ethnics or co-nationals over others when distributing public goods. The expectation of ethnic preference and discrimination works the other way, too: voters prefer parties led by co-ethnics or co-nationals, citizens prefer co-ethnic or co-national officeholders. To summarise this part, ethnic mobilisation has many different roots, some of which stem from the social status of an ethnic group, while others stem from its role in the social and political system of the state. These reasons do not all occur in every case. Rather, they should be perceived in the wider context of ethnic mobilisation as a social phenomenon.

The process of ethnic mobilisation stems from a long history of political organisation along ethnic lines. In this process, leaders decide to speak for their ethnic group, thereby making the abstract idea of ethnic belonging a somewhat more tangible reality and engaging the members of this group in political action (Vermeersch 2011). This political action encompasses not only voting behaviours but any kind of political behaviour, including ones that do not deal with voting. The study of political mobilisation outside electoral behaviours has its roots in political sociology and the study of social movements.

Peter Vermeersch presents four different theoretical perspectives on ethnic mobilisation, stemming from broader literature of social movements:

- the 'culturalist' perspective, which emphasises the significance of strong subjective bonds and values within ethnic groups for shaping the lines of ethnic mobilisation;
- the 'reactive ethnicity' perspective, which uses an economic perspective to argue that the primary cause of ethnic mobilisation lies in the coincidence of ethnic bonds and relative deprivation, based on the unequal distribution of resources;
- the 'competition' perspective, which focuses on ethnic leaders making rational calculations about their identity and invoking ethnicity in their struggle for resources and power, based on the conflict of interests between different social groups;
- the 'political process' perspective, which emphasises the role of the macro-political context, encompassing the institutional environment and the dominant political discursive context (2011).

Three stages of ethnic mobilisation can be recognised. In the first stage, activists must work to achieve the consolidation of a shared understanding of ethnic group membership. In the second stage, the movement party must associate this solidarity with specific grievances suffered by the targeted community. Finally, the aggrieved but cohesive ethnic community must undergo a process of actualisation that links the emerging awareness of injustice to a specific course of action (Van Morgan 2006, 455). The last stage leads to ethnic conflict.

In ethnically divided societies, the politicisation of ethnicity has sometimes been recognised as a threat to democracy. For example, Horowitz argued that when the conflict is based on ethnic lines, the group that gets the majority and rules is likely to dominate other groups (2014). He also presented two models of amelioration, called consociationalism (based on Lijphart 1977) and centripetal. The first model is based on developing agreed guarantees, such as proportional participation in government and minority vetoes. The second model usually includes incentives for developing interethnic coalitions and interethnic majority rule. And as far as the main focus is on preventing ethnic exclusion and, consequently, the probability of ethnic conflict, both models should be seen as ways to achieve the same goal. Conversely, when we look from the perspective of representation of ethnic group interests, we may need something different. Obviously, both the models mentioned above may serve in societies where at least two groups are large.

Minority parties can be seen as political representatives of the minority groups. Their main role lies in voicing the political interests of their group and promoting the achievement of goals that are important for the minority group. These goals may be diverse, but three of the most important ones are usually: recognition of the minority, preservation of its distinctiveness and ensuring a non-discriminatory policy. In scholarly literature, it has also been established that having a political party as a minority representative and the existence of political inclusiveness (a guaranteed seat for the minority in the Parliament or election facilitation) in the state tools have a positive impact on the Satisfaction with Democracy (SWD) of members of minority groups. Consequently, inclusive ethnic politics can have a stabilising effect on democracy (Ruiz-Rufino 2013).

1.6 New Social Movements

In the study of ethnic mobilisation, it was already noted that: "[s]ometimes the mobilization of people into non-electoral and non-institutionalized types of public action may lead to new and stable political interest cleavages. These interest cleavages, in turn, may serve as a new basis of electoral mobilization" (Vermeersch 2011, 3). This is the reason why the methodology of studying social movements will be applied in this case, along with a conventional study of voting behaviours.

The political process model of social movements sees them as political phenomena. These phenomena are based on the existence of social inequality, which leads groups excluded from participation in the decision-making process to undertake rational attempts at mobilisation in order to execute their interests, using methods that are not only institutional (McAdam 2008, 20). The rise of a movement is connected to the existence of a structure of opportunities and external determinants. In the structure of opportunities, we can single out the existence of grievances or other reasons for the protest, the existence of interests and groups that are able to articulate them, organisation and structure. The first phase is the creation of basic organisational potential, which depends on the number of members of organisations ready to engage in a movement, the potential to recruit new ones, the existence of a strong bond of solidarity, a communication network and the emergence of leaders. The second phase is an increase in the awareness of the political situation and the existing means to change it. This phase is mostly symbolic and leads to shaping public opinion. In the last stage, the movement becomes a political actor and takes part in the political process (at least, as an organised protest movement). The existence and evolution of the movement depend on the reaction of the establishment, creation of alliances and outcomes of the movement.

New social movements are concentrated on the problems of values and ideologies (Buechler 2008). Their character is still political but is also cultural. The inequality fundamental to their emergence is usually symbolic: living under a dominant culture and having no say in the reproduction and creation of culture. In many cases, social movements are linked to a need to represent other (non-dominant) cultures, views and ideologies, which otherwise would remain in the shadows, in the area of private life. The political challenge to the state is based on challenging the dominant culture it represents and reproduces and its authorities. This leads to demands for change in the social and cultural life of society as a whole. In this way, the movement still is political in its nature. The role of symbols and awareness becomes much more important, but this does not mean that other political demands cannot be raised. New social movements are also defensive in their nature, and the defence is usually concerned with the identity (non-dominant culture) on which they are based.

Modern ethnic movements can be classified as a type of new social movement. They are usually based on cultural differences, identity protection and real or perceived discrimination. As time goes by, they can become political actors and create political representation. As a result, they can be studied through the models created for research into new social movements. Firstly, we should study the potential causes for protest: discrimination, past or present grievances, the group's identity and its potential to lead to the movement. Afterwards, organisational potential should be investigated: existing organisations, membership in the organisations and in the group, the group's elites and leaders of the movement. Finally, the extent to which the social and political environment plays a role in the movement should be analysed: political opportunity, potential to create alliances within and outside the state, and potential benefits, which can come from taking part in the movement. As was already noted, the last stage of the movement is its institutionalisation, which usually leads to the emergence of political parties.

1.7 Regionalist and Ethnoregionalist Parties

A political party is defined as a permanent association of citizens, based on free membership and a programme willing to occupy (through the process of elections) politically decisive positions in the state in order to implement ideas for resolving the main problems of society (Heywood 2010, Sokół & Żmigrodzki 2005). The Polish *Political Parties Act*, in Art. 1 para. 1, states that: "a political party is a voluntary organisation, using a defined name, whose purpose is participation in public policy through democratic means in order to shape the policy and participate in the exercise of public authority". In para. 2, it states that: "a political party can enjoy the rights guaranteed by law after registration".[1] As a result, the legal existence of a political party starts after its registration as such by the Court. However, in political science, the term 'political party' does not require any legal form of organisation, which means that it is possible to analyse other types of associations as long as they meet the criteria included in the former definition, even though they do not meet the legal criteria included in the legal definition of a political party (Wojtasik 2012, 48). In many cases, the term 'proto-party' is used for such organisations, especially at the stage when it is unclear whether an emerging organisation will take part in elections (Lucardie 2002).

Scholars use the term 'party family' for a group of parties with similar programmes and ideologies. One such family includes ethnoregionalist parties, among which we can distinguish regionalist parties, ethnic parties and

---

1 Dz. U. 2011.155.924 with amendments.

ethnoregionalist parties. Regionalist and ethnoregionalist parties are recognised as belonging to one family, distinguished by Lieven de Winter. He defined them as parties that demand a political reorganisation of the existing nation-state power structures (de Winter 1998, 204). Regionalist parties can be characterised by a demand for more regional power, a lack of interest in becoming nation-wide, not representing the interests of the whole population of the state and aspiring to the government of and for the region. Factors contributing to the creation of a regionalist party usually include peripheral distinctiveness and grievances suffered from the centre, organisational resources and the external situation enabling them to take action. Ethnoregionalist parties may also be defined as: "referring to the efforts of geographically concentrated peripheral minorities which challenge the working order and sometimes even the democratic order of a nation-state by demanding recognition of their cultural identity" (Müller-Rommel 1998, 19). Some scholars make a distinction between regionalist and ethnoregionalist parties, defining the former as "formations with a region-based electorate and mobilisation resources, or as formations representing sub-national (regional) interest communities exercising party functions to the full extent in a regionally defined operating space (...)" (Strimska 2002). The name 'regional party' can also be found in the literature. These are understood as parties with a social and political base located in one region but concerned with nation-wide issues, not necessarily promoting regional interests (e.g., CSU) (Seiler 2005, 21). Due to the fact that, for the time being, Polish literature on the issue does not sufficiently differentiate between these topics, the terms are used in accordance with the definitions quoted above.

In some works, the term 'regional nationalist parties' is used to describe this kind of organisation. Its phenomenon is based first upon the consolidation of regional solidarity; second, the politicisation of identity-related grievances; and third, the actualisation of the targeted community in support of the nationalist party (Van Morgan 2006, 453). This term, in my view, can only be used in cases where the existence of a nation (usually a stateless-nation), nationalism and a national movement can be confirmed. This means that regional nationalist parties can constitute a specific form of an ethnoregionalist party, but not all ethnoregionalist parties can be defined as 'regional nationalist'.

De Winter further classified regionalist parties into protectionist, autonomist and national-federalist (1998, 204). These categories were further divided by Régis Dandoy into sub-categories: protectionist – conservative and participationist; decentralist – autonomist and federalist, confederalist; secessionist – independentist, irredentist and rattachist (2010, 207). He also categorised ethnoregionalist parties according to their demands (soft, mild and radical) and the sub-categories were divided according to the nature of the demands. Some scholars categorise these parties along the left-right axis (Seiler 2005, 23), though it is not a dominant trend, and, in order to do so, parties must hold a significant position in a party system.

Regionalist parties aim at the modification of the vertical allocation of power between centre and periphery in different fields of policy-making (culture, identity policy, economic and taxation policy, etc.). They usually have fewer but more specific programs. By the success of regionalist parties, "we refer not only to electoral results, but also to government participation (success in office) and actual political output (policy success). In fact, it is on policy success, that we shall focus the most: the achievements of regionalist parties in terms of changing collective decisions" (Mazzolleni & Müller 2016, 1). This view is shared in the present book.

An ethnic party can be characterised as one that champions the interests of an ethnic group. Non-ethnic and multi-ethnic parties are also recognised in the literature. An ethnic party in such a context is the party championing the interests of one or of a set of ethnic groups (Chandra 2011, 155). According to Lech Nijakowski an "ethnic party is a social organisation (also association), which is the official representative of an ethnic or national group with the aim of participation in exercising public authority on every level. The candidate of such a party being voted for is not perceived by his/her electorate as a professional, but rather as a member of an ethnic or national group" (2006, 36). In the case of ethnic parties, issues linked to a particular ethnicity constitute central problems. In addition, it (usually) receives its support from the members of a targeted ethnic group. Indicators that allow us to classify parties within this group include, among others:

– party name – ethnic parties usually take the name of the ethnic group or include its historical land in its name;
– explicit appeals – ethnic parties use ethnicity to raise demands and receive voter support;
– position on explicit issues – in their position on particular issues, ethnic parties usually favour the ethnic groups they represent;
– implicit activation of ethnic identities – sometimes, ethnic parties use the identity of the group, which they represent implicitly, raising the demands which are not openly in favour of the group, but which will benefit it;
– group votes – an ethnic party receives votes from the members of one ethnic group more frequently than from members of another ethnic group (Chandra 2011).

Consequently, when there is evidence of both appeals both in programmes, names or activation of the target group(s), the party can be categorised as ethnoregionalist. This is especially in the case when the ethnic group is heavily concentrated in one (usually peripheral) region.

However, the existence of ethnic, regionalist and ethnoregionalist parties in a political system leads to some concerns in the scholarly literature. Firstly, as to ethnic parties, the so-called outbidding effect was described and disputed by Chandra (2005). The outbidding effect, in short, refers to the situation when two polarised groups compete politically on the one-dimensional political axis with two radically opposite ends. In this situation, political parties promoting a more centric political programme are likely to be outbid by more radical parties, and this may lead to the destabilisation of democracy. It was further suggested that ethnic parties are prone to the outbidding effect because the political axis is based on gains for one ethnic group, and they emerge in societies where ethnicity is politicised and creates political division. But, Chandra argued that ethnicity, especially in a constructivist approach, is multidimensional and fluid. Moreover, in today's world, as was argued above, individual choice is much less dependent on belonging to a certain group than it is on the particular programme presented in concrete elections, which suggests that it is unlikely that the political competition will be located only on a one-dimensional political axis.

As to regionalist parties, a very similar argument was made by Bracanti (2005). His study on government (on the state-level) stability, when regional parties are involved, showed that the presence of regional parties might increase the chance for government instability, which, in turn, undermines democracy. Although the term 'regional party' is vague, Bracanti's further arguments indicate that it is regionalist parties that demand some type of autonomy, which may have this 'destabilising effect' on government. He suggests a few reasons for this situation. First, because regionalist parties tend to focus on one axis of political competition (which we would identify as the centre-periphery axis) and this makes it hard to find a compromise in such a limited political field. Second, because regionalist parties demand autonomy, which can be seen by the state-wide parties and central institutions as a demand to diminish their political power. As to the second argument, Bracanti showed in his study that the claim of a regional community for autonomy does not necessarily have the 'destabilising effect', especially when the same claim is incorporated by a state-wide party. As to the first argument, as in the case of ethnic parties, regionalist parties may have more focused and limited programmes, but they are rarely one-dimensional and based purely on the centre-periphery axis because the interests of regional communities are not.

Finally, a recent study by Heinisch, Massetti and Mazzoleni (2019, 279–281) outlined the relations and the fine line between ethnoregionalist ideology and populism. They concluded that "[a] common denominator is found in their equation of 'the people' with certain ideas of ethnos and territory and their antagonistic relationship with elites, including both internal elites and those external to the territory in question". This is far from saying that all ethnoregionalist parties are populist, but the study shows that over time and space, at least in Europe, some primarily ethnoregionalist parties have adapted various programmes that can be categorised as populist.

1.8 Issue and Value Voting – Theory

In contrast to the Lipset-Rokkan theory of structural (cleavage) voting behaviours, new theories about the reasons behind individual and group voting still seem to be in the development phase. The need for a theory with more explanatory power in an ever-changing world started with the contestants to the Lipset-Rokkan theory, who argued that since the 1980s, at least, we can observe the process of voter dealignment. Dealignment indicates that the explanatory power of the social structure over voting is diminishing (Knutsen 2018, 3). Later, the concept of realignment was introduced, suggesting that new cleavages emerge in societies and lead to a change in the party system and political parties themselves. Also, it was argued that voting behaviour might be better explained not by social structure but by the conflict over values and ideologies. Some authors, especially those who emphasise the role of post-modernism, are ready to state that the role of individual choice of particular programmes in particular elections may be a better explanation for voting behaviours in modern societies.

Additionally, it was argued in the literature that traditional parties, especially in well-established democracies, tend to take positions that diminish political polarisation (their programmes have become increasingly similar). At the same time, new political parties, usually identifying strongly with one ideology (Radical Right, New Left parties), emerged and entered political competition, taking part of the more radical electorate from mainstream parties (Kitschelt 2000). Kitschelt also suggested that: "[p]olitical alignments in post-communist polities thus tend to be multidimensional in that they involve (1) considerations of economic (re)distribution, (2) considerations of political governance (civil and political rights, exclusiveness and inclusiveness of political participation), and (3) the management of ethnocultural identities and diversity" (2015).

Furthermore, the work by Oscar Mazzoleni and Sean Müller, related indirectly to party strategy and directly to the problem of the success of ethnoregionalist parties, showed that this success is mostly connected to a limited programme (including, most importantly, the allocation of influence on public policy and allocation of public funds in a vertical axis: centre-periphery, dominant – non-dominant culture) (2016, 1).

To summarise, drawing from the new approaches to studying party systems, the theory of structural voting based on the clear-cut opposition of interests of large-scale groups may not be the only or best explanation for the emergence of the ethnoregionalist movement in Upper Silesia. The question of whether the evolution of the political potential of the ethnoregionalist movement in Upper Silesia is a consequence of the consolidation and revelation of an existing cleavage (hidden during the reign of Socialism in Poland) or whether it is an example of a new political movement, based on the approach of a social movement with one, strong ideology and a limited political programme, constitutes an interesting theoretical problem for this work.

I will argue here that in the case of a centre-periphery axis, we can observe its evolution towards the inclusion of ethnic demands rather than de- or realignment. In most cases, voting behaviour is based on belonging to a particular social group located on a periphery (regional community) but also on ethnic identity (and demands for its preservation/recognition), which is seen here as an individual choice. This way, the most promising results in understanding voter behaviour would come from combining both structural voting and values voting approaches.

1.9 Communities and Nationalism

The social and political movements, organisations and parties described above explicitly or implicitly appeal to some kind of community. These communities are based on a common identity, interests and goals. Here, I define three types of communities: regional community, ethnic group and nation. There are many theories on which the definitions of an ethnic group and nation are based: nowadays, ethnosymbolism and constructivism seem to be the most popular and are elaborated below.

The doctrine of ethnosymbolists, in the approach of Anthony D. Smith, shows that: "a nation is a named human community, residing in a perceived homeland and having common myths and shared history, distinct public culture and common law and customs for all members" (2010, 13). An ethnic group (or ethnic community), on the other hand, is: "a named human community connected to a homeland, possessing common myths and ancestry, shared memories, one or more elements of a shared culture, and a measure of solidarity, at least among the elites" (Smith 2010, 13).

In the constructivist doctrine, there are also many different views. According to Benedict Anderson, a nation can be considered an imagined community, united by a "deep, horizontal comradeship" (1983, 7), whereby national co-fellows are believed to constitute a 'natural' entity. A nation is imagined as both inherently limited and sovereign. In this theory, the idea of nation is illustrated in the census, the map and the museums, which represent the people, their domain and the legitimacy of the nation's ancestry (Anderson 1983, 164). The constructivist theory of ethnicity was presented by Phillip Yang, among others. In his theory, ethnicity is socially constructed, partly on the basis of ancestry or presumed ancestry and, more importantly, by a given society, which implies that the interests of an ethnic group determine ethnic affiliation and that ethnic boundaries are relatively stable but undergo changes from time to time (Yang 2000, 48).

The main difference between these two kinds of communities in the ethno-symbolist approach is based on the public-private division. A nation is defined by having developed public culture, while an ethnic community has elements of shared (private) culture. Furthermore, a nation, according to this definition, should have a common law and customs, which bind all its members. At the same time, an ethnic group should have some measure of solidarity. Nations occupy defined territories – homelands – while ethnicities have only symbolic bonds to their territory. In the constructivist doctrine, the difference lies in the existence of a nation-state. A nation is not only an ethnic group, bound by presumed ancestry, common interests and affiliation but also a community imagined as limited and sovereign within a nation-state.

Smith defined the concept of nationalism, and in his work, the concept has a few meanings:

– a process of formation or growth of nations (narrow sense);
– a sentiment or consciousness of belonging to the nation;
– a language and symbolism of the nation;
– a social and political movement on behalf of the nation;
– a doctrine and/or ideology of the nation, both general and particular (which encompass the idea of national autonomy, national unity and national identity) (2010, 5).

Anderson sees nationalism mostly as official (state-) nationalism, which is a conscious, self-protective policy linked to the preservation of a state's (imperial) interests. Consequently, nationalism is an ideology in which communities are imagined as nations (Anderson 1983, 159).

Michel Billig presented another theory of nationalism. He suggests that the "whole complex of beliefs, assumptions, habits, representations and practices" which (re)produce national identity are reproduced in the banal realm of everyday life as part of the "endemic condition" of nations (Billig 1995, 6). Tim Edensor also studied the reproduction of national identity, mostly in popular culture (2002, 12), where cultural forms and practices are sometimes used without due reflection. Everyday life reflects the common understanding, practice and knowledge of people who take part in practices and create patterns. Nationalism, in this sense, is 'how things are' and 'how we do things', as understood by common people (Edensor 2002, 19). Scholars also developed terms such as 'regional nationalism' and 'regional minority nationalism'. Both refer to the demands of regionally concentrated ethnocultural groups (stateless nations) for a state of their own (Olsson 2009).

An ethnographic group is defined as a community that lives in a small region (area) of a state, whose culture is believed to be a part of the national culture, is mainly folkloristic and uses the local dialect of the national language. They can evolve into an ethnic group (Mucha 2005, 17).

A regional community is a population of a region. The people creating it are functionally bonded to the region and each other. They have common interests and some form of identity, usually consciously reproduced. In most cases, a regional community is represented by a regional authority with different degrees of public power, in which case, a regional community becomes a political community and develops regional policy along with political organisations.

Nationalities could be conceptualised as non-spatial cultural communities endowed with various forms of non-territorial rights. However, nationality claims, with their assertion of self-governing rights, are more than mere claims for cultural recognition – indeed, in some places, their cultural content is rather small. Yet, they do entail territorial autonomy, and the territory becomes important in many ways. Nationality movements seek to exploit existing opportunities in the form of regionalism, minority rights, regimes and nationalism (Keating 2004, 373). In this meaning, the term encompasses many different communities, from ethnic groups to developed nations.

1.10   Ethnic Identity and Ideology

Individual and collective identity is a dynamic social construct, defined by the past, present and future. In its basic meaning, identity signifies:

- 'sameness' – being the same person manifesting a continuation of oneself;
- 'distinctiveness' – being unique and separate from the others (Bokszański 2005, 37).

Postmodernity and the times in which we live have changed our perception of identity. The earlier paradigms saw the individual as a member of a social group, which shaped his/her identity and social status. Today, we agree that the individual creates his/her identity consciously and by choosing from the many options available. Nevertheless, social bonds and group dynamics still have a strong influence on one's choices and, consequently, identity (Zygmunt 2015, 120).

Collective identity is the consequence of social interactions (intentional and unintentional). It depends on processes "in which the attribute of 'similarity' among its members, as against the strangeness, the differences, the distinction of the other, is symbolically constructed and defined" (Eisenstadt & Giesen 1995, 74). The boundaries are constructed based on three types of symbolic codes: primordial (original, natural differences between ethnic groups), civic (observance of rituals, traditions and rules of a group) and the relation of the collective subject to the sacred (any kind of universal idea, which can be carried by the culture in a missionary fashion). Also, identity is created in the process of the development of a movement by collective actors, who usually aim at a redefinition of their place in the society and social order. It can be defined as the creation of a collective subject, in which the bonds of the group with 'important' and 'unchanging' values play the most important part (Bokszański 2005, 63). They are established as an act of the group's self-definition and its perception by outsiders.

There is a general agreement that every culture is located in a particular space – it always belongs and comes from 'somewhere' (Burszta 2015, 4). This is why the link between ethnic groups, their cultures and the territory in which they live is so strong. The relationship is built on a few factors: the landscape becomes a typical imagining of home, ways of living are connected to the land and its possibilities, the culture is connected to the changing of seasons and the nature of a particular locality. On the other hand, the ethnic group changes the landscape and nature to its needs and binds its development to a particular locality.

Ethnic identities "rather than being 'primordial' phenomena radically opposed to modernity and the modern state are frequently reactions to processes of modernisation" (Eriksen 2010, 13). Ethnicity is the enduring communication of cultural differences between groups considering themselves to be distinct. Therefore, it is relational and also situational – the ethnic character of a social relationship depends on the situation and context (Eriksen

2010, 69). Ethnicity, in many cases, is perceived as continuity with the past, but many scholars have regarded utility as the main variable in accounting for the maintenance of ethnic identity, regarding identity as contingent on ethnic political organisation, which is formed in situations of competition over scarce resources. However, notions of utility are themselves cultural creations, so the boundary between that which is useful and that which is meaningful becomes blurred.

The clarity of ethnic differences becomes even more complicated in the case of ethnopolitics, where, in order to communicate its distinctiveness, representatives of the group must adopt the culture and language of the majority. This is why, in order to negotiate with the state (centre), one needs to lose his/her ethnicity first (Eriksen 2010, 156). The paradox sometimes leads to undermining the existence of the ethnic distinctiveness of the group itself.

According to one of the pioneers in the field of research in ethnopolitics, "(...) in modern and transitional societies – unlike traditional ones – politicized ethnicity has become the crucial principle of the political legitimation and delegitimation of systems, states, regimes, and governments and at the same time has also become an effective instrument for pressing mundane interests in society's competition for power, status, and wealth" (Rothschild 1981, 2). Ethnicity is socially relevant when people notice and condition their actions on ethnic distinctions in everyday life. Ethnicity is politicised when political coalitions are organised along ethnic lines or when access to political or economic benefits depends on ethnicity (Fearon 2006, 853). Primordialists assume that certain ethnic categories are always socially relevant and that political relevance follows automatically, while modernists see ethnic groups as political coalitions formed to advance the economic interests of members (or leaders). Firstly, shared language and culture make it easier for political entrepreneurs to mobilise 'intragroup' rather than across ethnic groups. Secondly, ethnic and administrative boundaries tend to coincide, and modern goods, like schools, electricity and water projects, tend to benefit people in a particular location. Lobbying for these goods along ethnic lines is thus natural (Fearon 2006, 860).

Therefore, the role of ethnicity in politics and policy in ethnicity should not be underestimated. Ethnicity can be transformed into ethnic, ethnoregionalist or nationalist ideology, defined as a set of "ideas and beliefs (whether true or false) which symbolise the conditions and life-experience of a specific, socially significant group or class. (...) [Which moreover] attends to promote and legitimise the interests of social groups in the face of opposite interests" (Eagelton 1991, 29).

32   CHAPTER 1

1.11   Communities and International Law

Granting rights to communities has its roots in ancient philosophy. In classic philosophy, the logic was simple: because an individual exists within a community, he or she can only fully thrive in that community. Due to the fact that natural order is based on society (Strauss 2012, 138) and it is in human nature to live in a state (political organisation) (Aristotle 2003), the community deserves protection as well. This idea is continued today by communitarian philosophers. Communitarians point out that the obligations of an individual derive from the culture of a community: as a result, what is good for an individual is good for people and the community. Moreover, the issue of roots is raised, which means that our lives are only narrations, deeply based in collective narrations – traditional, historical and social – and an individual is not separated from his or her social context (MacIntyre 2007, 221).

Collective human rights are understood today as rights given to the individual, but either aiming at the protection of a community or able to be exercised only by communities (Mik 1992, 231). Examples of such rights include: the right of the people to self-determination, the right to recognition and protection of identity, the rights of minorities and the right to develop in accordance with local circumstances (UNESCO 1989, 5). The aim of these rights is the protection and empowerment of individuals forming part of a community. It should be distinguished from so-called 'solidarity rights' in the concept of Karel Vasak, which aim at the protection of the common good of all humanity (Plis 2014, 46) – e.g., the right to a healthy and clean environment.

Peoples are defined in two ways: first, as a territorial community, and second, as a community of people with common features. In order to be able to exercise its rights, a community needs to:
– have bonds beyond citizenships,
– be identified by outsiders and by its members as a community,
– have institutions or means to express its identity,
– be able to choose legitimate representatives (Barten 2015, 3).

The *nation* is usually the sovereign in the state, based on constitutional principles. In this meaning, it is understood as a political community (Kranz 2010, 20). In the work of the International Law Commission, the terms of 'nation' and 'state' have been used alternatively.[2] The same can be observed in the *Charter of the United Nations* from 1945. But the same cannot be said about the

---

2   See: *Yearbook of International Law Commission* I session 1949, UN 1956, p. 67.

term 'people'. In the *Charter*, the terms 'nation' and 'people' are used in different contexts and meanings.

The right of peoples to self-determination as a legal principle was recognised for the first time in the *Charter of the United Nations*, which stated in art. 1 para. 2: "to develop friendly relations among nations based on respect for the principle of equal rights and self-determination of peoples (...)". Later, United Nations General Assembly [UNGA] resolution 1514 (XV) art. 2 stated that: "all peoples have the right to self-determination; by virtue of that right they freely determine their political status and freely pursue their economic, social and cultural development". Also, the *International Covenant on Civil and Political Rights* from 1966[3] and the *International Covenant on Economic, Social and Cultural Rights* from 1966[4] reaffirmed in art. 1 par. 1 that: "All peoples have the right of self-determination. By virtue of that right they freely determine their political status and freely pursue their economic, social and cultural development".

Crucial for the understanding of the principle is UNGA resolution 2625 (XXV): "by virtue of the principle of equal rights and self-determination of peoples enshrined in the Charter of the United Nations, all peoples have the right to determine freely, without external interference, their political status and to pursue their economic, social and cultural development, and every State has the duty to respect this right in accordance with the provisions of the Charter". But the actions undertaken by UNGA did not end in the 1970s. Resolutions titled: *The Importance of the Universal Realization of the Right of Peoples to Self-Determination and of the Speedy Granting of Independence to Colonial Countries and Peoples for the Effective Guarantee and Observance of Human Rights* were issued from 1970 till 1988, only to be replaced by the series *Universal Realization of the Right of Peoples to Self-Determination* issued till today.

The Committee on the Elimination of Racial Discrimination, in its recommendation regarding self-determination, drew the distinction between internal and external methods of the realisation of this right. The internal aspect is explained as follows: "the rights of all peoples to pursue freely their economic, social and cultural development without outside interference. In that aspect, there exists a link with the right of every citizen to take part in the conduct of public affairs at any level. In consequence, Governments are to represent the whole population without distinction as to race, colour, descent or national or ethnic origin".[5]

---

3   UNTS, vol. 999, p. 171.
4   UNTS, vol. 993, p. 3.
5   CERD. 1996. *General Recommendation No 21: Right to Self-Determination.* para. 4.

It is also commonly accepted that the right of peoples to self-determination was introduced in order to enable peoples to conduct their own affairs and to remove barriers in these actions (Saul 2011, 619). It was also recognised by the International Court of Justice in a few advisory opinions [AO]. Firstly, in *Namibia AO*[6] and in *Western Sahara AO*.[7] Two later opinions, *Palestinian wall AO*[8] and *Kosovo AO*,[9] were issued outside the colonial context.

The means of exercising the right of the people to self-determination depends on the subject and its situation. Some of them refer to nations and peoples (including the indigenous population), such as:
– the right to choose a government and to take part in governance (self-government),
– the right to benefit from natural resources,
– the right to economic, social and cultural development (right to recognition of customs),
– the right to equality and recognition.

Some of the means refer only to peoples (including indigenous), such as:
– the right to autonomy (territorial and non-territorial), especially in situations of ethnic conflict,
– the right to the creation of their own state (mostly in the context of decolonisation and dissolution of the country),
– the right to secession (in extraordinary circumstances – usually when the right to participation in government or other human rights are not observed or when the state accepts the wish of a part of its population),
– the right to rebellion (in extreme circumstances when basic human rights are systematically violated).

'Minority' is even harder to define. There is no legally binding definition of a minority in international law, and few definitions were proposed during the works of United Nations bodies (Capotorti 1977, 96; Chernichenko 1997). A further proposition of a definition of the term was included by the Parliamentary Assembly of the Council of Europe *Text of the proposal for an additional protocol to the Convention for the Protection of Human Rights and*

---

6 *Legal Consequences for States of the Continued Presence of South Africa in Namibia (South West Africa) notwithstanding Security Council Resolution 276 (1970)*, Advisory Opinion ICJ, Reports 1971, para. 52.

7 *Western Sahara*, Advisory Opinion ICJ, Reports 1975, para. 59.

8 *Legal Consequences of the Construction of a Wall in the Occupied Palestinian Territory*, Advisory Opinion ICJ, Reports 2004.

9 *Accordance with International Law of the Unilateral Declaration of Independence in Respect of Kosovo*, Advisory Opinion ICJ, Reports 2010.

Fundamental Freedoms, concerning persons belonging to national minorities (1993) in art. 1:

> For the purposes of this Convention, the expression "national minority" refers to a group of persons in a state who:
> a. reside in the territory of that state and are citizens thereof;
> b. maintain long-standing, firm and lasting ties with that state;
> c. display distinctive ethnic, cultural, religious or linguistic characteristics;
> d. are sufficiently representative, although smaller in number than the rest of the population of that state or of a region of that state;
> e. are motivated by a concern to preserve together that which constitutes their common identity, including their culture, their traditions, their religion or their language.

However, the definition of the term has not been included in any treaty. In many works, the term 'national minority' is used to describe a minority living in a nation-state, not necessarily a group having a kin-state outside the borders of the state in which they live (Preece 1998, 29). Only one legal definition of a minority is included in the non-binding document of the Central European Initiative called CEI *Instrument for the protection of minority rights* from 1994.

Today, the recognition of minorities is no longer only within the discretionary power of states, but it must be based on objective and subjective criteria included in legal documents (UN Office of the High Commissioner for Human Rights 2010, 3). The main characteristics of a minority group are: ethnicity, separate culture, traditions and customs, religion or language, and the cultivation and protection of a separate identity. The last criterion is auto-identification – the consciousness of individuals – in creating the collective identity of a community, connected to the will to have a representation of its interests (Janusz 2011, 26–32). Minority exists *de facto*, regardless of its recognition *de iure* (Janusz 2011, 44).

Protection of minority rights is guaranteed in the universal and European legal system. United Nations General Assembly resolution 47/135 *Declaration on the Rights of Persons Belonging to National or Ethnic, Religious and Linguistic Minorities* from 18 December 1992 (A/RES/47/135) art. 1 states that:

> 1. States shall protect the existence and the national or ethnic, cultural, religious and linguistic identity of minorities within their respective territories and shall encourage conditions for the promotion of that identity.

2. States shall adopt appropriate legislative and other measures to achieve those ends.

Four general conditions for the protection of minority rights are: the protection of existence, the prohibition of exclusion, the prohibition of discrimination and the prohibition of assimilation.[10] Many duties of states were included in specific conventions (some of which are negative obligations):

- prohibition of extermination (*Convention on the Prevention and Punishment of the Crime of Genocide* from 1948);[11]
- prohibition of exclusion (*International Covenant on Civil and Political Rights* from 1966, *Convention on the Reduction of Statelessness* from 1961);[12]
- prohibition of assimilation (*International Covenant on Civil and Political Rights* from 1966);
- prohibition of discrimination (*International Convention on Elimination of All Forms of Racial Discrimination* from 1965).[13]

The United Nations Committee of Human Rights, in its commentary to art. 27 of International Covenant on Civil and Political Rights, pointed out that in order to protect minority culture, language or religion, states might be obliged to undertake positive actions to protect the identity of a minority group, the rights of peoples belonging to it and the possibility to cultivate their separateness.[14] This can be applied in the fields of culture, education and political participation, as stated in conventions:

- UNESCO *Convention from 2003 for the Safeguarding of the Intangible Cultural Heritage*[15] (scope of the Convention – art. 1 and art. 2 – indicates that the Convention protects all communities and individuals);
- UNESCO *Convention from 2005 on the Protection and Promotion of the Diversity of Cultural Expressions*[16] (art. 2 demands equal respect for minority and indigenous cultures);
- UNESCO *Convention from 1960 against Discrimination in Education*[17] (art. 5 demands existence and states' support for minority schools and conducting classes in minority languages).

---

10   *Commentary of the Working Group on Minorities to The UN Declaration on the Persons Belonging to National or Ethnic, Religious and Linguistic Minorities*, UN 2005, para 23.

11   UNTS, vol. 78, p. 277.

12   UNTS, vol. 989, p. 175.

13   UNTS, vol. 660, p. 195.

14   CCPR. 1994. *General Comment no. 23 (50)*.

15   UNTS, vol. 2368, p. 3.

16   UNTS, vol. 2440, p. 311.

17   UNTS, vol. 429, p. 93.

REGION, ETHNICITY AND POLITICS 37

In the European system, the organisations that have undertaken steps towards protecting minorities include: the Organisation of Security and Co-operation in Europe (OSCE) – previously, until 1995, the Conference on the Security and Co-operation in Europe (CSCE), the Council of Europe (CoE) and the European Union (EU).

In the OSCE, the system *Document form Copenhagen* from 1990 should be mentioned, where, in Part IV, the so-called 'human dimension' in rules of protection of minorities was included. The rights of the members of minorities are as follows:
- the right to choose to belong to a minority;
- the right to freedom from discrimination;
- the right to express freely, preserve and develop their ethnic, cultural, linguistic or religious identity and to maintain and develop their culture in all its aspects, free of any attempts at assimilation against their will;
- the right to the protection of ethnic, cultural, linguistic and religious identity of minorities on their territory and create conditions for its promotion;
- the right to be consulted in its own matters;
- the right to learn the official language or languages of the state concerned and have adequate opportunities for the instruction of their mother tongue or in their mother tongue, as well as, wherever possible and necessary, for its use before public authorities;
- the right to the teaching of history and culture in educational establishments, taking into account the history and culture of national minorities;
- the right to effective participation in public affairs, including participation in the affairs relating to the protection and promotion of the identity of such minorities;
- the recommendation for establishing local or autonomous administrations corresponding to the specific historical and territorial circumstances of such minorities and in accordance with the policies of the state concerned.

These rules were confirmed in a number of documents: *Charter of Paris for the New Europe*, 1990; *The Challenges of the Change*, Helsinki 1992 (which established the High Commissioner on National Minorities); *Towards the Genuine Partnership in the New Era*, Budapest 1994.

The main instrument of the Council of Europe is *The Framework Convention for the Protection of National Minorities* from 1995,[18] which, in art. 1, states: "The protection of national minorities and of the rights and freedoms of persons belonging to those minorities forms an integral part of the international

---

18   ETS No. 157.

protection of human rights, and as such falls within the scope of international cooperation". Furthermore, art. 2 demands good faith in the application of the Convention in a spirit of understanding and tolerance. One of the most important rights, which stems from the Convention, is embodied in art. 4:

1. The Parties undertake to guarantee to persons belonging to national minorities the right of equality before the law and of equal protection of the law. In this respect, any discrimination based on belonging to a national minority shall be prohibited.
2. The Parties undertake to adopt, where necessary, adequate measures in order to promote, in all areas of economic, social, political and cultural life, full and effective equality between persons belonging to a national minority and those belonging to the majority. In this respect, they shall take due account of the specific conditions of the persons belonging to national minorities.
3. The measures adopted in accordance with paragraph 2 shall not be considered to be an act of discrimination.

The *European Charter for Regional or Minority Languages*[19] of the Council of Europe from 1992 is another instrument concerned with the rights of persons belonging to minorities. In art. 1, the definition of regional or minority language is included. The term means a language that is "traditionally used within a given territory of a state by nationals of that state who form a group numerically smaller than the rest of the state's population; and different from the official language(s) of that state; it does not include either dialects of the official language(s) of the state or the languages of migrants". The Convention is to be applied to all minority and regional languages. Art. 7 states that its principles are:

- the recognition of the regional or minority languages as an expression of cultural wealth;
- the respect of the geographical area of each regional or minority language (...);
- the need for resolute action to promote regional or minority languages in order to safeguard them;
- the facilitation and/or encouragement of the use of regional or minority languages, in speech and writing, in public and private life;

---

19   ETS No. 148.

- the maintenance and development of links, (...) between groups using a regional or minority language and other groups in the State employing a language used in identical or similar form, as well as the establishment of cultural relations with other groups (...);
- the provision of appropriate forms and means for the teaching and study of regional or minority languages at all appropriate stages;
- the provision of facilities enabling non-speakers of a regional or minority language living in the area where it is used to learn it if they so desire;
- the promotion of study and research on regional or minority languages at universities or equivalent institutions.

The legal system of the European Union did not create its own system of protection of the rights of persons belonging to minorities. Nevertheless, the prohibition of any form of discrimination is present in its system. One of the examples is art. 21 para. 1 of the *Charter of Fundamental Rights*[20]: "any discrimination based on any ground such as sex, race, colour, ethnic or social origin, genetic features, language, religion or belief, political or any other opinion, membership of a national minority, property, birth, disability, age or sexual orientation shall be prohibited". The Council Directive 2000/43/EC of 29 June 2000 *implementing the principle of equal treatment between persons irrespective of racial or ethnic origin*[21] further developed the scope of the non-discrimination principle in European law, even before the *Charter of Fundamental Rights* was adopted.

In international law, we are faced with many problems as to the application of the provisions of treaties and resolutions in the field of the rights of communities and persons belonging to them. Firstly, due to the lack of a definition of terms, such as people and minority, there are always concerns about the application of the provisions in a particular case. Recognition of these communities as subjects of international law (to the extent foreseen in the treaties) is within the authority of the state and, sometimes, the international community or its institutions (like the International Court of Justice). Secondly, the rights and duties stemming from international law are usually open to interpretation and can sometimes be abused by states. An obligation to implement treaties in good faith does not change that. Thirdly, the question remains and will probably remain whether the instrument for the protection and empowerment of minorities and peoples foreseen in international law is enough to prevent the discrimination, assimilation and disappearance of cultural heterogeneity.

---

20   OJ 2012/C 326/02.
21   OJ L 185, 24.7.1996, p. 5.

40   CHAPTER 1

Furthermore, it should be kept in mind that the same group may be recognised both as a people for the purpose of the right to self-determination and as a minority for the purpose of protection under minority rights.[22]

1.12   Communities and Polish Law

The Republic of Poland is bound by international law and ratified Conventions. Most of the legal acts described above are binding in Poland, and some of the provisions were implemented into Polish law.

Article 35 of the *Constitution of the Republic of Poland* from 2 April 1997[23] provides that:

1. The Republic of Poland shall ensure Polish citizens belonging to national or ethnic minorities the freedom to maintain and develop their own language, to maintain customs and traditions, and to develop their own culture.
2. National and ethnic minorities shall have the right to establish educational and cultural institutions, institutions designed to protect religious identity, as well as to participate in the resolution of matters connected with their cultural identity.

In 2004, work on the *National and Ethnic Minorities and Regional Language Act* in Parliament took place. When the project was presented on 3 December 2004, "especially emotional was the voice of Senator Kazimierz Kutz, who called the draft of the National and Ethnic Minorities and Regional Language Act shameful, due to the fact that Silesians were not recognized there as an ethnic minority. He stated that we have here a camouflaged anti-Silesian act, which ruled out the cultural, regional and ethnic distinctiveness of Silesians. His stance spurred a public debate about the status of Silesians" (Łodziński 2005, 13; my translation).

In the end, the *National and Ethnic Minorities and Regional Language Act* from 6 January 2005[24] was accepted. In art. 2, definitions and a list of national and ethnic minorities are included:

---

22   *Commentary of the Working Group on Minorities to the United Nation Declaration of Rights of Persons Belonging to National or Ethnic, Religious and Linguistic Minorities,* UN 2005, para. 15.

23   Dz.U. 1997, NR 78 poz. 483. Official translation: Sejm RP. n.d. "The Constitution".

24   Dz.U. 2005. 17. 141 with amendments.

1. A national minority, pursuant to the Act, is a group of Polish citizens, which meets all of the following requirements:
   - is less numerous than the rest of the population,
   - is essentially different from the rest of the population, because of language, culture or tradition,
   - pursues to preserve its own language, culture or tradition,
   - is conscious about its own historical national unity and pursues its expression and protection,
   - its ancestors resided in current territories of the Republic of Poland for at least 100 years,
   - identifies itself with a nation living in a sovereign State.
2. The following are recognised as national minorities:
   - Belarusians,
   - Czechs,
   - Lithuanians,
   - Germans,
   - Armenians,
   - Russians,
   - Slovaks,
   - Ukrainians,
   - Jews.
3. An ethnic minority, pursuant to the Act, is a group of Polish citizens, which meets all of the following requirements:
   - is less numerous than the rest of the population,
   - is essentially different from the rest of the population, because of language, culture or tradition,
   - pursues preservation of its own language, culture or tradition,
   - is conscious about its own historical ethnic unity and pursues its expression and protection,
   - its ancestors resided in the current territories of the Republic of Poland for at least 100 years,
   - does not identify itself with a nation living in a sovereign State.
4. The following are recognised as ethnic minorities:
   - Karaites,
   - Lemkos,
   - Romas,
   - Tatars.

The Kashubian language is recognised as a regional language in art. 19 and enjoys the same rights as the languages of minorities.

Art. 5–18 embodies the rights of persons belonging to national and ethnic minorities and, to some extent, communities using a regional language:

- assimilation and discrimination are forbidden;
- persons belonging to officially recognised national and ethnic minorities can use their native language: they can exchange information in the native language. Moreover, they have a right to the native spelling of names and can teach and learn the minority language or in the minority language;
- in the cases where a minority is more than 20% of the population of a municipality, the minority language can be used in official communication with municipal officials and next to the official names of streets and municipalities, and names in the native language of a minority can also be used;minority organisations can receive budget funding for: cultural institutions, events and minority art, preservation of cultural identity, publishing of books and periodicals, supporting TV programmes and radio auditions, protection of places connected to the minority culture, existence of libraries and archives, education, promotion of the knowledge about minorities.

Other rights are guaranteed in the fields of education, public media and the electoral system. According to the *Educational System Act* form 7 September 1991[25] art. 13, the school enables students to preserve their national or ethnic, linguistic or religious identity, especially by teaching the language, history and culture. Textbooks may be funded from the state budget. Also, activities towards the promotion of knowledge about national and ethnic minorities, their language, history, culture and religion will be undertaken by the minister.

The *Radio and Television Act* from 29 December 1992[26] art. 21 states that public television and radio shall respect the needs of the persons belonging to minorities by broadcasting programmes in the languages of minorities. Art. 30 includes the obligation to enable members of organisations representing minorities to participate in the committees of programmes broadcasting programmes for minorities.

According to the *Electoral Code* from 5 January 2011[27] art. 197, only national minorities can take advantage of privileges concerning the election threshold. National minorities are recognised in art. 2, para. 2 of the National and Ethnic Minorities and Regional Language Act.

The last National Census was conducted in Poland in 2011 in accordance with the *National Census 2011 Act* form 4 March 2010.[28] In art. 2, the legal definitions

---

25   Dz.U. 1991. 95. 425 with amendments.
26   Dz.U. 1993. 7. 34 with amendments.
27   Dz.U. 2011. 21. 112 with amendments.
28   Dz.U. 2010. 47. 277 with amendments.

REGION, ETHNICITY AND POLITICS 43

of the terms used in the Act were used. One of them was the definition of nationality (para 6) as: "belonging to a national or ethnic group is understood as declarative, based on the subjective belief and individual characteristic of every person, explaining his/her emotional, cultural or ancestral connection to a specific nation or ethnic group". In the individual forms presented to the citizens in the surveys for the purpose of the Census, a list of nationalities (also beyond the recognised minorities and majority) was presented.

1.13   Region, Ethnicity and Politics – Conclusions

Ethnicity and politics are two entangled social phenomena. Both of them influence each other and the social order in a given society. This relationship is not always explicit and clear-cut – many other phenomena coincide with them and are sometimes hard to exclude from the study. The outcomes of this relationship, although diverse, are usually relevant for social order. The present study, which aims to discover the ways in which interaction between ethnicity and politics occurs and determine the outcomes thereof, must be interdisciplinary in nature and thorough. The summary presented below is not outlined in chronological order but is instead based on a study of the system that emerges from the relationship between these two social phenomena.

Firstly, there may be a relationship between ethnic and regionalist ideologies. In this case, when an ethnic group is concentrated on a specific territory, two kinds of interests and demands are raised. What they have in common is that they are usually voices of opposition against centralised and assimilatory politics. This is the case for the ethnic group because it represents a non-dominant culture, struggling to survive and resist assimilation, but also because ethnic lines may represent political lines of favour and discrimination. It is also a case for a regional community, because to effectively take part in the political decision-making process and distribution of resources in a centralised state, in many cases, it must demand its decentralisation and a vertical division of power.

Secondly, when an ethnic or regional community recognises that its interests are different from the interests of the centre (majority group), it aims at its articulation and puts forward demands. This is when ideology is developed. Ethnoregionalist ideology is a set of views about the state of conditions of life and experiences of an ethnic group – also constituting a regional community – that advocates for its interests and their legitimisation and promotion.

Thirdly, based on this ideology, political mobilisation might take place. If it is successful, a social movement emerges. At this point, ethnic conflict arises, which can assume different manifestations, including purely peaceful ones. A social movement becomes representative of the interests of a group. After some time, it can become institutionalised, and organisations, including political parties, may emerge from it. In this process, new political subjects arise. If the phenomenon is persistent, long-lasting and on a relevant scale, it leads to the highlighting of cleavages based on centre-periphery opposition. This is the moment when the political system of the state is changed and, consequently, a party system evolves. The political behaviours of people, at least to some extent, depend on ethnicity and solidarity within an ethnic group.

Lastly, these phenomena occurred and occur in many states, including those in Europe. Because it is always related to a less numerous, politically weaker and usually discriminated group, it requires legal protection. This is why international law in this field was developed. In heterogeneous societies, the only way to preserve social order is to develop ways in which different groups of people can coexist, regardless of their differences. This model allows society to stay intact and empower diverse groups of interests. Politics in such a society must allow for the representation of the ethnic majority and minorities through legal means, simultaneously preserving the existence of the society as a whole. This is why the role of the appropriate law is so crucial.

CHAPTER 2

Political Situation in Upper Silesia

2.1 Upper Silesia – Definition, Names, Borders

Upper Silesia is a part of the (macro-)region of Silesia. Today, Silesia is located in the south-western corner of Poland and the northern part of the Czech Republic (some scholars define a small part of the eastern territory of the Federal Republic of Germany as a part of Silesia as well). For a long time, Silesia was divided into two regions: Upper and Lower Silesia (with the border on the so-called *przesieka* – a natural, geographical division on a line from the point south-east from Nysa, along Nysa Kłodzka and Stobrawa to Prosna). But in the XX century, a new sub-region, Opolszczyzna or Śląsk Opolski, also called Mittle-Schlesien (Middle Silesia), started to be outlined in the middle between the two older regions. The complicated history of the region led to the creation of other divisions of the Upper Silesia region, firstly in the XVIII century after the Silesian Wars – Austrian Silesia and Prussian Silesia. Then, during the inter-war period the region was divided again into: Czech Upper Silesia, German Upper Silesia and Polish Upper Silesia.

Today, Upper Silesia can be defined as a region on its own. Still, it is divided into three administrative units, one of them in the Czech Republic – Moravskoslezký Kraj – and two of them in the Republic of Poland – the Opolskie and Śląskie Voivodeships. All of the units within Poland are urban rather than rural, especially the Śląskie Voivodeship (77% of the population lives in urban areas).[1] The people who live there are employed in industry (today, about a third) and more than half in services.[2] Still, it should be kept in mind that neither of these administrative units encompasses exclusively historical Upper Silesian territories. Moravskoslezký Kraj is a unit combining Moravian and Silesian lands, the Opolskie Voivodeship encompasses Lower Silesian territories as well, and the Śląskie Voivodeship encompasses territories of Małopolska (Lesser Poland): part of Wyżyna Krakowsko-Częstochowska (the Częstochowa part of the Polish Jura, called the Częstochowa Upland), Zagłębie Dąbrowskie (the Dąbrowa Basin) and Żywiecczyzna (the Żywiec Area).

---

1 GUS (Główny Urząd Statystyczny). 2018. "Ludność w miastach i na wsi".
2 GUS (Główny Urząd Statystyczny). 2017. "Pracujący w gospodarce narodowej według grup sekcji".

© ANNA MUŚ, 2022 | DOI:10.1163/9789004466456_004

It is extremely hard to point out the capital of the region. Historically, this role was played by Opole, Racibórz and Opava. Today, the biggest city of the region in the Republic of Poland is Katowice, the capital of the Śląskie Voivodeship, and in the Czech Republic, it is still Opava. The region has as many names as the languages used there are numerous. In Silesian, it is *Górny Ślūnsk* (also written: *Gůrny Ślůnsk* or *Wirchnie Ślōnsko*), in Czech – *Horní Slezsko*, in German – *Oberschlesien* and in Polish – *Górny Śląsk*. Historically, the Latin name – *Silesia Superior* – was also used. Most of the remarks presented below relate to Polish Upper Silesia, especially the Śląskie Voivodeship.

Silesia is and was a borderland, which changed its shape throughout the centuries. In the beginning, the name was used for the territories around Wrocław, but as early as the Middle Ages, it encompassed territories of more than a dozen duchies. Afterwards, the borders of the region changed in tandem with changes in the Kingdoms and then Republics to which it belonged. The distinction between Upper and Lower Silesia was already used in the Middle Ages. Today, the region of Upper Silesia is divided into two states and three administrative units. Still, the name 'Upper Silesia' is used for six sub-regions (Hannan 2005, 144): in the Czech Republic – Hulčin, Opava Silesia and part of Cieszyn Silesia (called by Poles *Zaolzie*); in Poland – Katowice Silesia, Opole Silesia and the rest of Cieszyn Silesia. However, a strict demarcation of the borders of these sub-regions themselves is controversial.

Upper Silesia is an ethnically and culturally diversified region. The majority of the population in Polish Upper Silesia consists of Poles. This identification is declared in the Opolskie Voivodeship by 88% of the population, whereas 82% declare it as the only one. In the Śląskie Voivodeship, the percentages are 91% and 82%, respectively. The second-biggest community consists of Silesians. This identification in the Opolskie Voivodeship is declared by 10.5% of the population, while 4% declare it as the only one. In the Śląskie Voivodeship, Silesian identification is declared by 16% of the population, while 7% declare it to be the only identification. The German national minority constitutes a smaller community. In the Opolskie Voivodeship, 8% of the population declares itself as German, while 3% declare it as their only identification. In the Śląskie Voivodeship, 1% of the population declare themselves as German, while only 0.2% see it as their only identification. Czechs constitute an even smaller minority in the Śląskie Voivodeship.[3]

---

3   GUS (Główny Urząd Statystyczny). 2015. "Tabl. 54 Ludność województw według identyfikacji narodowo-etnicznych w 2011 roku".

POLITICAL SITUATION IN UPPER SILESIA

The total population of the German minority in Poland was determined to be 147,814 (0.4% of the population of Poland), of which 144,238 (98%) people hold Polish citizenship.[4] Most of them live in the Opolskie (53%/78,595) and Śląskie (24%/35,187) Voivodeships.[5] The total population of Czechs in Poland was determined to be 3,447 (0.1% of the population of Poland), of which 2,833 (82%) hold Polish citizenship. The biggest concentration of the Czech minority is in the Śląskie Voivodeship (20%/704). The total population of Silesians in Poland was determined to be 846,719 (2.2% of the population of Poland), of which 846,192 (almost 100%) held Polish citizenship. Most Silesians live in the Śląskie (85%/722,143) and Opolskie (13%/106,375) Voivodeships.

The administrative units of the region play an active part in the creation of European regions and international relations at the regional level. The Pradziad-Pradĕdwas Euroregion was created in 1997, and the Opolskie Voivodeship, along with the Olomoucký Kraj (Czech), has been part of it ever since. The Silesia and Śląsk Cieszyński-Tĕšínské Slezsko Euroregions were created in 1998, and the Śląskie Voivodeship has taken part in this cooperation since the beginning, along with the Moravskoslezký Kraj (Czech). The Śląskie Voivodeship has been part of the Beskidy-Beskydy Euroregion since 2000, along with the Małopolskie Voivodeship, Slovakian Žilinský Kraj and the Czech Moravskoslezský Kraj. The Śląskie and Opolskie Voivodeships have been members of the European Grouping of Territorial Cooperation TRITIA since 2013.

2.2 Upper Silesia – Subregions

As was said above, Upper Silesia is an ethnically and culturally diversified region. But this diversification is not the only one. In general, the term 'Upper Silesia' is a simplification. Five sub-regions were highlighted above: Hulčin, Cieszyn Silesia, Katowice Silesia, Opava Silesia and Opole Silesia. The reason for this division and differences between sub-regions will now be elaborated.

Hulčin is situated between the city Opava in the west, the river Opava in the south, the river Odra in the east and Płaskowyż Głubczycki in the north. It was a part of the Duchy of Opava in the XIII century, and for many years, it shared the fate of Opava Silesia until the Silesian wars in the XVIII century. Then, in 1742, in the course of the First Silesian War, the Treaty of Breslau was negotiated

---

4 MSWiA (Ministerstwo Spraw Wewnętrznych i Administracji). n.d. "Charakterystyka mniejszości narodowych i etnicznych w Polsce".

5 GUS (Główny Urząd Statystyczny). 2015. "Tabl. 54 Ludność województw według identyfikacji narodowo-etnicznych w 2011 roku".

between Maria Teresa of the Habsburg dynasty and Frederick II Hohenzollern. While most of the Opava Silesia lands remained under Habsburg rule, the lands north from the Opava river were transferred to Prussia's rule. Thus, it became part of the so-called Prussian Silesia. In the XIX and at the beginning of the XX century, it is estimated that 90% of the population of Hulčin was ethnically Czech but used, as they themselves called it, the Moravian language and German language, and referred to themselves as *Moravci/Morawzen/Mährer* (Nowak 2011a). The sub-region was incorporated into Czechoslovakia in 1918 and was then annexed by Nazi Germany in 1938, along with the so-called Sudetenland after the Munich Agreement. Since 1945, Hulčin has been part first of Czechoslovakia and then of the Czech Republic. However, especially between 1945 and 1947, there was a border conflict between Czechoslovakia and the Republic of Poland over some of the land in the borderlands within Cieszyn Silesia and Hulčin. The definitive border treaty between both states was signed very late, in 1958. In 1945, in Hulčin, almost a third of the population declared German national identity, but in 1946, it was about 2%. This decrease mostly happened due to the evacuation at the end of the war, and then the expulsion carried out by the authorities after the war. Although a large part of the population left for Germany after the Second World War, some inhabitants stayed in Hulčin. However, during the time of the socialist regime in Czechoslovakia, they were put under pressure to assimilate, especially because the dominant confession in the sub-region had been Catholic.

This higher percentage of people belonging to the Catholic Church is still visible in two districts of Moravskoslezský Kraj, historically belonging to the Hulčin sub-region: Hulčin (32%) and Kravaře (44%) (while in the whole Czech Republic, it is 10%).[6] Inhabitants of Hulčin call themselves *Moravci* (from the Czech term *Morava*) or *Prajzáci* (from *prušáky* – inhabitants of Prussian Silesia, in contrast to *císařáků* – inhabitants of Austrian Silesia, especially Opava Silesia). This is why, although historically, Hulčin lands were connected to Silesian duchies, the inhabitants of this sub-region cannot be categorised as Silesians.

Cieszyn Silesia started to develop at the end of the XIII century, when the Duchy of Cieszyn was created (separate from the Opole-Racibórz Duchy). The borders of the sub-region are: in the west – the rivers Ostravica and Odra, in the north – the river Wisła, in the east – the river Biała and in the south – the mountains, Beskidy. Historically, it was first part of the Kingdom of Poland. Since the XIV century, the territory belonged to the Bohemian Crown and, later,

---

6   čsú (Český Statistický Úřad). 2014. "Náboženská víra obyvatel podle výsledků sčítání lidu".

POLITICAL SITUATION IN UPPER SILESIA

the Habsburg dynasty. *Prima facie*, its history is similar to other Upper Silesian lands, but this is not entirely true. Firstly, during its time in the Kingdom of Poland, under the Bohemian Crown and even under Habsburg rule, the Duchy was continuously ruled by dukes and duchesses from the Piast dynasty (from Mieszko I of Cieszyn – 1252–1315 – until the time of the last duchess – Elisabeth Lucretia – 1599–1653). Secondly, since the first half of the XVI century, the religion of the Duchy was Lutheran, but after the death of the duchess, when the Duchy fell under the direct rule of the Habsburg dynasty, Leopold I Habsburg led a grand, coercive Counter-Reformation programme which faced substantial resistance from his subjects in the second half of the XVII century (Spyra 2012, 44–56). Still, by the beginning of the XVII century, the repressions against the Protestants softened. Thirdly, after the Silesian Wars, it stayed under Habsburg rule, constituting part of Austrian Silesia (sometimes called East Silesia at the time). Fourthly, in 1910, Poles constituted 55% of its society, Czechs 27% and Germans 18%; at the same time, 22% of inhabitants were of Evangelic confession. Fifthly, before the Great War and during the war against the Austro-Hungarian Empire, two national movements – Polish and Czech – raised territorial demands, and the movements also started a dispute between themselves as to the rights of any nation to territories of Cieszyn Silesia. After the Great War and the dissolution of the Austro-Hungarian Empire, this led to border conflict between the II Republic of Poland and I Czechoslovak Republic, which ended in 1920 when Cieszyn Silesia was divided along the river Olza/Olša (after which, the territories of Cieszyn Silesia in the Czech Republic started to be called *Zaolzie* by Poles). Sixthly, it is not a unified sub-region, and differences between the Bielsko area (historically, along with villages around it, called 'the language island' because it was heavily populated by German-speaking inhabitants – about 20% of the population), the Cieszyn/Těšín area, the Frysztat/Fryštát area and the Frydek/Frýdek area.

This is why social divisions and the social landscape in Cieszyn Silesia are significantly different from other Upper Silesian lands. Historically, even until today, a dialect of the Polish language exists in the sub-region, which also differs from the Silesian language typical for Opole and Katowice Silesia. In Cieszyn Silesia, there is also a social, colloquial division between people who are from Cieszyn Silesia (*stela*) and came there later (*niestela*) (Bortliczek 2019). Furthermore, in opposition to Cieszyn Silesia and the idea that it is a unified sub-region, stands the area around Bielsko-Biała (not only historical Silesian lands but also lands belonging historically to Żywiecczyzna – historical Małopolska lands), which, in the XX century, started to be called *Podbeskidzie*, leaving the name of Cieszyn Silesia behind. Also, part of Cieszyn Silesia, which is called *Zaolzie* by Poles (part of the Cieszyn/Těšín, Frysztat/Fryštát and Frydek/Frýdek areas) is today significantly more under the influence of Czech culture. Inhabitants of Cieszyn Silesia (especially the Cieszyn/Těšín area) are sometimes called *cesaroki* or *cysaroki* (the name comes from the Polish word *cesarz* – the emperor – and signified subjects of the emperor from Habsburg dynasty; the second version comes from *cysorz* – a dialectical version of the word). The religious diversity also looks different in Cieszyn Silesia. In Poland, about 0.2% of the inhabitants declare themselves as Evangelicals of the Augsburg confession, in the Silesia Voivodeship, it is 1.1%,[7] and for the Cieszyński district, it is 18%.[8]

Opole Silesia is a sub-region of Upper Silesia with its western border on *przesieka*, southern border on the Eastern Sudetes, and northern border on the river Prosna. And what about the eastern border of the sub-region, the border with Katowice Silesia? Well, it is the hardest (perhaps even impossible) to define. This is because, historically, the heart of Upper Silesia in Poland was the Opole Duchy (XII–XIII century) and its eastern border was on the rivers Przemsza, Brynica and Liswarta. The problem is that this is the eastern border of Upper Silesia, which, in its eastern part, encompasses Katowice Silesia. So, the border between Opole Silesia and Katowice Silesia must be drawn more to the west. Still, it was not historically fixed, and I only attempt to draw a general demarcation line here. It would probably go a little bit to the west from the river Odra and then north from the river Ruda (resembling the western borders of the Duchy of Racibórz). Later, at the level of the Rybnickie lake, the border would go straight north all the way up to the river Liswarta (resembling the western borders of the State Country of Bytom). So, the lands west from this line would constitute Opole Silesia and east from it – Katowice Silesia. Historically, Opole Silesia, along with the Racibórz lands, was the centre of political power in the part of Upper Silesia that laid within the borders of the Kingdom of Poland. Later, in the XV century (when the lands were already part of the Bohemia Crown), the Duchy of Opole-Racibórz was partially restored, but within different borders. After the start of the XVI century, the Duchy was ruled directly by the Habsburg dynasty until 1742, when, in the course of the First Silesian War and the Treaty of Breslau, Opole Silesia became part of Prussian Silesia. After the Great War and the plebiscite, Opole Silesia remained a part of the Weimar Republic. It became part of Poland after 1945. In the years 1945–1949, it is estimated that about 0.5 million people were relocated

---

7 GUS (Główny Urząd Statystyczny). 2015. "Tabl. 74 Ludność województw według przynależności do wyznania religijnego w 2011 roku".

8 GUS (Główny Urząd Statystyczny). 2015. "Tabl. 75 Ludność powiatów według przynależności do wyznania religijnego".

to Germany (sometimes forcefully) from Silesia in Poland, and a large part of them was still living in Opole Silesia up until the end of the Second World War. It is estimated that after the Second World War, only about two-thirds of the population of Opole Silesia stayed in the sub-region (including some people with German national identification). Soon after the war, people from the so-called *Kresy Wschodnie* (the Polish eastern borderlands during the inter-war period; today, parts of Ukraine, Belarus and Lithuania) were relocated to Opole Silesia. Additionally, people from neighbouring voivodeships (Kieleckie and Krakowskie) moved to Opole Silesia.

Today, Opole Silesia can be characterised by the existence of a Silesian ethnic minority (about 10% of the population), German minority (about 8% of the population) and a group of Poles, whose families came from *Kresy Wschodnie* (Kisielewicz 2015). This is why we can distinguish at least a few social groups. *Kresowiacy/Kresowianie* is a term referring to people who came to Silesia from *Kresy*, but today, it is sometimes used for their descendants as well. The term *chadziaje* (from the term *chazjaj* used by *Kresowiacy* to signify the landlord) also refers to the same group of people. *Hanysy* is a term used in reference to people who can be considered Silesians. It comes from the German name Hans and demonstrates the close relationship between Silesian and German culture. Its opposite is the term *gorole* – people from outside Upper Silesia, not of Silesian origin, speaking the Polish language. It probably comes from the term *górale* – the Polish term for highlanders from Podhale and Żywiecczyzna – because historically, this was the first group of people who came to Upper Silesia in the early industrialisation era in great numbers, looking for jobs. Later, as groups from Central Poland and Galicja (Kielecczyzna and Małopolska) started to become more predominant migrant workers in industrial parts of Upper Silesia, the term evolved to *gorole*. Interestingly, nowadays, both terms are used in Upper Silesia, and the term *górale* (nowadays used only for highlanders) is less pejorative than *gorole* (nowadays used for the rest of the Poles). Furthermore, aside from the Silesian culture and German minority culture (including bi-lingual names), a distinctive culture (especially traditions and collective memory) is cultivated by Kresowiacy and is still present in the sub-region.

I have purposefully left two sub-regions of Upper Silesia for the end. The borders of Katowice Silesia were already described above in the section on Opole Silesia. Both sub-regions also share a history but for a few differences. The first should probably be the existence of the State Country of Bytom (Kuzio-Podrucki 2014) and the State Country of Pszczyna (Polak 2014), which together constituted the better part of Katowice Silesia. Additionally, Katowice Silesia is known as a land rich in minerals, metals, coal and mining. Indeed, the first gold mines existed there as early as the XIV century and the first mines of silver in the XII century. Lead, copper, solder and iron were also acquired there in the late Middle Ages. Already in the XIII century, mining had transformed from open-pit mining to shaft mining. In the XV century, ironworks were established in the area. Also, in the XIII-XIV century, the miners started to change from farmers working from time to time in mines to professional miners, gathered in organisations resembling guilds, and their work was based on a set of regulations. Still, because farming was the main branch of the economy at the time, the region was rather poor. The situation started to change in the XVI century with reforms applied in the State Country of Bytom and the Duchy of Opole-Racibórz, which revived and grew the industry in the sub-region. In the XVI century, coal mines were established in Katowice Silesia, but this branch of mining only developed fully in the XVIII century, later becoming the trademark of the region. The economic growth of the region in the XVIII and XIX centuries and large-scale industrialisation and urbanisation projects led to the transformation of the sub-region into a modern, profitable land, and one of its most valuable resources was black coal. New ironworks were also established in the XVIII century in the sub-region. Along with industrialisation, new technologies came to the region: the steam engine, railways and, typical for this sub-region landscape, nearby industrial facilities built by large cities and their residential districts (e.g., the city Königshütte – today part of the city Chorzów – was built near the mine *König* and the ironwork *Königshütte*). Also, today's centre of the sub-region, Katowice, gained an important role in the XIX century when the railway was built and the headquarters of the growing industrial complex was located there (Greiner 2011). At the same time, the traditions, privileges and specific lifestyle of miners and their families evolved into the forms known until the second half of the XX century. In the inter-war period, most of the sub-region became part of the II Republic of Poland as the *Śląskie Województwo Autonomiczne* (Silesian Autonomous Voivodeship). After the Second World War, the whole sub-region was incorporated into Poland, and its autonomous status was revoked. Similar to Opole Silesia, many inhabitants of German origin left the sub-region during the evacuation at the end of the war, were expelled after the war by authorities or left on their own.

Today, Katowice Silesia is in one voivodeship with parts of three sub-regions of Małopolska – *Wyżyna Krakowsko-Częstochowska, Zagłebie Dąbrowskie* and *Żywiecczyzna*. Still, more than 15% of its inhabitants declare themselves as Silesians, and the population of the German minority constitutes 1% of the total population. However, the historical eastern border on the river Brynica (between Silesia and Zagłebie Dąbrowskie) is still symbolically present in prejudices and today symbolises the difference between groups of people living on

POLITICAL SITUATION IN UPPER SILESIA 53

its western riverbank – *hanysy* – and on its eastern riverbank – *gorole*. But for people from neighbouring sub-regions, there are additional pejorative names. People from the Częstochowa area are sometimes called *medalikorze* (a reference to a religious medallion – Częstochowa is one of the most important centres of Catholic Church in Poland) by Silesians, while *Zagłymbioki* is a term used for people from Zagłębie Dąbrowskie. Katowice Silesia is also home to the Upper Silesian ethnoregionalist movement and a witness to the revival of the Silesian language, which is used more and more often in the public space.

Opava Silesia's western and southern borders lie on the rivers Biele, Moravice and Odra, which also constitutes its eastern border, while the northern border is mountains – Sudets. Opava Silesia is also a complex sub-region. The Duchy of Opava was separated from Moravia in the XIII century and, for a time, belonged to one of the lines of the Přemyslid dynasty. In the XV century, the Duchy was ruled by Jiří z Kunštátu a Poděbrad, and his son. Later, in the XVI century, it belonged to the duke of the Duchy of Cieszyn. In the XVII century, it was given to Karl I, Prince of Lichtenstein. Within the Duchy of Opava, the Duchy of Krnov was also a separate Duchy (which, for a time, belonged to the House of Hohenzollern), but it was merged with Duchy of Opava into one Duchy by Karl I. In the XVIII century, the Hohenzollern titles to lands in the Krnov, Racibórz and Opole areas were one of the motives for the attack of the King of Prussia, Frederick II, on Silesia. Still, most of Opava Silesia remained under the rule of the Habsburg dynasty after the Treaty of Breslau (1742). The sub-region belonged to Austrian Silesia, and Opava became its capital. During the inter-war period and after the Second World War, Opava Silesia was a part of the I Czechoslovak Republic. After the Second World War, the Germans left the sub-region during an evacuation, were expelled from what can be called Czech Silesia (Opava Silesia, part of Cieszyn Silesia and Hulčin) by the new authorities or left on their own. Work camps and relocation camps were also created for people of German origin (Nowak 2011b). All in all, the German population of Czech Silesia was reduced significantly by up to 80%.

The lands around Bruntál/Freudenthal in Schlesien should also be described separately because the area was separated from the Duchy of Krnov in the XV century. It first belonged to the Lords of Vrbno and Bruntál and then was given by the emperor Ferdinand II to the Teutonic Order (one of the reasons for this was the Counter-Reformation actions undertaken by the Habsburgs). However, those lands were still considered part of Austrian Silesia. This status quo lasted until the inter-war period. Most of the population of the area was German, and it was annexed by Nazi Germany in 1938 along with the so-called Sudetenland after the Munich Agreement. In 1945, by the decree of the President, Edvard Beneš, the Teutonic Order was dispossessed. Today, in Opava Silesia, a German minority still exists, though it is not numerous. The population of Opava Silesia is mostly Czech and Moravian, with only a few people declaring themselves to be Silesian. The distinctiveness of the sub-region within the Czech Republic is mostly based on the historical region and tradition of the existence of the regional community.

2.3 Upper Silesia – Historical Remarks

As a border region, Silesia has witnessed many border shifts and formed part of three different states in its history.[9] The core of the population has remained in its family motherland, but each historical event brought new waves of migrants and immigrants. This is why the Silesian community was multicultural from early on in its existence (Kamusella 2007, 7). Some historians claim that Silesia became part of the Great Moravia State in the IX century, although this is still disputed. Certainly, during the process of the formation of the first Slavic states in Central Europe in the X century, most of the Silesian region became part of the Duchy of Poland, which was ruled by the Piast dynasty. In the XII-XIII century, during the Polish Fragmentation, the Silesian branch of the Piast dynasty constituted one of the most powerful of all the Polish duchies. At the same time, the first wave of German colonisation began.

In the XIV century, Silesian dukes pledged their reverence and submission to John the Blind (Luxemburg). King Casimir the Great (Kazimierz Wielki) confirmed this in 1356 in Prague, and the Duchy of Silesia became part of the Kingdom of Bohemia. At the end of the XV century, Silesia, like other Bohemian and Hungarian territories, was ruled by the Jagiellonian dynasty, with King Vladislaus (Władysław) II at the helm. It was also a time when many Silesian lords and their people became Protestant. After 1526, according to the Vienna treaty (1515), Czech and Hungarian lands came under Habsburg domination. After the Silesian wars (1740–1763), this region was divided into two: Austrian and Prussian. In the XIX century, a boom in industrialisation began. The industrial landscape became a symbol of the region. Although the upper tiers of society were German, workers and farmers were still Slaves, and their language at the time was referred to by the Germans as 'wasserpolnisch', mainly because it differed from the high Polish of the inhabitants of central Poland. In the XIX century, the German administration launched Kulturkampf, a programme

---

9 The remarks below refer mostly to the part of Upper Silesia that is today within the Republic of Poland.

POLITICAL SITUATION IN UPPER SILESIA

originally aimed against the Catholic Church, while in the regions under German control, the programme was directed against Polish culture as well (Popiołek 1972, 70–165).

During the Great War, most of the inhabitants of Silesia fought for the German Army. Conversely, Polish-orientated groups saw the emergence of nationalist movements. After the war, during the Vienna Peace Conference, the question of Silesia (mostly Upper Silesia) was the cause of conflict between Germany, Poland and Czechoslovakia, which were under construction at the time. In 1919, the decision to hold a plebiscite was taken: most of the region was to decide on their state membership in a vote in accordance with the self-determination principle. The first military conflict in Upper Silesia in 1919 was spurred by social issues as well as national affiliation conflicts. The next military conflict in Upper Silesia in 1920 was a result of an aggressive Polish and German nationalist campaign before the plebiscite to make Silesians decide whether they were Polish or German (although most of them did not feel any national affiliation). The vote took place in 1921, but its results did not satisfy the parties, and a third military conflict in Upper Silesia broke out in May. Then, in 1921, the League of Nations ended the border conflict by granting Lower Silesia and parts of Upper Silesia to Germany and the rest to Poland. Additionally, in 1918, the conflict between the newly restored Republic of Poland and the Republic of Czechoslovakia began. The object of the conflict was the borderland territories of Upper Silesia (mostly Cieszyn Silesia), which were interesting to both states. Initially, the idea of a plebiscite was suggested, but in the end, the League of Nations and both parties agreed to leave the decision to the Conference of Ambassadors, which was to draw a demarcation line. The decision was made on 28 July 1920 (Masnyk 2011, 219–238). The *Constitutional Act that included the Organic Statute for the Śląskie Voivodeship* was adopted on 15 July 1920, and it provided future Silesian authorities with legislative, administrative and fiscal powers (Ciągwa 1988). It came into force in 1922 in the part of the region that became the Polish Śląskie Voivodeship (part of Upper Silesia). After 1922, many officials and workers came to Silesia from central Poland. They depreciated Silesian speech and culture, and most Silesians felt that their position in their own home-region was under threat (Wanatowicz 2011, 239).

On 1 September 1939, the Second World War, which was also waged in Silesia, broke out. The German Army occupied most of the region of Silesia by 3 September. In 1939, these lands became part of the Third Reich. The Deutsche Volksliste was introduced in 1941, and many Silesians were compelled to sign and were given a category (most of them were given III group) (Kaczmarek 2011, 255–260). Some Silesians took an active part in the Nazi regime, but it was not a dominant group. The region was exploited by the military industry and underwent partial destruction during the war. In the winter of 1945, the Soviet army took over Silesia from Nazi occupation (Czapliński 2002, 408–425). Afterwards, heavy repressions on civilians took place: many Silesians were incarcerated, sent to work camps, dispossessed and publicly humiliated. They were treated as Germans or a 'nationally uncertain element'. The years 1945–1950 are referred to as the so-called Upper Silesia Tragedy (Dziurok 2015, 9). Also, at this time, a migration of people from Silesia to Germany (also referred to as resettlement) took place. This was followed by the forced resettlement of people from Galicja and Wołyń – the border-regions of Poland and Ukraine – to Silesia. The composition of Silesian society had radically changed (Dziurok & Linek 2011, 271–275).

During the regime of the Polish Peoples' Republic (1945–1989), the region was used as an industrial base for Poland. Industrialisation progressed gradually. Silesians, their culture and language began to disappear due to a programme aimed at making Poland a mono-ethnic state. The fact that Silesians differed from the Poles inhabiting central Poland was the reason for repressions (prohibition of the use of the Silesian language at schools, a new narration of Silesian history and destroying German cultural heritage along with any signs of Silesian culture, with the exception of state-controlled folklore).

The separate administrative units encompassing the Polish Upper Silesia region were already present during the Polish Fragmentation, when several duchies existed in the territory. However, after becoming part of the Bohemia Crown, it was unified. Afterwards, during Prussian rule, a new administrative unit emerged, followed by changes in the administrative regime. In 1815–1922, Upper Silesia became part of the *Regierungsbezirk Oppeln* (German administration). Starting in 1922, part of it became the Silesian Autonomous Voivodeship (Polish administration). After the Second World War, another part was also included in the so-called 'Regained Lands' – former German lands given under Polish administration as a result of the Berlin Declaration from 2 August 1945. In 1946, the Śląskie Voivodeship was created (also referred to as the Śląsko-Dąbrowskie Voivodeship at the time). In 1950, its name was changed to the Katowickie Voivodeship. In 1975, it was divided into three voivodeships: Bielskie, Katowickie and Częstochowskie. Since 1998 (in force since 1999), the newly created Śląskie Voivodeship has covered the core part of it.[10] As to the Opolskie Voivodeship, in 1946, the Wrocławskie Voivodeship was created, and, at the same time, some of the districts from Opolskie became

---

10   *Basic Three-level Territorial Division of the State Act* from 24 July 1998. Dz.U. 1998. 96. 603 with amendments.

POLITICAL SITUATION IN UPPER SILESIA 57

part of the Śląskie Voivodeship. In 1950, the Opolskie Voivodeship was created. In 1975, a single Voivodeship covering lands of Middle Silesia was created in its place, also called the Opolskie Voivodeship. The borders of the Opolskie Voivodeship today were created in 1998. The debate on the borders of Upper Silesia in Poland still continues. Nevertheless, as a region, it is an important base for the Silesian movement. Regional borders, based on the regional and ethnic identity of its inhabitants and restoration of the autonomy for the region, are core demands in a contemporary political debate concerning the region.

2.4 Inter-War Period in the Silesian Autonomous Voivodeship

Even before the Great War, the conflict between the rising Polish and German nationalisms was growing in Upper Silesia, and both sides achieved moderate success (Gehrke 2011, 212–213). But a bigger part of society was referred to as 'nationally indifferent' (Karch 2018) and 'local' (Wanatowicz 2004, 153) and had no connection to either national movement. This group can be referred to as Silesians or Upper Silesians. After the Great War, at the Peace Conference in Paris in 1919 (but even as early as 1918), a political conflict between Czechoslovakia, Germany and Poland was waged for these territories (Szpotański 1922, 65–66). To resolve the conflict, the British Prime Minister, Lloyd George, suggested holding a plebiscite, which was contested by Germany and Poland. In the end, the decision to organise the plebiscite was set in art. 88 of the Annex to Section VIII, Part III *Treaty of Peace between the Allied and Associated Powers and Germany*, signed in Versailles on 28 June 1919.[11]

However, the tension between the German and Polish movements in Upper Silesia was so high that it led to military conflicts in Upper Silesia in 1919 and 1920. Radicalism and aggressive campaigns were constantly present prior to the plebiscite (Masnyk 2011, 224). To gain an advantage, the parties to the conflict offered new political solutions for the territory of the plebiscite. As early as 17 September 1919, the Prussian Landtag adopted an Act, which created the provinces of Lower and Upper Silesia. On 16 May 1920, Reichrat (the Council of the Reich) passed a resolution proposing that within two months from the German administration taking over the region, a referendum should be held to decide whether Upper Silesia should remain part of Prussia or become an

---

11   See: Library of Congress. n.d. "Treaty of Peace between the Allied and Associated Powers and Germany".

independent land. The referendum was held on 3 September 1922, and the majority voted that the region should remain part of Prussia (Schattkowsky 1994). The opponent – the Republic of Poland – adopted the *Constitutional Act that included the Organic Statute for the Śląskie Voivodeship* on 15 July 1920.[12]

By that time, when both nation-states were proposing different offers and promises, a new idea was raised and voiced: 'Silesia for Silesians' (Szramek 1934, 35; Schattkowsky 1994). In the region, three political groups were present at the time: Poles, who agitated for Poland, Germans, who agitated for Germany, and indigenous Silesians, who were at least partially nationally indifferent (Karch 2018). Few organisations were established by that time. In 1919, the Związek Górnoślązaków – Bund der Oberschlesier (Alliance of Upper Silesians) was founded in Bytom. Its initiators were Ewald Latacz and the brothers Jan and Tomasz Reginek, who promoted adding a third question to the plebiscite, which was to be about the creation of the independent Free Region of Upper Silesia (Wolny Górny Śląsk – Freeistaat Oberschlesien) (Kulik 2014). It was also an attempt to maintain the unity of the region at a time when the representatives of the Entant had already agreed to the division of the region.

After the plebiscite in 1921, no one was content with the results. In May, the third Silesian military conflict broke out. This conflict was an attempt to change the decision concerning the demarcation line proposed by international institutions. But some politically active citizens proposed peaceful solutions, such as holding a new plebiscite with a third option – an alternative, which included the creation of a bi-national micro-state in Upper Silesia (Szramek 1934, 26). Although this did not happen, the mere emergence of such ideas could be referred to as the first Silesian political awakening.

At the same time, in Cieszyn Silesia, the *Śląska Partia Ludowa* [śPL] (Silesian Peoples Party) (founded in 1909) become a popular political force. Its leader, Józef Kożdoń (Josef Koždoň), became the mayor of the Czech part of Cieszyn (which lay inside the borders of Czechoslovakia) from 1921 to 1938 (until the Polish military invasion on Zaolzie). In 1938, the śPL was removed from the list of legal organisations.

The Autonomous Silesian Voivodeship (the Polish part of Upper Silesia) became part of the Republic of Poland on 20 June 1922. The new political system introduced in 1920 by the *Constitutional Act including the Organic Statute for the Silesian Voivodeship* from 15 July 1920 immediately came into effect. It created three autonomous institutions: the *Sejm Śląski* (Silesian Parliament), the *Rada Wojewódzka* (Voivodeship Council) and the *Skarb Śląski* (Silesian

---

12   Dz.U. 1920. 73. 497.

Treasury). The *Sejm Śląski* gained legislative competences in many areas of life, but the most important right invested in it was the right to create and adopt a Constitution for the Voivodeship, which was to be later signed by the President of the Republic of Poland (although this never happened). The Silesian Parliament was also competent to decide which Polish Acts and Laws would apply in the Voivodeship (in the area of its competences). The Voivodeship Council was an executive organ, with a representative delegated by the Polish Executive at its head. The Silesian Treasury was a fiscal organ. It is estimated that three-quarters of the wealth generated in the voivodeship remained in the voivodeship (Wolny 1920). In the area of judicature, an administrative branch was created separately for the Śląskie Voivodeship. The autonomy status was annulled by the communist authorities on 6 May 1945 by the *Constitutional Act Annulling the Organic Statute for the Silesian Voivodeship*,[13] but it had ceased to exist *de facto* since the beginning of the Second World War. What is interesting is that in the original wording of the *Constitutional Act including the Organic Statute for the Silesian Voivodeship* from 20 July 1920, changes in the scope of legislative powers or self-government of regional authorities demanded the consent of the *Sejm Śląski* (art. 44). This was changed by art. 81 para. 3 of the *Constitution of the Republic of Poland* from 23 April 1935. Art. 44 now stated that from then on, changes to the *Organic Statute* could be introduced by a State Act, and this article in the changed form was used by communist authorities in the Act from 6 May 1945.

Still, there was no uniform vision of how the autonomy in the voivodeship was to work. In the period from 1922 to 1926 (the Piłsudski *coup d'etat*), the Christian Democrats formed the main political force in the Silesian Parliament, headed by the leader of the Uprising and main politician during the time of the plebiscite, Wojciech Korfanty. In that time, the main ideology consisted of the need to unify the Śląskie Voivodeship with the rest of the state, leaving the idea of autonomy as a temporary measure for the voivodeship (Marcoń 2009, 79). After 1926, autonomy became the main point of contention between the opposition (ChD) and a new political force – *Sanacja* (Sanation), represented by the voivode, Michał Grażyński. While Grażyński believed that autonomy should be reformed and changed in accordance with the requirements of a new political system in Poland, the opposition tried to adhere to the existing rights and laws as closely as possible to avoid losing the shred of political independence the voivodeship had despite the centralisation and unification policy of the *Sanacja* (Marcoń 2009, 81). The main tool of political conflict became

---

13   Dz.U. 17. 92. 1945.

60 CHAPTER 2

the need to pass the "Silesian Constitution", constituting an act defining the organisation of the main Silesian institutions and the relationships existing between them (Marcoń 2009, 62–69). The split between the political forces was so deep that, in the end, the new law was never passed.

2.5 Silesian Harm (or Upper Silesian Harm)

One of the most important social phenomena connected to the collective memory of the indigenous population of Upper Silesia – the Silesians (mostly in the area historically referred to as Prussian Upper Silesia and later, Polish Upper Silesia) – is the so-called 'Silesian harm' or 'Silesian injustice'. The collective memory, in this case, should be seen as a narration about the past, the process of its reproduction and interpretation (Kansteiner 2002, 188). "Tadeusz Kijonka, a local poet and – what is important for us – an activist engaged in the protection of Silesian culture, long ago expressed his views about the issue, stating that: the so-called <Silesian harm> (...), one can long talk about old resentments, complexes and complications of this issue. It is not a new issue, and even more, it is not a problem that is easy to solve. Because of this, it is worth revisiting accurate and thorough diagnoses (...) from the years before the Second World War (...) warning of the impending downfall. This can be followed by an assessment of the old prejudices and accusations of separatism. Afterwards, the war added fire to old accusations of separatism, particularism and national indifference of a significant part of the population, which created new dramatic barriers, resentments and divisions, perfidiously exploited by manipulators and dodgers (...). It was accompanied by (...) a neglecting attitude towards local traditions, expressed by different sorts of 'kulturtragers'" (Kijonka 1988 after Gerlich 1994, 5; my translation). 'Kulturtrager' is a name used in Upper Silesia and comes from the German word 'Kulturträger', meaning a carrier of culture, a person who imposes culture and values on other communities or who transmits culture.

The Silesian harm is a phenomenon connected to the past of the region: its complications, lack of stability and dynamic changes in social structure. Until recently, the Silesian narration about the phenomenon was only communicated unofficially – intimately, usually within a family (Copik 2014, 35). This is why the collective memory of Silesians can be described as a 'secretive memory', hidden from public discourse (Hajduk-Nijakowska 2010, 74). At the same time, it is one of the most powerful factors of integration within the ethnic group (Wanatowicz 2004, 212). This memory survived for generations in the indigenous population of Upper Silesia. It became an element of the

POLITICAL SITUATION IN UPPER SILESIA · 61

auto-identification of those who did not live during the times and events leading to the emergence of the Silesian harm (Czapliński 2006, 65). It seems as if new layers of interpretation and resentment were laid throughout the time, and each generation saw the Silesian harm differently, though its core was still not forgotten.

Some scholars, such as Michał Smolorz (2013, 118), date the genesis of the phenomena as early as the XVII century, when Silesian lands were destroyed and transformed during the Counter-Reformation lead by the Habsburg dynasty. Another author, Marek Czapliński, sees its beginning in the XVIII century, when the Silesian region became part of Moravia and lost its privileges as a 'Kraj' administrative unit (2006, 60). It seems more likely, though, that for the average Silesian, it was not until the inter-war period that the feelings of harm became visible and conscious. This was the time of the plebiscite, the military conflict in Upper Silesia and the hatred shown by both sides in the conflict, which was based on national affiliation. The community, which had existed more or less peacefully before the Great War and had prospered, was influenced by nationalism after the war (Czech, Polish and German) to the extent that it affected most parts of everyday life (Novikov 2015). Then, after 1922, in Polish Upper Silesia, waves of immigrants came from other parts of Poland with different cultural baggage, a 'pure Polish' culture and a lack of knowledge about the Upper Silesian social environment. After the Second World War, the alienation and conflict between the Silesian and non-Silesian parts of society in this territory were strengthened by prosecutions connected to the *Deutsche Volksliste*, the relocation of a large part of the population from former Polish territories in the east, and the Communist Party policy, which favoured people from Zagłębie Dąbrowskie, who were already traditionally disliked by Silesians (due to regional labour migration, which dated back to the XIX century).

"Today, the so-called Silesian harm is fuel for protest movements, which manifest their disagreement with what is happening in Silesia".[14] Thus the role of this phenomenon was summarised by journalist Marek Twaróg, and one cannot but agree with his statement. The feeling of harm had turned into a strength, which aimed to change the social and political situation of the population of Upper Silesia. This evolution is outlined by Elżbieta Anna Sekuła, who recognised the emergence of the 'RAŚ generation' (2009, 358). This is a generation of young people, who declare themselves to be Silesians, aim to change the political status of their group and region, live in the Silesian culture, use the Silesian language and, above all, are proud of it. It is thanks to them that

---

14   My translation.

Silesian social and political movements thrive and have gained the ability to advocate for the interests of Silesians. This can be observed in the rising number of Silesian ethnic (or national) declarations in support of Silesian autonomy and initiatives aimed at the recognition of the Silesian minority. But the growing bonds of solidarity, understanding of common interests and a need for their articulation, promotion of culture and language, as well as the growing number of Silesian events, are also indicators that something has changed in the region. Today, being Silesian has turned into a strength, not a weakness.

2.6   Upper Silesia as a Periphery

Pursuant to the *Basic Three-level Territorial Division of the State Act* from 1998, two administrative units were created in the territory of historical Upper Silesia: the Opolskie and Śląskie Voivodeships. Also, on the local level, a series of districts and municipalities were introduced as administrative units. Art. 15 para. 1 of the *Constitution of the Republic of Poland* states: "the territorial system of the Republic of Poland shall ensure the decentralization of public power". This article relating to self-government is specified in Art. 163: "local government shall perform public tasks not reserved by the Constitution or statutes to the organs of other public authorities". It should be recalled that in Polish legal terminology, the term 'local' refers only to districts and municipalities. Therefore, regional institutions of self-government (voivodeship institutions) do not lie within its scope. Territorial self-government has become part of public authority, not as a sovereign, but based solely on statutory law (Kociński 2007, 11). It was also recognised by the doctrine that the legal presumption of the authority of self-government does not encompass acts of *iure imperii*, which need specific justification in material law (Kociński 2007, 14). A further limitation is related to the territorial scope of its authority.

Pursuant to the *Municipality Self-Government Act* from 1990,[15] the scope of the authority of the municipality encompasses all public affairs on the local level if they are not in the scope of the authority of other organs (art. 6). The organs of the municipality include the council and *wójt/prezydent miasta* (one-person executive organ) (art. 11a). Pursuant to the *District Self-Government Act* from 1998,[16] district authorities can only act in the scope of the defined public affairs entrusted to them (art. 4). There is no legal presumption in the Act as to

---

15   Dz.U. 1990.16. 95 with amendments.
16   Dz.U. 1998. 91. 578 with amendments.

its authority. Organs of the district include the council and the executive, with the *starosta* at its head (art. 8). The organs of self-government on the regional level include the *Sejmik* (regional council) and the executive, with a *Marszałek* at its head (art.15).[17] The governmental (centralised administration) organ of the Voivode also represents the state government and its affairs in the region.[18] Self-government institutions pursuant to the *Voivodeship Self-Government Act* from 1998 encompass in their scope of authority all public affairs on the voivodeship level that do not lie within the scope of the authority of governmental administration (art. 2). The scope of activity of the organs belonging to this unit are mostly administrative (art. 11, art. 14). The Sejmik can determine the main goals of international cooperation and take part in international regional associations. The foreign policy of the voivodeship must be in accordance with the state policy and lie within the scope of its competences (art. 75, art. 76).

In the scope of their authority, local and regional organs can issue enactments of local law. They are foreseen by the Constitution in art. 87 as: "a source of universally binding law of the Republic of Poland in the territory of the organ issuing such enactments". The municipality, district and voivodeship can issue such enactments regarding their own organisation and associated issues. Additional competences rest with the municipality and district in situations requiring special acts to restore public order. In this case, such enactments may be issued (art. 40 of *Municipality Self-Government Act* and art. 41 *District Self-Government Act*, respectively).

Pursuant to the *Incomes of Units of Territorial Self-Government Act* from 2003, the incomes of units of territorial self-government include: own income, general subsidies, purpose grants, funds from foreign sources (non-refundable), funds from the budget of the EU and other sources (art. 3).[19] For the purpose of the present study, only own income will be further elaborated. In this category, we can find the following sub-units: share of public income from taxes and fees, income of institutions established by the unit, income from the assets of the unit, inheritances and donations, interest and others (art. 4, art. 5 and art. 6). The share of the overall income was 49.7% in municipalities, 63.5% in cities, 33.5% in districts and 41.8%[20] in voivodeships. In the case of the Śląskie Voivodeship, 53.3% of revenue constituted own income (including EU and

---

17   Dz.U. 1998. 91. 576 with amendments.
18   Dz.U. 2009. 31. 206 with amendments.
19   Dz.U. 2003. 203. 1966 with amendments.
20   GUS (Główny Urząd Statystyczny). 2015. "Tabl. 9. Wpływy z podatków PIT i CIT w dochodach jednostek samorządu terytorialnego".

foreign funds).[21] In the case of the Opolskie Voivodeship, 47.2% of the revenue constituted own income (including EU and foreign funds).[22] On the basis of these numbers, it is easy to see that voivodeships are dependent on centralised public financing in their activities. Still, the Śląskie Voivodeship produces 13% of the Polish GDP, while the Opolskie Voivodeship produces 2%.[23]

Elections, which take place in Poland, pursuant to the *Electoral Code* from 2011 art.1, include:

- elections to the Sejm and Senat (every four years),
- presidential elections (every five years),
- elections to the European Parliament (every four years),
- elections to self-government bodies (every four years),
- elections of the municipal executive (wójt/prezydent miasta) (every five years).[24]

Pursuant to the *Electoral Code*, during elections to the Sejm, electoral districts are created (at least seven deputies are chosen in each), which can encompass the whole territory of a voivodeship or part of it. Their borders cannot cross the borders of districts and voivodeships (art. 201). Lists of candidates can be submitted by the political party electoral committee, the coalition electoral committee or electoral committees of voters. There were six electoral districts in the last election (2015) in the Śląskie Voivodeship (65 deputies were elected there) and one in the Opolskie Voivodeship (12 deputies).[25] The electoral threshold for the lists of a single party or committee of voters is set to 5% and 8% for coalitions (art. 196).

Pursuant to the *Electoral Code*, in the elections to the Senate, the whole territory of Poland is divided into 100 districts, and only one senator is elected in each of them. The borders of the electoral districts cannot cross those of districts created for the purpose of the elections to the Sejm (art. 260). Candidates can be proposed by political party electoral committees, coalition electoral committees or electoral committees of voters. In the last elections (2015), 13 senators were elected in the Śląskie Voivodeship, and three senators were elected in the Opolskie Voivodeship.[26]

---

21   Tabl. III Dochody budżetu o województwa śląskiego w 2015 roku, Sprawozdanie roczne z wykonania budżetu województwa śląskiego w 2015 roku, załącznik 1 do uchwały nr 541/103/V/2016 Zarządu Województwa Śląskiego z dnia 23 marca 2016 roku, at 113.

22   Sprawozdanie roczne z wykonania budżetu województwa opolskiego w 2015 roku, załącznik do uchwały nr 1887/2016 Zarządu Województwa Opolskiego z dn. 28 marca 2016 roku, at 9.

23   GUS (Główny Urząd Statystyczny). 2015. "Produkt Krajowy Brutto".

24   *Electoral Code* from 5 January 2011. Dz.U. 2011. 21. 112 with amendments.

25   PKW (Państwowa Komisja Wyborcza). 2015. "Wyniki wyborów do Sejmu RP 2015".

26   PKW (Państwowa Komisja Wyborcza). 2015. "Wyniki wyborów do Senatu 2015".

Pursuant to the *Electoral Code*, in presidential elections, the whole state constitutes an electoral district. Candidates for the office of president require the signature of at least 100,000 citizens (art. 296). Pursuant to the *Electoral Code*, during elections to the European Parliament, more than one deputy can be elected in every electoral district (art. 328). Electoral districts can be created from one or more voivodeship or from its part (art. 340). The threshold is 5% (art. 335). In the elections of 2014, the Śląskie Voivodeship constituted one electoral district (seven deputies elected), and the Opolskie Voivodeship created an electoral district with the Dolnośląskie Voivodeship (six deputies were elected).

During the elections to self-government bodies (municipality, district and voivodeship councils), pursuant to the *Electoral Code*, electoral districts encompass parts of a municipality (art. 417). In municipalities that are not cities, one person is chosen in every district, while in cities that have the competences of a district, five to ten people are chosen (art. 418). In this case, committees must achieve at least 5% of the votes in the city (art. 416). Lists of candidates can be submitted by political party committees, coalition committees, organisation committees or electoral committees of voters (art. 399). Electoral districts are also created in elections to districts, with three to ten persons chosen in each of them (art. 453). In elections to the Sejmik, a district or districts constitute an electoral district (art. 462). In each, five to 15 persons are chosen (art. 463). Seven districts were created in the Śląskie Voivodeship and five in the Opolskie Voivodeship.[27]

For the purpose of elections to the office of wójt/prezydent miasta, the whole municipality (city) forms an electoral district. Candidates can be proposed by political party committees, coalition committees, organisation committees or electoral committees of voters (art. 478).

In sum, voivodeships were created in Poland without regard for historical and cultural regions. They have a connection to them only occasionally (e.g. by way of the name). As a result, in the case of administration, public finances and elections, we can speak only about artificial administrative units, not about regions, which complicates clarity of thought. In general, self-government units are entrusted with some administrative competences and share in public authority, but only to a small extent. Furthermore, they are financially dependent on centralised public funds. In elections to European and central Polish institutions, the influence of territory depends on the size of the population. This is why the Śląskie Voivodeship, with a population of

---

27   PKW (Państwowa Komisja Wyborcza). 2014. "Wyniki wyborów samorządowych – Sejmiki".

4,630,366 (12.0% of the state population) and the Opolskie Voivodeship, with a population of 1,016,212 (2.6% of the state population)[28] have significant political potential – 17% of deputies to the Sejm and 16% of senators are elected from these voivodeships.

2.7 Upper Silesians

The first problem to be addressed rests with the name of this population. The group lives in the region of Upper Silesia and, as was already mentioned, the region constitutes only a part of the wider region of Silesia. It would seem that the group should consequently be called 'Upper Silesians', and indeed, some scholars use this name. However, the popular belief, which is shared by some scholars, is that the common name for this group is 'Silesians'. Such an approach can be justified primarily due to the fact that the term 'Lower Silesians' is not used. This is why, in the remainder of the study, both names (Silesians and Upper Silesians) are used interchangeably, without any prejudice. The group refers to itself as *Ślūnzoki/Ślonzoki* (in some parts *Szlonzoki*), while the Czech name for the group is *Slezané*, the German name *Schlesier*, and the Polish name is *Ślązacy*.

In Poland, there is endless debate about the identity and status of the Silesians. Are they an ethnographic group, as was stated by the Polish government in February 2016 in its opinion to the citizens' legislation initiative on the modification of the *National and Ethnic Minorities and Regional Language Act* from 6 January 2005, which was submitted to the Sejm on 27 August 2014?[29] Or should they instead be considered as an ethnic group, as many Polish scholars perceive them (Nijakowski 2004, 155; Szczepański 2004, 114; Wanatowicz 2004, 212; Kijonka 2016, 8)? If they are an ethnic group, are they also a nationality (which seems to be a logical consequence of the former statement)? If we agree that they constitute an ethnic group, by that definition, they are a minority as well. So, why are they not recognised as such? This situation was already commented upon by the EU Network of Independent Experts on Fundamental Rights, which stated that: "(…) the other Member States, some of which, while accepting that minorities exist on their territory, restrict the notion only to certain groups (…) while other groups are being excluded from that notion

---

28   GUS (Główny Urząd Statystyczny). 2013. "Tabl. 3 Ludność według płci i gęstości zaludnienia oraz województw w 2011 roku".

29   Sejm RP. 2014. "Obywatelski projekt ustawy o zmianie ustawy o mniejszościach narodowych i etnicznych oraz o języku regionalnym, a także niektórych innych ustaw".

POLITICAL SITUATION IN UPPER SILESIA

which, arguably, should be recognized as applicable to them (for instance (...) the Silesian minority in Poland)" (2005, 10–11). Furthermore, the *Third Opinion on Poland*, adopted on 28 November 2013 by the Advisory Committee of the Framework Convention for the Protection of National Minorities, states in point 206 that: "diverging opinions remain as to the options available regarding protection of the Silesian identity and language". The *Forth Opinion on Poland*, adopted on 6 November 2019 by the same Committee, goes even further in points 25–26: "the Advisory Committee reiterates that it is part of its [State's] duty to assess whether the approach taken to the scope of application does not constitute a source of arbitrary or unjustified distinctions among communities with regard to access to rights (...) that it has consistently encouraged authorities to take an open and inclusive approach (...) that establishing a closed list of national minorities falling under the protection of the Framework Convention is not in line with the right to individual free self-identification (...)". Finally, in point 27, it states that: "[i]n this light, the Advisory Committee strongly regrets that no progress has been made regarding the requests for recognition of the Silesians as an ethnic minority and Silesian as a regional language". A citizens' legislation initiative on the modification of the *National and Ethnic Minorities and Regional Language Act* from 6 January 2005 was also submitted to the Sejm on 27 August 2014, which aimed at the recognition of the Silesian ethnic minority and the Silesian language as a regional language.

Are they then, ultimately, a stateless nation? This was debated by some authors in *Nadciągają Ślązacy. Czy istnieje narodowość śląska?* (Nijakowski 2004; Szczepański 2004; Kwaśniewski 2004), but also by, e.g., Małgorzata Hołomek, who seemed to be concerned that some people might feel like they belong to the Silesian nation (2014, 168). For the remainder of the study, a moderate approach is taken. Silesians are recognised as an ethnic group and, as a result, as a minority (in accordance with the thesis presented in the first chapter stating that a minority exists *de facto* regardless of its recognition *de iure*) and nationality (in accordance with the National Census from 2011 and the legal definition of the term included therein). Obviously, Silesians may also be seen as a regional community, which does not contradict the previous statement but is based on a different perspective. The question of whether they also constitute a stateless nation, as well as the question about their legal recognition, will emerge further on in the study.

As was already mentioned, the total population of Silesians in Poland was determined to be 846,719 (2.2% of the total population of Poland). Of those surveyed, 376,600 (45% of all Silesian declarations) said they were of Silesian nationality exclusively. Since 2002, when 173,153 (0.4%) people declared Silesian identity, this number increased almost five-fold (GUS 2004, 35). There

68   CHAPTER 2

may be a few reasons for this situation: first and foremost – in the census from 2002, each person could choose only one national or ethnic identification, while in the census from 2011, it was possible to choose two (complex identity). Moreover, many social and cultural minority organisations prepared information programmes and encouraged people to choose a minority with which they identified (Gudaszewski 2015). Still, the numbers have been questioned by regional and ethnic leaders, who claim that there were problems during the census, and the number was lower than in reality. Some scholars estimate that as many as 1.5 million ethnic Silesians live in the historical region of Upper Silesia (Smolorz 2013, 54). In the Czech Republic, only about 12,000 (0.1% of the population of the Czech Republic) people declared themselves as Silesians in 2011, and the number has decreased almost four-fold since 1991 (0.4%/44,446).[30] Silesians constitute 15.6% of the population of the Śląskie Voivodeship and 10.5% of the Opolskie Voivodeship.[31]

The language of Silesians is also a complicated issue. The Polish government, in its opinion from 2016, stated that Silesian is a dialect of the Polish language. Scholars developed the term 'ethnolect' for the family of Silesian dialects, which are distinguishable from the Polish language but have not yet developed a standard version of the Silesian language (Tambor 2010). However, Silesians themselves have pressed for Silesian to be recognised as a regional language. This became evident in October 2010, when a group of Members of the Parliament presented a legislative initiative to modify the *National and Ethnic Minorities and Regional Language Act* from 6 January 2005 by adding Silesian as a regional language.[32] This initiative was evaluated by four experts: Grzegorz Janusz, Jolanta Tambor, Bogusław Wyderka and Marek S. Szczepański. All of them (with the opinion of Grzegorz Janusz being noticeably vague) approved the modification and stated that Silesian deserves the protection required of regional languages, though every one of them presented different reasons. Another legislative initiative with the same goal was presented to the Sejm on 21 February 2020 by a group of MP s led by Monika Rosa.[33]

According to Ethnologue, Silesian is an Indo-European language belonging to the West Slavic group and the Lechitic subgroup (ISO code: szl).[34] Silesian is

---

30   ČSÚ (Český Statistický Úřad). 2016. "Tabl. 1–16 Obyvatelstvo podle národnosti podle výsledků sčítání lidu v letech 1921–2011".
31   GUS (Główny Urząd Statystyczny). 2015. "Tabl. 54 Ludność województw według identyfikacji narodowo-etnicznych w 2011 roku".
32   Sejm RP. 2011. "Druki Sejmowe VI kadencja – druk 3835".
33   Sejm RP. 2020. "Projekt Ustawy No: EW-020-98/20".
34   Ethnologue. n.d. "Silesian", Languages of the World.

POLITICAL SITUATION IN UPPER SILESIA

used by 529,377 people (1.4% of the population of Poland) and 63% of Silesians, who usually speak Polish as well.[35] Today, Silesian is not taught in schools (only a few teachers conduct additional classes about Silesia and Silesian). However, this situation is partially going to change. Since the 2016/2017 school year, lessons about Silesia and the Silesian language have been introduced to schools in Rybnik. However, in the next school years, it is foreseen that this may spread to other Silesian cities.[36] NGO s also conduct lessons in the Silesian language (in cooperation with the Muzeum Śląskie and the Górnośląski Park Etnograficzny). Furthermore, the most popular manual of this language – *Gōrnoślōnski ślabikŏrz*[37] – was recently published. In the Czech Republic, most Silesians speak Czech. Only 909 people (8% of the population of Silesians) declared their language as 'other' or 'not identified' in the 2011 census, but this does not necessarily imply that the mother tongue of those persons is some version of Silesian.[38]

The issue of religion is much easier to elaborate upon. The dominant religion of Upper Silesians in Poland is Roman Catholicism (90.5%/766,347). Silesians also belong to the Evangelical Church of the Augsburg Confession (1%/8,668), Jehovah's Witnesses (0.2%/1,774) and Pentecostal Church (0.1%/ 416),[39] which mirrors the religion declarations in Polish society in general, with the only difference being a higher number of Silesians belonging to the Evangelical Church of the Augsburg Confession.

To sum up, in terms of identity, Silesians are neither Czechs nor Germans nor Poles. They are Silesians, a separate ethnic group, a minority in Poland and the Czech Republic. Some of them also identify themselves as Germans or Poles. It can be assumed that the size of their population is underestimated, possibly by far. The group is highly concentrated in the historical region of Upper Silesia. Their language is Slavic, with Czech, Polish and German influence and it is still widely used among the group.

---

35 GUS (Główny Urząd Statystyczny). 2015. "Tabl. 20 Ludność według rodzaju i liczby języków używanych w domu w 2011 roku".

36 See: Portal Samorządowy. 2016. *Śląsk – nowy przedmiot edukacja regionalna*; Demokratyczna Unia Regionalistów Śląskich. n.d. "Rechtōr. Forum Regionalistów Śląskich".

37 Pro Loquela Silesiana. n.d. "O nas".

38 ČSÚ (Český Statistický Úřad). 2016. "1-17 Obyvatelstvo podle národnosti a mateřského jazyka podle výsledků sčítání lidu v letech 1970, 1991, 2001 a 2011".

39 GUS (Główny Urząd Statystyczny). 2015. "Tabl. 45 Ludność według identyfikacji narodowo-etnicznych oraz przynależności wyznaniowej w 2011 roku".

2.8 Upper Silesians in Scholarly Literature

One of the first sociological works about Upper Silesia was published in 1934 by Emil Szramek. His *Śląsk jako problem socjologiczny. Próba analizy* was one of the milestones in the analysis of the population of the region. He created the term 'corner region' and 'borderland character of people' to describe the complicated situation of the population in Upper Silesia, living for centuries under the changing influence of different states and powers.

One of the earliest works on the topic of Upper Silesia, which was published just after the transformation, is a book by Mirosława Błaszczak-Wacławik, Wojciek Błasiak and Tomasz Nawrocki, *Górny Śląsk szczególny przypadek kulturowy*, from 1990. The book elaborates on the Silesian culture and society in the historical context, paying special attention to the particular characteristics of the region and its complicated history. A few years later, the book *Ethnic Minorities & Ethnic Majority*, edited by Marek S. Szczepański, was published. In this book, general and particular topics are considered. There are a few chapters about Silesians or chapters that refer to this group. The book was published at the time when a political debate about Upper Silesia was fuelled by works concerning new law on the administrative division of Poland and the role of self-government.

The book, which was the result of international cooperation on the issue of Silesia and Silesian identity, was published in 2006 and titled *Dynamika śląskiej tożsamości*, edited by Marek S. Szczepański and Janusz Janeczek. The problems of Polish Upper Silesia, as well as Czech Upper Silesia, were considered in the book. The identity of Upper Silesians was considered in the historical, cultural and social context. Problems of the role of community, its categorisation and consequences of its development were elaborated in the international context. The problem of categorisation of Silesians and possible consequences of their recognition as a nation is elaborated by Jacek Wódz and Kazimiera Wódz (2004). Extensive reflections on the identity of Silesians (ethnic and regional) may also be found in *Dylematy regionalnej tożsamości. Przypadek Górnego Śląska* by Marek S. Szczepański and Anna Śliz. The problems of definition of identity and its categorisation were discussed therein. In their work, the authors recognised that in the case of Upper Silesians, regional identity is connected to ethnic identity, though not in every instance.

An extensive summary of sociological publications on the topic of Silesia was made by Teresa Sołdra-Gwiżdż in her *Socjologia wobec Śląska – jedność czy wielość* in 2010. She outlined paradigms present in the field of Silesian studies. The 'Western and Northern Lands' paradigm was presented first, which stressed

POLITICAL SITUATION IN UPPER SILESIA   71

the achievement of the assimilation of the people living there. The issue of connections with Germany and migration thereto was also an important point for this paradigm. Many of the earliest works in this paradigm can be referred to as 'polonocentric'. The second paradigm was called 'multiculturalism'. In this paradigm, it has been shown that there are many cultures that influenced the development of the region and are still present there. Sometimes they did so through conflict, but usually, influence and development were achieved through diversity. The third paradigm is the 'borderland region'. It is one of the earliest developed paradigms, in which problems regarding the localisation of the region and the consequences of historical changes are elaborated. Cultural differences and diversity are especially important for this stance. The last paradigm can be referred to as 'industrialisation, urbanisation and modernisation'. This stance analyses Silesian society from the point of view of changes and development relating to the wider sphere of processes. It became especially important during and after the transformation of Poland's political and social system, which had a strong influence on Upper Silesian society.

The results of the 2002 and 2011 National Censuses were elaborated in many books. Two works are of particular interest: a chapter by Piotr Wróblewski from 2015 and a book by Justyna Kijonka from 2016. In the former, the role of the censuses was analysed in the context of Silesian symbols and the development of organisations of the Silesian community. The influence of the results of the censuses on the legitimacy of claims voiced by organisations claiming to represent the Silesian ethnic group (sometimes nation) was elaborated. In the latter, the attitude towards censuses and their results was analysed, along with some problems that emerged when they were administered (such as the refusal of the persons conducting the censuses to mark Silesian nationality, even when the respondent said he/she was Silesian). The author paid special attention to the diverse attitudes among Silesians towards the consequences of censuses, especially the census from 2011.

Furthermore, Silesians as a group and their political behaviour were analysed to some extent in the book *Mniejszości w wyborach. Wybory mniejszości*, edited by Janusz Mieczkowski. In particular, the role of the Silesian minority in past elections was studied, along with Silesian organisations and their political campaigns. Unfortunately, the book described the relations between the Silesian and German minorities in a confusing manner, sometimes melding the two separate groups into one. Maintaining clear distinctions between the behaviours of the Silesian and German minorities and their representatives (even if the minorities cooperate closely in the Śląskie Voivodeship) is one of the hardest tasks we face today.

2.9 (Upper) Silesian Movement

The Silesian movement is an example of ethnic and regional mobilisation. It is a social movement that developed in the early 1990s in Upper Silesia and is still evolving. Its three main groups of goals include social, cultural and political issues. Social goals were most important in the 1990s during the transformation of Poland's economy, when the main industries in Silesia were shut down or sold. However, goals such as the elimination of unemployment or social exclusion are still present. Cultural goals aim at increasing the attention paid to characteristic features of the region and encompass the protection of Silesian culture and prevention of its disappearance, recognition of Silesians as an ethnic minority and Silesian as a regional language, and organisation of regional events and institutions. Within the movement, there is disagreement as to the status of the Silesian group: some believe that they are an ethnic group, while others that they are a stateless nation. Moreover, some historical events and processes are interpreted differently by organisations within the movement. Last but not least are the political goals, which divide organisations within the movement. In general, the goal that binds all of the organisations within the movement is the need to take responsibility for the Upper Silesian region through its population and its representatives. What differs is how each organisations suggests they should achieve this goal. On the one hand, there is a group of organisations that aims to introduce a new political system in Poland that will make it possible to establish an autonomy of regions, including Upper Silesia. Before this goal is achieved, though, their plan is to remain political participants of the existing political system. On the other, there is a group of organisations that believes that the decentralisation of public authority as it is today is enough to achieve the goals of the movement, as long as the means that are available to achieve this end are used to the maximum possible extent. The first significant collective actors, which developed the movement in the 1990s, were the *Związek Górnośląski* (Upper Silesian Union) and the *Ruch Autonomii Śląska* (Silesian Autonomy Movement) (previously the *Ruch na Rzecz Autonomii Śląska*). At the same time, two German minority organisations were created in Upper Silesia: *Towarzystwo Społeczno-Kulturalne Niemców Województwa Śląskiego* (Social and Cultural Society of Germans of the Śląskie Voivodeship) (1990) and *Niemiecka Wspólnota "Pojednanie i Przyszłość"* (German Community "Reconciliation and Future") (1991).

Since its beginning, the Silesian movement has evolved, and it presumably will continue to evolve in the future (Wódz 2012). Initially (1990–1996), when the first organisations were created, some of their representatives took part in elections and held public offices in the region. In the second phase

POLITICAL SITUATION IN UPPER SILESIA

(1996–2003), the main debate concentrated on the registration of the *Związek Ludności Narodowości Śląskiej* (Union of People of Silesian Nationality). This process ended in 2004, when the European Court for Human Rights ruled in favour of a decision of the Polish State, which hindered the union's registration as an association (the main reason was that, according to the Court, part of its name 'narodowości', meaning 'nationality', could in the future lead to the organisation claiming it should take part in parliamentary elections with the privilege granted for national minorities recognised by the Polish State).[40]

The third stage (2003–2009) started with the membership of the *Ruch Autonomii Śląska* in the European Free Alliance and was connected to increased activity on an international level. This period marked the second wave of the creation of Silesian organisations. Some of them were created as specialised organisations: *Pro Loquela Silesiana Towarzystwo Kultywowania i Promocji Śląskiej Mowy* (Pro Loquela Silesiana Society for Cultivating and Promoting Silesian Speech) (2007), *Tôwarzistwo Piastowaniô Ślónskij Môwy "DANGA"* (Association for Cultivating Silesian Speech "DANGA") (2008) and the *Fundacja "Silesia"* ("Silesia" Foundation) (2009). In this period, the *Stowarzyszenie "Przymierze Śląskie"* (Association "Silesian Alliance") (2005), associations promoting further cooperation and integration within Silesian movements, were created. The creation of this association may also be perceived as the first split within the movement, as it evolved from the local groups *Związek Górnośląski* in Tarnowskie Góry and *Związek Ślązaków* (Union of Silesians) (2006). The creation of the *Ślónskŏ Ferajna* (Silesian Band) (2009) may be seen as a further split within the movement (it evolved from a local group of the *Ruch Autonomii Śląska* in Mysłowice), but it is perceived by its creators as a specialised organisation promoting German-Silesian heritage in the region.

The fourth stage started in 2010 and lasted until 2017. In 2010, RAŚ took part in elections to decentralised bodies and won three seats in the Sejmik of Śląskie Voivodeship.[41] Later, it took part in the ruling coalition with the *Platforma Obywatelska* (Civic Platform; one of the state-wide parties) in the Śląskie Voivodeship. Some authors believe that from that moment, the organisation should be categorised as a proto-party, even though legally, it is registered as an association (Wódz 2015, 26). The third wave of the creation of Silesian organisations took place when specialised organisations were created: *Pomocna Dłoń – Krystyn i Sympatyków* (The Helpful Hand – Christina and Friends) (2011), *"Silesia Schola" Stowarzyszenie na rzecz Edukacji Regionalnej* ("Silesia

---

40   Gorzelik and Others vs. Poland. ECHR. Application No. 44258/98. Judgement from 17 February 2004, para. 106.

41   Sejmik of Śląskie Voivodeship – regional council, self-government body.

Schola" Association for Regional Education) (2012) and *Demokratyczna Unia Regionalistów Śląskich* (Democratic Union of Silesian Regionalists) (2015). Two organisations aimed at further integration within the movement were also created: *Stowarzyszenie Osób Narodowości Śląskiej* (Association of Persons of Silesian Nationality) (2011) and *Initiative der kulturelle Autonomie Schlesiens* (Initiative for the Cultural Autonomy of Silesia) (2011) – which is also an organisation of the Silesian diaspora in Germany. As a result of a deep split within the movement, the *Stowarzyszenie "Nasz Wspólny Śląski Dom"* (Association "Our Common Silesian Home") was created in 2012. In 2017, two regional parties – *Ślonzoki Razem* (Silesians Together) and the *Śląska Partia Regionalna* (Silesian Regional Party) – were founded, and in 2018, they were registered as political parties in accordance with Polish law. Arguably, these events mark the beginning of the fifth stage of the development of the movement.

Consequently, organisations within the Silesian movement today may be categorised into four groups (in accordance with the manner of their creation and initial goals):

- protagonist – organisations that developed the Silesian movement in the 1990s,
- specialised – organisations whose goals are limited to certain fields within the movement: language, charity, regional education and promotion,
- integration – organisations that chose to form platforms of cooperation around different issues revolving around the goals of the movement,
- dissident – organisations that were created as a result of a split (mostly from protagonist organisations) within the movement.

As to the character of the movement, Piotr Wróblewski (1998) was the first to use the term 'regional nationalism', which was later used by other authors. Nevertheless, today, all the main actors of the movement agree that Silesians constitute an ethnic group rather than a nation, which means that nationalism cannot be the right term for the movement. The unfortunate term 'nationality' used in relation to Silesians started a long-lasting debate, which led to the emergence of opposite theories. Yet, the term nationality does not mean that there must be a nation – it can also refer to an ethnic group. This is especially true given that, according to Polish law, the term national minority means a minority that has a kin-state, and ethnic minority means a minority without such a state. This leads to the conclusion that we can stop being afraid to use the term minority. Nevertheless, the Silesian movement should instead be categorised as an ethnoregionalist movement with ethnic (socio-cultural but also political) and regional (political and territorial) goals.

The Silesian movement, as a social movement, can be analysed in three dimensions: solidarity, resources and opportunity. Solidarity means the

POLITICAL SITUATION IN UPPER SILESIA

ideology binding the members of the community and activists of the move-ment. It does not necessarily need to be ethnicity – it can equally be ecology or gender. This ideology needs to be developed on the foundations of social or political situations, usually connected to discrimination or a new social issue. As a result, grievances suffered by the group represented by the movement constitute a very interesting and important part of any analysis of the issue. Resources consist of the size of the population represented by the movement, previously existing organisations and structures, methods of recruitment, and other resources, such as financing. Opportunity consists of the social, eco-nomic or political situation of the movement and its political environment. Political systems, which favour civic participation, extreme economic circum-stances, a tolerant society and political changes, are usually positive stimuli for the evolution of a social movement.

As to solidarity, the development of the Silesian movement was connected to the syndrome of Silesian harm. It led to the emergence of a new narra-tion about regional, local and 'ours' – Silesian (Trosiak 2016, 202), because "Silesianism is a context, evoked by space, time, history, patterns of behaviour and of thought. Through individual and familial experience, which takes into account the past and present, it is possible to understand what 'Silesianism' means" (Kunce 2007, 67; my translation). One of these experiences is Silesian harm, which evolved from a stigmatising element to one of the reasons for social mobilisation. This conversion was mentioned by Randall Collins: "a suc-cessful social ritual operating in the collective gathering of a social movement is a process of transforming one emotion into another. The ritualized sharing of instigating or initiating emotions which brought individuals to the collective gathering in the first place (outrage, anger, fear, etc.) gives rise to distinctively collective emotions, the feelings of solidarity, enthusiasm, and morality which arise in group members' mutual awareness of their shared focus of attention" (2001, 29). There are positive elements of solidarity: the belief that Silesians understand each other, usage of the common language, common values and customs. In the common mindset of Silesians, being a community was always important because there were always 'others', and usually, the culture of the 'others' was the dominant one, holding public authority and power.

The second element, resources, consists of at least four elements: popu-lation, previous organisations, structure and financing. These will be elabo-rated in detail below. First, the structure of financing the movement will be explained. Pursuant to the *Political Parties Act* from 1997[42] art. 28, parties that

---

42 Dz.U. 1997. 98. 604 with amendments.

created electoral committees alone and gained at least 3% of votes in the elections to the Sejm and parties that created coalition committees and gained 6% have a right to a subsidy from the state budget. However, as previously stated, there are only very young political parties in the Silesian movement. Organisations that form the Silesian movement are usually registered as associations. The *Associations Law* from 1989[43] foresees many sources of funding (art. 33–35): membership fees, donations, inheritance, income from activities (also economic ones), income from assets, public charity and purpose grants from public funds (budget or budgets of self-government units).

In terms of political system and opportunities, after 1989, in Poland, a few ethnic and regionalist parties, proto-parties and quasi-parties were created, or there were plans to create them:

– *Towarzystwo Społeczno-Kulturalne Mniejszości Niemieckiej na Śląsku Opolskim* (1989-) creates the *Mniejszość Niemiecka* Electoral Committee, which was very successful in elections (also state-wide) in the 1990s and today has one representative in the Sejm (the obligatory seat for the German minority) and can be categorised as a proto-party;

– *Białoruskie Zjednoczenie Demokratyczne* (1990–2004), registered as a political party, took part in a few elections, especially in the 1990s;

– *Blok Wyborczy Mniejszości* (Ukrainians, Lithuanians, Slovaks and Czechs), created for the purpose of parliamentary elections in 1991;

– *Kaszëbskô Jednota* (2011), a member organisation of the EFA since 2016, registered as an association, but can be categorised as proto-party;

– *Kaszubska Partia Narodowa* (2005), the idea of creating an ethnoregionalist party was not successful;

– *Obywatelski Krąg Łemków* (1990) – *Rusiński Demokratyczny Krąg Łemków "Hospodar"* (1991), registered as a political party, active in the 1990s, absent today;

– *Partia Rozwoju Pomorza* (2006), the idea of creating a regionalist party was not successful;

– *Związek Kaszubsko-Pomorski* (1956) (quasi-party), members of the Association take part in elections to decentralised bodies, but the Association has never had to take part in elections (Mieczkowski 2014, 182–185);

– *Regionalna Mniejszość z Większością* (2017) a political party of the German minority.

Additionally, after 1989, following the transformation of the political and economic system in Poland to a fully democratic one, an opportunity appeared

---

43   Dz.U. 1989. 20. 104 with amendments.

POLITICAL SITUATION IN UPPER SILESIA

for the representatives of minorities. As was presented above, this opportunity was only partially taken advantage of by the minority organisations. Even if political projects emerged, they were usually undermined and even attacked by Poles and Polish authorities. One reason for this state of affairs is the political thesis, which claims that the Polish Nation (citizens of the Polish State) is ethnically and nationally homogeneous, and although it permits for the existence of regional and local differences, these cannot carry any political significance. However, the reality is very different. Some communities bind cultural and political claims together. The Upper Silesian case is a good example (Wódz 2012, 2). The political and social conflict between the representatives of the more active and demanding communities and the Poles and Polish authorities is ongoing. A few examples of this are presented below, where concrete examples of actions of representatives of the Silesian minority are elaborated.

2.10   History of the Movement

There was a movement before the Great War and during the inter-war period, which was similar in some ways to the modern Silesian ethnoregionalist movement, in that it was based on the discontent of the indigenous population (Madajczyk 2005, 113). However, the discontent was connected to the political and social situation of the Silesian population in its region, as it pointed to different 'others' and existed for different reasons.

The *Śląska Partia Ludowa* [ŚPL] (Silesian Peoples Party) was founded in February 1909 in the Austrian part of Silesia (mostly Cieszyn Silesia). A year later, the Association – Silesian Peoples Union – was also founded. Józef Kożdoń became the leader of the ŚPL, and it issued the newspaper "Ślązak". The programme of the party was based on the idea of "Silesia for Silesians". Its policy was to promote the indigenous population of this part of Silesia and preserve its distinctiveness: its language, traditions and culture. The programme included the need for cooperation with the state structures – the Austrian- and German-speaking inhabitants of the region. It promoted learning the German language in order to be able to communicate with these institutions (Dobrowolski 1972, 53–54). After 1918, the ŚPL promoted the idea of the neutralisation of Silesia and the creation of a republic under the protection of the League of Nations or under the protection of the newly-created Czechoslovakia (Dobrowolski 1972, 57). After the incorporation of a part of Silesia into Czechoslovakia, the ŚPL advocated for autonomy status, and Kożdoń became the mayor of the Czech part of Cieszyn. In 1921, the ŚPL had as many as 3,500 members, according to its own data (Dobrowolski 1972, 197).

During the rise of the Nazis in Czechoslovakia, the most radical right-wing of śPL began collaborating with them. After the Polish army invaded their lands in 1938, the śPL was dissolved (Dobrowolski 1972, 213).

The *Związek Górnoślązaków* (Alliance of Upper Silesians) was founded in 1919. Its leader was Edward Latacz, and it issued the newspaper "Der Bund-Związek". During the plebiscite in the former German part of Upper Silesia, it advocated for the creation of a Free State of Silesia under the protection of the League of Nations. It promoted the idea of adding a third question to the plebiscite, asking if Upper Silesia should become an independent state. At the conference of ZG in 1921, 337 delegates took part from 198 local groups (Dobrowolski 1972, 82–83).

The *Związek Obrony Górnoślązaków* [ZOG] (Union for the Protection of Upper Silesians) was founded in 1925. Its leader was Jan Kustos, and it promoted the idea of "Upper Silesia for Upper Silesians", which was important during the migration of peoples to this region from other parts of Poland. It advocated for more competences for autonomous institutions and strict observance of the the *Constitutional Act that included the Organic Statute for the Śląskie Voivodeship* from 1920. In particular, it aimed at more autonomous competences in the field of economics and culture. Its leader explicitly confirmed the existence of 'minorities of people' next to 'national minorities' and indicated that Upper Silesians belong to the former category (Dobrowolski 1972, 167). From 1927, ZOG cooperated with Wojciech Korfanty against the new authorities – the *Sanacja* (Sanation). In 1932, the leader – Jan Kustos – died, which led to the dissolution of the organisation after a few years (Dobrowolski 1972, 183).

Some scholars point out that the organisations making up the Silesian movement make references to the time before the Great War and inter-war period in their programmes and narration of history, and especially to the so-called 'ślązakowski' movement in Cieszyn Silesia (śPL) and the activity of Jan Kustos and his *Związek Obrony Górnoślązaków* in the Śląskie Voivodeship (Sekuła 2009, 59). Some go even further and use the term 'ślązakowcy' for today's activists in the Silesian movement (Trosiak 2016, 18). This reference indicates the historical continuity of the movement and ideological sameness of the organisations, although such a thesis is certainly far-fetched. A general similarity of goals (with a categorical exclusion of separatism and radical ideas such as "Silesia for Silesians") or a general sameness of location of activities (although today, they concentrate in old Prussian Silesia – the central part of the Śląskie and eastern part of the Opolskie Voivodeships) do not justify the use of this terminology. Although this short presentation indicates that scholars see a continuity of ethnoregionalist movements in Upper Silesia in the XX century, historical and modern movements are different.

However, there is a possible time-gap in the activities of ethnoregionalists in Upper Silesia between 1939 and 1989. The evolution of ethnic and national attitudes in the region was studied by Maria W. Wanatowicz. Firstly, she indicates that as early as the 1950s, some activities associated with Upper Silesian particularism were undertaken. In particular, the *Der Deutsche Kampfbund Oberschlesien* was founded, which aimed at separation of Silesia from Poland and distributed badges with the sign "Komitet Wyzwolenia Śląska" ("Committee of Liberation of Silesia") (Wanatowicz 2004, 101). Claims for the restitution of autonomy were also raised (e.g., during miner strikes in Katowice in 1957 that started after the liquidation of miners' insurance, which was their insurance facility) (Wanatowicz 2004, 115–116). Secondly, she connects the emergence of organised opposition in the 1970s and 1980s with the growth of general discontent in society. She points out that a shift in scholarly research on Silesia started in the 1980s, aimed at a more neutral and objective study of the region than that inspired by Polish Peoples' Republic propaganda and a deeper understanding of the existence of social phenomena of the indigenous borderland population of Silesians, still classified as 'nationally indifferent', became the goal for some scholars (Wanatowicz 2004, 126–129).

The 1980s were already described as special in the region: "in Upper Silesia (...) since the fall of the 80s, (...) a spontaneous process of articulation of regional and ethnic identity existed, which was mirrored in the institutionalisation of the Silesian movement. A process of becoming the subject by the Silesian indigenous population developed on a scale not known before" (Gerlich 1992, 35; my translation). The decade is a very interesting turning point marking the start of a process that contested the idea that Poland is an ethnically homogeneous state (an idea promoted by the Communist regime in the late 1940s). During the time of the Polish Peoples' Republic, only certain forms of folklore approved by the *Polska Partia Robotnicza* [PPR] (Polish Workers' Party) and later the *Polska Zjednoczona Partia Robotnicza* [PZPR] (Polish United Workers' Party) were present, and no separate interests and identities could have been articulated. For Poles during this time, Silesians were just Poles, perhaps with some strange customs, traditions and a dialect – no regional or ethnic particularism could have been approved. If any existed, they were to be assimilated with Polish culture and become extinct (Wanatowicz 2004, 19–25). It was not until the 1980s when some tendencies, like regionalism and decentralisation, saw the light of day.

At the beginning of the 1980s, an idea arose to create the *Klub Inteligencji Katolickiej* [KIK] (Catholic Intellectuals Club) in Katowice. KIK was one of the few legal organisations not run by the state during the socialist era in Poland. However, Silesia was a particularly important region for the authorities, and no sign of opposition could develop there. As a result, the authorities only allowed the creation of KIK in Katowice in 1981, after explicit support from the Catholic Church and NSZZ "Solidarność" for the initiative. The KIK in Katowice was also special because one of its statutory goals became the development of Silesian regional culture (Przewłoka 2016, 111). The organisation wanted to include the problems and situation of the indigenous population of the region in their programme from the very beginning. As early as 1981, KIK in Katowice organised an exhibition, in which the narration of Silesian history was different from the official one and outlined Silesian identity (Przewłoka 2016, 116). The KIK in Katowice was part of a movement encompassing the whole state, but the older KIKs in Warsaw and Krakow knew and accepted the particular role it could play for Silesians and Silesian culture. Still, according to its creators, Silesians were seen as part of the Polish Nation, and the whole opposition movement in the 1980s had a state-wide character (Przewłoka 2016, 167). Yet, at the same, it was the KIK in Katowice that organised meetings and lectures about the role of Wojciech Korfanty, his long-lasting argument with Michał Grażyński and the *Sanacja* (Sanation) and other controversial issues between Silesians and Poles. In 1988, the KIK in Katowice had 1,430 members (Przewłoka 2016, 187). But what is most interesting is the fact that many of its members became the founders of the *Związek Górnośląski* in 1989 (Prof. Andrzej Klasik, Wojciech Czech and Józef Buszman to name a few).

One of the few scholars who tried to elaborate on the history of change in Upper Silesia is Marian G. Gerlich, who started his study of the issue in the early 1990s as an ethnographer. In his study, the story of one of the activists goes back as far as 1987: "Silesians were oppressed for years. We needed to answer the most basic questions to ourselves – to know where we come from and where we are going. We could not wait any longer and still not be free. We do not need 'kulturtrager', we need to take things in our own hands" (Gerlich 1992, 37–38; my translation). This statement indicates that even back then, there was an awareness of the existence of the separate interests of this group and the need to take steps towards the empowerment of the Upper Silesian indigenous population. Gerlich indicated that the newspaper article by Andrzej Klasik from 7 February 1988 published in "Gość Niedzielny" was the first public expression of the programme of the Silesian movement. The article was titled "Tożsamość Górnego Śląska". Andrzej Klasik later became the chairman of the *Związek Górnośląski*, which was registered on 30 June 1989. Its founders, apart from Klasik, included Józef Buszman, Idzi Panic, Jerzy Wuttke, Jan Rzymełka, Janusz Wycisło and Stanisław Tkocz, among others.

POLITICAL SITUATION IN UPPER SILESIA

The year 1989 was significant in the development of the Silesian movement. Gerlich points out, e.g., the article of Stanisław Bieniasz, a Silesian writer, which was published in November of 1990 in the Parisian "Kultura", titled "O autonomię Górnego Śląska". The author stated that "Upper Silesia is boiling (...). All of a sudden, it was revealed, that diverse groups of the population exist, which have different interests and which are opposed to the interests of other groups".[44] This statement indicates that not only different interest groups but also political and social actors, who were able to articulate them, existed back then. The year 1989, and especially the parliamentary elections held at the time, became a symbol of the change – of the transformation of the political system in Poland. For Upper Silesians, this time was significant for two reasons. Firstly, the collective awareness of living through similar experiences and rapid changes appeared. Secondly, Silesians believed that their actions, especially the strikes in the region in 1988, played an important role in transformation, which led to pride resulting from belonging to a regional community (Gerlich 2010, 60–67).

The first political programme of the *Ruch Autonomii Śląska* was published by Antoni Kositz in 1991 in the "Jaskółka Śląska". The headline article was titled "Autonomia – jedynym wyjściem" ("Autonomy – the only way"), which became the basis for RAŚ's activities during the first few years and presented the attitude of the indigenous population, which saw itself as a separate entity from the German and Polish Nations – a population that created a community on its own and claimed the right to self-government with extensive competences and the autonomy of the region. The *Ruch na Rzecz Autonomii Śląska* was founded on 13 January 1990, but the *Ruch Autonomii Śląska* was formally created a year later. Its first chairman was Paweł Musioł.

2.11 European Context

A study of any ethnoregionalist movement leads to a temptation to put it in a wider perspective and to compare it with other, similar movements. The temptation is even greater when the studied movement is less well known and less studied. However, at the same time, we must keep in mind that just as ethnic groups and regions are different, ethnoregionalist movements may share some features, too, while having many differences.

---

44   My translation.

In the end, I decided to write a whole subchapter and make an attempt at a structured approach. As I have mentioned before, the Upper Silesian ethnoregionalist movement makes claims and demands in three areas of public policy:

– ethnic, which may also be called cultural (the recognition of the ethnic minority by law; the recognition, preservation and promotion of the Silesian language);
– political (autonomy for this particular region or all regions in Poland, which is now a unitary state);
– economic (the preservation of Silesian industry and workplaces, mostly in heavy industry but also for some time now as part of a process of transforming the regional economy to a more environmental-friendly one).

All of those areas are taken into consideration. However, to start with, even if one decides to compare only those movements within the contemporary and former European Union states, it is still hard to define how many of them should be analysed and why those specific ones. It could be said that because this study is focused on ethnoregionalist organisations, one should pay special attention to the cases of movements represented among members of the European Free Alliance because the *Ruch Autonomii Śląska* (Silesian Autonomy Movement) is one of them. But still, the list would be very long. This is why this analysis can only serve to put the Upper Silesian ethnoregionalist movement in the wider context and why it is by no means considered an in-depth study.

Arguably, the best-known movements that can be considered ethnoregionalist are the Catalan and Scottish movements. But, both movements are separatist (secessionist–independentist) in nature, so their political claims, even if they are also based on the idea of self-determination, are further-reaching than in the studied case (Swan 2020). Also, Catalans are considered a 'nationality' by Spanish law, and many Catalans consider their community to be a nation. Likewise, in most cases, Scots consider themselves a nation. Consequently, the differences between those movements and the Upper Silesian ethnoregionalist movement are substantial. Still, the Upper Silesian movement and the Catalan movement have in common a strong emphasis on the economic strength of the region, and with the Scottish movement, there is a similar recognition of the value of integration within the European Union and the opportunities that it presents for ethnoregionalists.

There are also other separatist (secessionist–independentist) movements. An example of such a movement is the one on Åland Island. However, a larger part of the population there identifies itself with another state – Sweden – although the island is under the sovereignty of Finland. Consequently, there is no issue of a separate ethnic group. Still, one can say that by coincidence, Silesia shares a similar history with Åland Island in the inter-war period, more specifically, at the end of the Great War. At that point, the decision about the fate of Åland Island was also made as a result of an international arrangement.

The Bayer ethnoregionalist movement not only operates within very different state structures (federations), but it is also separatist in its programme. The same could be said about the Flanders ethnoregionalist movement and the Basque ethnoregionalist movement, which in both cases represent groups that consider themselves nations.

Additionally, there are movements and organisations of national minorities with programmes focused on the preservation and promotion of language and culture. There is the Slovenian movement in Austria, the Hungarian movements in Romania, the Russian movement in Latvia, the German movement in Denmark and the Slovenian movement in Italy, to name only a few. Again, none of these is concerned with a separate ethnic group that has no kin-state. Consequently, unlike Silesians, those national minorities are often also protected by international law (through bilateral treaties between the kin-state and the host state) and exist in different circumstances.

One rather obvious comparison can be made with another ethnoregionalist movement from Central Europe, namely the Moravian movement in the Czech Republic. The comparison has already been made by me in the past (Muś 2019), so I will only provide a short summary here. Firstly, both movements are located in regions with a long history of some form of self-government or even self-rule. Secondly, both movements have and have had in the past political representation and parties, which presented autonomist programmes. The main difference lies in the emphasis on the ethnic component of the political programmes. Here, the Moravian movement should be categorised as more regionalist, while the Upper Silesian movement has strong ethnic (cultural and linguistic) demands.

Another similar movement can be observed today in the province of Friesland in the north of the Netherlands. The ethnoregionalist movement there is represented by the Frisian National Party [FNP]. Like in Upper Silesia, political demands there are concerned with the introduction of a federal system in the Netherlands with more autonomy for Frisians. Also, the movement has strong cultural (ethnic) and linguistic dimensions, but many members of the community regard Frisianness as a regional identity rather than a national identity (van der Zwet 2015). The FNP, like some organisations in Upper Silesia, also takes part in politics at regional and European levels.

Additionally, some similarities can be found between the Upper Silesian ethnoregionalist movement and the Lusatian movement in the Federal Republic of Germany. The territory where the ethnic group of Sorbs lives was divided: Upper Lusatia was incorporated into Saxony, and Lower Lusatia into

Brandenburg. Lusatian languages (Upper and Lower) belong to the group of West Slavic languages, and the preservation of the language and culture is the main goal of many Sorbian organisations. The language is still taught at schools, and the government of the Federal Republic of Germany guaranteed many rights for Sorbs, but internal migrations of the members of this ethnic group within Germany and widespread globalisation have been leading to a gradual decline of people using the Lusatian language (Szczepankiewicz-Battek 2017). For a long time, the main organisation of Sorbs was *Domowina* (an umbrella organisation of Sorbian societies), but today, a new ethnoregionalist organisation (and a political party since 2005) has become active, even on the European level – the *Lausitzer Allianz/Lužicka Alianca*. The party advocates for further decentralisation of the decision-making process and for the protection of the ethnic and linguistic separateness of Sorbs. It also takes part in district and municipal elections. While there are some similar goals between the Upper Silesian movement and the movement in Lusatia, the main difference is the pre-existing level of protection of Sorbian languages and culture and the federal system within Germany.

In France, the unitary system of the state allows some comparisons with Poland. Therefore, two regions and their movements seem especially interesting for the study, namely, Brittany and Corsica. In both cases, the historical identities are now in the process of revival, and there is a clientele for regionalism in politics (Pasquier 2016). The first region, Brittany, boasts two minority languages, namely Breton – a Celtic language – and Gallo – a Romance language – and has preserved its cultural distinctiveness. Historically, Brittany had remained an independent duchy for a long time and later became a privileged territory within France. In such a landscape was created *l'Union Démocratique Bretonne/Unvaniezh Demokratel Breizh*. The party was founded in the 1960s, and, from time to time, it has held seats in regional and municipal assemblies. It advocates for more autonomy for the region, preferably within a federal France. The second region, Corsica, became part of France in the second half of the XVIII century (before it had strong ties to Italy and even a short period of independence). In the 1970s, tensions between Corsican nationalists and the French government escalated. Corsica also has a distinctive culture. In terms of language practices, over the past 250 years, the population's first language has changed from Corsican, an Italo-Romance language, to French, largely thanks to language management strategies and economic incentives (Blackwood 2011). Still, the Corsican language is still strongly present on the isle. There are two nationalist parties advocating for the rights of the population of Corsica, the preservation of their culture and language, and autonomy, namely *Femu a Corsica* and *Partitu di a Nazione Corsa*. Both movements in France bear a

POLITICAL SITUATION IN UPPER SILESIA

strong resemblance to the Upper Silesian ethnoregionalist movement in their calls for the preservation of their separate culture and language and demands for autonomy in today's unitary states.

Finally, although it is possible to find some analogies between the Upper Silesian ethnoregionalist movement and some of Italy's ethnoregionalist movements, one should keep in mind that the latter operate within a state that is already deeply decentralised (regarding regionalism in Italy) (Lublin 2014, 285–286).

The comparisons made here should not be considered exhaustive. In today's Europe, there are many ethnoregionalist movements and minority rights movements, and it would take a separate study to analyse them all in-depth.

2.12   Political Situation in Upper Silesia – Conclusions

Upper Silesia is a specific region with a culturally diversified heritage and multi-ethnic society. Recognised and unrecognised minorities live there together, but it is the unrecognised Silesian minority that makes the region interesting for social and political science. The process of politicisation of this ethnicity started in 1989 (and perhaps even earlier) and has lasted until today, turning into the potential for political organisations and parties in the region.

The complicated history of the region has led to animosities and even open conflicts, especially in times of growing nationalisms. However, it has also led to tolerance, cooperation and the thriving coexistence of different groups of people. The history of Upper Silesia, and specifically the narration about this history, strengthens the bonds within the community in the region and intensifies the differences between the ethnic groups. Furthermore, historical conflicts in the region about the scope of autonomy, political system and national belonging of its inhabitants are still present in public debate and in the awareness of the community in Upper Silesia, laying the groundwork for research into the continuity of ethnoregionalist movements, albeit mostly symbolical ones. The revitalisation of the collective memory of the members of Silesian ethnic group also plays a significant role in political mobilisation.

The modern political situation of the region also leaves room for an ethnoregionalist movement. The economic and political importance of the region, with its limited administrative competences, drives political demands for a change in the allocation of power between the centre and periphery and between the dominant and non-dominant ethnic groups within the state. Today's Upper Silesian ethnoregionalist movement emerged after 1989 and was created at a time when society believed in great changes and the betterment of everyday life. The political transformation in Poland provided the opportunity for many voices to be heard and movements to be created, especially in the area of ethnic and regional policy. This movement was (and is) dynamic, rapidly evolving, and playing an increasingly more important political role in the region every day.

CHAPTER 3

Methodology

3.1 Aim and Object

The aim of this research is to study the political potential of the Upper Silesian ethnoregionalist movement by recognising the relationship between the ethnic (and, to some extent, regional) identity and political behaviours of the peripheral population. In the field of sociology of politics, there are many theories and explanations for political behaviours. For the purpose of this study, the theory of Martin Lipset and Stein Rokkan was used as the theoretical and, to some extent, methodological framework.

The aim of the study is to decide whether the territorial axis of the Lipset-Rokkan theory (centre-periphery opposition) can be applied to Poland as an explanation for the political behaviours of the population of a periphery. The object of the study is the features of the chosen region (Upper Silesia), such as the identity of its residents, its peripheral nature, and the influence of this peripheral nature on the political behaviours of the population.

The Upper Silesia region was chosen for this study for many reasons. First and foremost is its location as a borderland and the history of its role as a periphery. Second, one of two active and popular ethnoregionalist movements in Poland is based in Upper Silesia (the second is in the *Pomorze/Kaszuby* – Pomerania/Kashubia – region). Third, many variations of national, ethnic and regional identities can be seen there, which makes it an interesting study case (Szmeja 2017, 8).

The scope of the study encompasses the period from 1989 until December 2019. Still, some references to the historical events from before that time are present. Geographically, the study encompasses the region of Polish Upper Silesia, which is divided into two administrative units: the Śląskie and Opolskie Voivodeships. The research was based on a study of the political behaviours of persons with the right to vote who make up the population of the part of Upper Silesia in the Śląskie Voivodeship.

3.2 Research Questions and Hypothesis

The general research questions are:

© ANNA MUŚ, 2022 | DOI:10.1163/9789004466456_005

- How can the political potential of the Upper Silesian ethnoregionalist movement be evaluated?
- Is the theory of Martin Lipset and Stein Rokkan useful for the study of the Upper Silesian ethnoregionalist movement?

The specific research questions are:

- What is the relationship between the peripheral identity and the political programmes of organisations representing the population of the periphery?
- What is the relationship between the peripheral identity and political behaviours of the community of the periphery?
- Was the centre-periphery opposition present in the past?
- Based on which elements does the community of Upper Silesia create its own identity?
- How do organisations representing the community of Upper Silesia create their ideologies?
- How do organisations representing the community of the periphery behave in the sphere of policymaking?
- Is the centre-periphery opposition present in the political programmes of organisations representing the Upper Silesian community?
- How popular are the organisations representing the Upper Silesian community among the members of the Upper Silesian community?

The main hypothesis of the study assumes that evaluation of the political potential of the Upper Silesian ethnoregionalist movement is possible based on such criteria as:

- The popularity of the organisations representing the movement,
- The existence of a widespread understanding of the role of ethnic and regional identity,
- The social, economic and legal circumstances of the Upper Silesian ethnoregionalist movement.

In the case of Poland, the circumstances for the development of territorial countercultures and social cleavage based on the centre-periphery opposition occurred on a large scale. Consequently, the territorial axis in the classic Lipset-Rokkan hypothesis can be applied to studies on voter alignment and the party system.

The specific hypothesis of the study assumes that:

- The peripheral identity influences the aims, scope and language of the programmes of ethnoregionalist organisations.
- Peripheral identity is one of the determinants of the political behaviours of the Upper Silesian population. For a smaller part of the population, it is the most important determinant of political behaviour.

METHODOLOGY

- The centre-periphery opposition has been present in Upper Silesia since the inter-war period.
- The identity of the community is based on many determinants, the most important being:
  - language,
  - customs and traditions,
  - separateness from the dominant culture,
  - common memory distinctive from the history known to the dominant culture, stereotypes about itself.
- The ideologies of organisations representing the community of Upper Silesia are created in one of two ways: in opposition to the dominant culture or promoting a specific variation of the dominant culture.
- Organisations representing the community of Upper Silesia represent many different approaches to politics:
  - some of them take an active part in the elections,
  - some of them have representatives in state-wide parties,
  - some of them try to influence politics and policy from the outside.
- The centre-periphery opposition is present in the political programmes of some of the organisations representing the Upper Silesian community.
- Support for ethnoregionalist organisations is related to the ethnic identity of a person.

3.3   Terminology and Indicators

'Politics' is defined in many different ways. Some define it as leadership and power over resources (Weber 1926; Lasswell 1936). Another group of definitions indicates that politics is a social activity aimed at the creation, preservation and betterment of the general rules and conditions of living in a society (Heywood 2010, 4). In this book, both understandings of what politics is and, consequently, what is political, are used. As a result, the term 'political' will henceforth encompass every action (individual or collective) aimed at the creation, preservation and betterment of the general rules and conditions of living in a society. Political activity becomes necessary when a conflict of interest occurs among socio-political groups, making it impossible to regulate the behaviours of members of a given society. The word *potential* is defined as: "latent qualities or abilities that may be developed and lead to future success or usefulness" (*Lexico Oxford Dictionary* n.d.). The political potential is studied in three categories:

- electoral success – the potential to gain the assumed support of voters, preferably support which enables the electoral committee to gain seats,
- office success – the potential to gain seats as the result of elections or to be appointed to positions of authority within the political system,
- policy success – the potential to influence the policymaking process in order to change the political, social and economic situation of the represented population (Mazzoleni & Müller 2016).

Consequently, the potential for electoral success, office success and policy success of the Upper Silesian ethnoregionalist movement is studied in this book.

Political behaviour is understood as any form of individual or collective participation in political processes and every action with political consequences. The categories of political behaviour chosen for the study included:
- voting behaviour,
- participation in a political campaign,
- belonging to organisations that have political goals,
- participation in political protests,
- participation in initiatives that have direct political goals (Potulski 2007, 231).

Ethnicity was elaborated upon in the first chapter, so I will only make one remark here. The ethnic identity of an individual is understood in this book as an explicit or implicit belonging to a community recognised by the individual as a separate group based on ethnicity. Many different manifestations of this identity are possible: auto-identification, usage of language, following customs and traditions, a feeling of belonging to a community and perception of auto-stereotypes, and these will be used as indicators. Furthermore, a very important indicator for the study includes self-awareness and the perception of separateness, which can indicate the extent to which members of the group perceive themselves as different and, consequently, whether they see the need for political representation.

Political programmes (not only those prepared exclusively for elections but also other manifestos and postulates, along with declarations made by members of organisations) of ethnoregionalist organisations are studied in the context of their political goals and possible influence on public policy. The support of the target group for the plans and postulates of organisations constitutes an important part of the study.

3.4   Methods, Techniques and Tools

The research methods used for the study include content analysis, focus group interviews (qualitative methods), and a questionnaire (quantitative method).

METHODOLOGY

All these methods enable the researcher to answer the research questions provided above.

i) Qualitative method – content analysis, technique: categorisation, tool: categorisation key.

The method consists of the analysis of election results, membership in organisations, administrative data and press and internet resources. The key point for the selection and categorisation of data is whether it is concerned with the Silesian ethnoregionalist movement. For the purpose of content analysis, the websites and periodicals of the organisations have been studied. Political programmes, policy documents and manifestos are the key sources of information about campaigns, initiatives and protests. For the analysis of administrative data and statistics, the selection key is Silesian auto-identification. For the analysis of electoral results and political programmes, the results and postulates of ethnoregionalist organisations constitute the selection key. For the analysis of the official websites of organisations, documents produced by them and their periodicals, the selection key includes events important for the Silesian ethnoregionalist movement and politicisation of Silesian ethnic identity.

ii) Qualitative method – technique: focus group interviews (FGI), tool: unified scenario.

The method is conducted among members of chosen member-organisations belonging to the so-called *Rada Górnośląska* (Upper Silesia Council). One interview is held with 6–10 interlocutors in each of the chosen organisations. The aim of this part of the study is to provide a description of programmes presented by the organisations and gather information about the methods chosen for achieving their political goals and reasons for their actions (the most interesting are those regarding belonging to a community of the periphery and opposition to the centre). This part enables the researcher to create full descriptions of the organisations and their programmes and makes it possible to compare the studied organisations. The research is based on the approach of ethnomethodology, which aims at studying not only the meaning given by the actors to terms and actions but also hidden meanings and goals connected to the use of certain terms and actions (Babbie 2008, 330). This method is recognised as useful by Grzegorz Babiński, who points out that in the process of studying different cultures, the aim should be to understand it 'from the inside' – from the perspective of the respondents (2004, 14–16). The data is categorised, and the main issues for further study are identified. Conclusions drawn from this part will become one of the foundations for the construction of a questionnaire.

iii) Quantitative method – technique: questionnaire survey, tool: questionnaire. This method is used to determine how popular the political behaviours listed above are among the members of the studied population of the Śląskie Voivodeship. Three electoral districts constructed for the purpose of elections to self-government bodies in 2014 were chosen: the one with the highest number of votes for the *Ruch Autonomii Śląska*, the one with the second-highest number of votes, and one with a middling number of votes. The number of questionnaires administered corresponded to the population of particular districts. A comparative study of people declaring a peripheral identity and of people who do not declare it is conducted. This enables the researcher to study the influence of peripheral identity on the political behaviours of the respondents. It constitutes the main part of the study, as it shows whether the programmes and actions aimed at representing the interests of the periphery in opposition to the centre are popular in the given society and whether the territorial axis is relevant for the political behaviours of a wider group of people. This makes it possible to decide whether the cleavage based on the centre-periphery axis exists in Poland. The problem relating to the generalisation of conclusions based on studies of the most active and conscious members of the community – leaders of the movement – has already been recognised in the literature (Babiński 2004, 24). These kinds of generalisations are not properly justified and can lead to false conclusions in relation to social reality. The public data that already exists from research conducted by specialised institutions (CBOS, PGSW, POLPAN) does not provide sufficient information for the analysis of the research problem. It does not allow for the disaggregation of data to a regional level and does not include all of the organisations studied in the current project. As a result, the conclusions from the first phase of the empirical research part are confronted in the second phase to verify whether the features of interest are present in the given society and help determine how they are distributed.

3.5   Sampling

Existing data have been used for the purpose of content analysis. The results of two censuses in Poland from 2002 and 2011 are analysed to study the auto-identification of the population of Upper Silesia. Furthermore, the results of previous elections were analysed, specifically the parliamentary elections of 1991 and 2015 and elections to self-government bodies of 2001, 2006, 2010, 2014 and 2018. As to political documents and manifestos, official websites of the organisations studied here were used as the main sources of information. Additionally, a few of the following issues of the periodical "Jaskółka Śląska" have been studied to obtain information about campaigns and initiatives before 2010.

METHODOLOGY

For the purpose of the FGI, seven typologically representative organisations were chosen. They represent the diverse attitudes and ideologies present within the movement. The sample was chosen with significant regard for different ethnic identifications – German-Silesian, Polish-Silesian and Silesian – and their representation. Focus group interviews were conducted among the members of the following six member-organisations of the *Rada Górnośląska* (Upper Silesian Council):

Fundacja "Silesia" – the meeting on 11 April 2018,
Niemiecka Wspólnota "Przyszłość i Pojednanie" – the meeting on 9 March 2018,
Pro Loquela Silesiana – the meeting on 3 April 2018,
Ruch Autonomii Śląska – the meeting on 20 November 2017,
Ślōnskŏ Ferajna – the meeting on 28 June 2018,
Związek Górnośląski – the meeting on 10 October 2017.

For the questionnaire, the sample was chosen based on the non-probability, stratified sampling method (based on the population ratios between the chosen districts and on quotas, such as gender and age). This enables the researcher to select a sample that meets the requirement of typological representativeness (see Annex).

3.6 Procedure

The mixed research method was chosen for the study. The main reason for this was the need to triangulate data from the previous stage of the study in order to fully analyse the extent of the popularity of the studied phenomena. Additionally, some data was used as a basis for the development of tools for the stages of the study that followed.

The content analysis method was used first. The ethnic identity declarations from the censuses and electoral results formed the basis for choosing the procedure for conducting the questionnaire survey. Both the electoral results of the Electoral Committee of Voters *Ruch Autonomii Śląska* and the Silesian declarations determined the selection of specific constituencies in which the questionnaire survey was conducted. Content analysis was also chosen for selecting the most important protests and initiatives that influenced the Silesian ethnoregionalist movement. Furthermore, the analysis of political programmes and campaigns was based on a content analysis of documents prepared by the organisations examined here.

Second, focus group interviews were conducted among members (usually members of the respective boards) of the organisations. This part of the study primarily aimed at analysing the political programmes and plans of the organisations, but also the ways in which they understand and promote Silesian identity. The influence of ethnic identity on the political agenda of the organisations was studied on the grounds of FGI results. These results also played a role in the creation of the survey for quantitative research.

Lastly, a questionnaire survey was conducted among members of the Silesian community – the inhabitants of chosen constituencies. The main purpose of this part of the research was to determine the popularity of the claims, policies and political goals of the organisations within their target group – the population of Upper Silesia. Here, the popularity of chosen political behaviours was also studied, and some conclusions as to the relationship between ethnic identity and political behaviours were drawn from the results of this part of the research.

The methods were applied chronologically, and their results were essential for the next part of the research. This sequential mixed approach design allowed us to explore the research problem and extrapolate its results to the larger population (Kasprowicz 2016, 108).

CHAPTER 4

Political Organisations in Upper Silesia

4.1 Rada Górnośląska

There are many different organisations operating in Upper Silesia. The member-organisations of the *Rada Górnośląska* (Upper Silesian Council) are analysed in the present study. This umbrella organisation was founded on 16 May 2012 in Katowice. Its objective is to gather organisations that accept or advocate for:

- Formal recognition of Silesian nationality (ethnic group) by institutions of the Republic of Poland,
- Recognition of the Silesian language as a regional language,
- Introduction of regional education to all levels of education.[1]

The first eleven organisations presented below formed the Council in 2012, and three more were admitted later. One organisation left in 2016. As of 2019, there are 13 organisations:

- *Fundacja Silesia,*
- *Pro Loquela Silesiana,*
- *Przymierze Śląskie,*
- *Ruch Autonomii Śląska,*
- *Stowarzyszenie Osób Narodowości Śląskiej* – in liquidation,
- *Stowarzyszenie "Silesia Schola"* – suspended its activities at the end of 2017,
- *Ślonsko Ferajna,*
- *Towarzystwo Piastowania Mowy Śląskiej "DANGA"* – in liquidation,
- *Związek Górnośląski,*
- *Związek Ślązaków,*
- *Initiative der kulturelle Autonomie Schlesiens,*
- *Niemiecka Wspólnota "Przyszłość i Pojednanie",*
- *Pomocna Dłoń – Krystyn i Sympatyków,*
- (*Stowarzyszenie "Nasz Wspólny Śląski Dom"* – left in 2016).

Only member-organisations of the *Rada Górnośląska* that took part in the FGI (and *Stowarzyszenie Osób Narodowości Śląskiej*) are described in more detail below. The names of the organisations in this chapter are used in their original form. English translations have been provided by the author only for informational purposes.

---

1 Stowarzyszenie Osób Narodowości Śląskiej. 2012. "Powołano Radę Górnośląską".

© ANNA MUŚ, 2022 | DOI:10.1163/9789004466456_006

4.1.1 *Fundacja "Silesia"*

The *Fundacja "Silesia"* ("Silesia" Foundation) undertakes projects and activities that aim at promoting Upper Silesian culture, language, traditions and history. It advocates for the recognition of Silesians as an ethnic group and the Silesian language as a regional language. Moreover, it is concerned with changing the image of Silesia and Silesians in Polish society and promoting knowledge about the region.

The Foundation was created in October 2009 and was registered by the Court on 26 November 2009 (KRS[2] 0000342696). It was a time when Silesian regionalism had started to become stronger again – during the second wave of the creation of Silesian organisations (the phenomenon had first become popular around 1990). Many organisations were founded at that time in Upper Silesia. The founders planned to start an initiative that would promote Silesian regionalism in one of "the most Silesian" cities – Chorzów.

The Foundation is orientated around the ideology of ethnoregionalism. It promotes recognition of Silesians as an ethnic group and the Silesian language as a regional language. Moreover, it stresses the need for regional education and the promotion of knowledge about Silesian culture and its specific historical circumstances. Its activists advocate for deeper and more factual education about such events as the *Tragedia Górnośląska* (Upper Silesian Tragedy). The Foundation takes part in charity activities in the region. It must be stressed that the organisation does not take part in elections and does not support candidates or parties in any kind of election or day-to-day political activities. The only political goals of the Foundation are connected to changing the status of Silesians, their language and the historical policy in the region. Since 2015, the Foundation has not taken part in the works of the *Rada Górnośląska* as an act of opposition towards the politicisation of its activities and the policy of using it for the short-term political goals of the largest organisations that form it. The Foundation promotes organic work and gradual evolution through its actions. Its chairman supports the party *Ślonzoki Razem*.

According to its Statute, the goals of the Foundation include: the preservation of the region's heritage and natural environment; the promotion and preservation of Silesian culture and tradition; the promotion of Christian values; the protection of monuments and revitalisation of dilapidated neighbourhoods; activities serving education; activities for the integration of local communities; the promotion of the idea of civil society and human rights; counteracting the exclusion and marginalisation of discriminated groups. Its

---

2 National Court Register.

POLITICAL ORGANISATIONS IN UPPER SILESIA

funds come from founding capital, income from statutory activities, charity, donations and inheritance and income from assets, donations and subventions, but most of its income comes from statutory activity. The activities of the Foundation are based on the work of volunteers. It runs a regional shop in Chorzów. Books, gadgets, flags and printed clothes can be found there. All of its income is used for the statutory activities of the Foundation.

The flagship project of the Foundation is "Gŏdōmy po ślōnsku" ("We speak Silesian"), launched in 2012, which promotes awareness about people who speak Silesian and the use of Silesian in the public space. Stickers with the logo of the project are distributed to public offices, companies and other places – these mean that visitors can communicate there in Silesian. The project became very popular, and many offices, e.g., the City Hall in Chorzów, have decided to take part. Every year in June, a gala takes place, during which people promoting the Silesian language receive the "Kamraty Ślōnskiej Gŏdki" ("Friends of Silesian Language") award. The Foundation also organises the Upper Silesian Charity Ball. One of the goals of the Foundation is the promotion of Silesian choirs, folk groups and other cultural groups. It takes an active part in commemorations of the Upper Silesian Tragedy in Chorzów and other Silesian cities. The Foundation was an initiator of the creation of the monument commemorating the events of 1945, but the city council in Chorzów was not interested in the idea. In 2016, the Foundation erected the statue of Saint Florian – the patron saint of the city of Chorzów –located on the crossroad of Nomiarki St., Raciborska St. and 75 Pułku Piechoty St. Additionally, it co-organises a tournament of the traditional Silesian card game *Skat*, which is popular in Upper Silesia and is played almost exclusively in the region.[3]

4.1.2 *Pro Loquela Silesiana*

The *Pro Loquela Silesiana Towarzystwo Kultywowania i Promocji Śląskiej Mowy* (Pro Loquela Silesiana Society for Cultivating and Promoting Silesian Speech) is focussed on promoting Silesian language and culture. It also encourages people to use Silesian in the public space. In 2018, the Association merged with *Tôwarzistwo Piastowaniô Ślónskij Môwy "DANGA"* (Association for Cultivating Silesian Speech "DANGA").

The Association has been active since 2007 but was registered by the Court on 30 January 2008 (KRS 0000297625). This happened during the time when the Silesian movement was becoming increasingly popular and rapidly developing – the second wave of the creation of Silesian organisations. It has its

---

3 Fundacja "Silesia". n.d. "Ogólne".

own seat in Chorzów. In 2009, it was awarded the status of a Public Benefit Organisation. According to the regulations of the *Public Benefit and Volunteer Work Act* from 24 April 2003,[4] non-governmental organisations and other entities operating in the area of public benefit may apply for public benefit status. There are certain benefits and obligations stemming from this status. Pursuant to art. 3 para. 1 of the Act, activities addressing the general public conducted by NGOs in the area of public tasks defined in the Act qualify as public benefit activity. Some of its members are members of the *Śląska Partia Regionalna* as well.

The Association is orientated around the ideology of ethnoregionalism. It promotes the recognition of Silesians as an ethnic group and the Silesian language as a regional language. The Association took part in many projects dealing with the Silesian language. Since its creation, it has been cooperating with other Silesian associations, such as *Ruch Autonomii Śląska, Fundacja "Silesia"* and *Tôwarzistwo Piastowaniô Ślónskij Môwy "DANGA"* (Association for Cultivating Silesian Speech "DANGA"). It also takes an active part in the works of the *Rada Górnośląska*. Its members were involved in the Silesian Language Codification Committee, which existed in 2008–2009 under the leadership of Prof. Jolanta Tambor (UŚ). The Association cooperates with specialists from the University of Silesia, such as Prof. Jolanta Tambor and Prof. Zbigniew Kadłubek. It does not take an active part in elections or day-to-day politics.

Pro Loquela Silesiana, according to its Statute, exercises its public obligations by: organising conferences, gatherings and meetings concerning Silesian speech; publishing periodicals and books; producing TV and radio shows; gathering literature and granting public access to it; initiating and supporting activities that promote Silesian speech in the media and the public space; expressing opinions on matters concerning Silesian speech in the media, public space and press; settling problems arising in the area of Silesian orthography, grammar and lexis; expressing opinions about language norms; the popularisation of knowledge about Silesian speech through public events, exhibitions and activity on the Internet. According to its Statute, the goal of the Association is to take care of the status of Silesian language in Upper Silesian society and ensure its presence in the public sphere, promote knowledge about Silesia, support studies and works that aim to unify Silesian orthography, grammar and lexis, promote Silesian language in the media and publications, and support writers. The funds of the Association come from: membership fees,

---

4 Dz.U. 2003. 96. 873 with amendments.

inheritances and donations, subsidies, grants, other funds, and incomes from charity, business and publishing activities, but most of its income comes from publishing activity.

Pro Loquela Silesiana's main activity is the promotion of the Silesian language and participation in the creation of its written form with a suitable orthography. Moreover, in Poland, it promotes the concept of acknowledging Silesian as a language (ISO 639–3 code 'szl'). In order to achieve this goal, the Association has been collecting expert assessments on the topic of the Silesian language from the start. Members also take part in meetings with researchers and authorities on the subject. A Silesian handbook was created under the guidance of Prof. Jolanta Tambor in 2008–2009. The most important part of this work was to prepare a written version of the Silesian language, which had survived until today in spoken form but has rarely been used in writing. At the same time, the Association organised events and contests related to the Silesian language. One of them was: "U nos we Gody" ("At our place during celebration"). In 2008, the project "Wzrost potencjału PRO LOQUELA SILESIANA kluczem do poprawy stosunków społeczno-językowych na Górnym Śląsku" ("Growing potential of PRO LOQUELA SILESIANA as the key to the betterment of social and language relations in Upper Silesia") was launched. In 2009, the project "Śląski elementarz – przez oświatę do kultury regionalnej" ("Silesian handbook – through education to regional culture") was created. The latest initiative, "Poradzisz? Gŏdej!" ("Can you? Speak up!") aims at promoting the use of the Silesian language in the public sphere and in offices. The sign for the campaign, "Gŏdōmy po ślōnsku" ("We speak Silesian"), developed in cooperation with *Fundacja "Silesia"*, has been increasing its public presence. Members of the Association organised and conducted Silesian lessons during events like "Lekcyje ślōnskij gŏdki" ("Silesian lessons") in cooperation with the Silesian Museum in Katowice and "Akadymijŏ Ślōnskij Gŏdki" ("Silesian Speech Academy") in cooperation with the Upper Silesian Ethnographic Park in Chorzów. In cooperation with the PLS, the first websites, menus, manuals and brochures were created in the Silesian language and were used by private and public bodies. For example, they prepared the Silesian version of the system for Samsung. The Association acts in the event of public discrimination of persons using the Silesian language as well, e.g., in January 2017, in one of the clinics in Ruda Śląska.[5]

---

5 Pro Loquela Silesiana. 2017. "Stanowisko"; Pro Loquela Silesiana. n.d. "O nas".

4.1.3 *Ruch Autonomii Śląska*

The *Ruch Autonomii Śląska* (Silesian Autonomy Movement – RAŚ) is one of the biggest and most popular organisations in the region today. Some authors already classify it as a proto-party, or even a regional party, taking into consideration the role it has been playing on the Upper Silesian regional and political scene. The creation of RAŚ marks one of the beginning points in the development of the modern Silesian movement, but the organisation has evolved significantly throughout the years.

The Association was first founded in January 1990 as the *Ruch na Rzecz Autonomii Śląska* (Movement for Silesian Autonomy). The name was changed in 1991. While the decision to establish the Association was first made on 3 January 1990, it was re-registered on 27 June 2001 (KRS 0000021371). The organisation was created during the first wave of the creation of Silesian organisations. Its seat is located in Katowice, but it also has an office in Chorzów. A year before its establishment, another association – the *Związek Górnośląski* – was founded. These events mark the beginning of the modern Silesian movement. It must be kept in mind that the beginning of the 1990s was, generally speaking, a time of great change and transformation in Poland, which led to the emergence of many associations and organisations and the development of civic society.

The *Ruch Autonomii Śląska* is orientated around the ideology of ethnoregionalism. It promotes recognition of Silesians as an ethnic group and Silesian as a regional language. The Association advocates for the restoration of political autonomy for Upper Silesia, preferably in the form of the asymmetrical federalisation (regionalisation) of the state. Since 2003, the Association has been a member of the European Free Alliance. The political ideas and means of their introduction are presented in their main document: "Statut Organiczny Województwa Śląskiego" ("Organic Statute for the Silesian Voivodeship" – its project can be found on the RAŚ website). The project foresees the creation of a voivodeship from the districts belonging culturally, historically or economically to Upper Silesia. The Silesian Parliament is to be bicameral, i.e., with a *Sejm* (Lower Chamber) and *Senat* (Upper Chamber). There is to be a Silesian government with a President of the Ministers at its head, a Silesian Treasury, Silesian Administrative Court, Silesian Ombudsman and Silesian Council of Mass Media. The Silesian Parliament is to have legislative powers within the competences delegated to the Śląskie Voivodeship. The competences encompass, among other things: the organisation of decentralised institutions, the support of culture and science, education, social support, health, and many branches of the economy (agriculture, industry) and regional infrastructure.

POLITICAL ORGANISATIONS IN UPPER SILESIA

The Silesian Treasury is to be responsible for collecting and maintaining taxes and other sources of financing. Every year, the due share of Silesian income is to be sent to the Polish Treasury. The Silesian Administrative Court is to judge in accordance with the laws and acts (Polish and Silesian) in the Statute and in accordance with Silesian laws. Some of its members are members of the *Śląska Partia Regionalna* as well.

According to the Statute, the Association aims to achieve the autonomy of the regions in Poland without changing the existing borders of the state or independence claims. Any person who accepts the goals of the Association may become a member. The goals of the Association include: autonomy for Upper Silesia in the form of further decentralisation of the Republic of Poland; strengthening the regional identity of the inhabitants of Upper Silesia and other regions; the development of active citizen attitudes among Silesian inhabitants; undertaking actions that aim to protect the natural environment and cultural heritage; the promotion of human rights and civic freedoms, the promotion of European integration and the development of relations and cooperation between societies; maintaining cultural and economic contacts with the Silesian diaspora and supporting their emotional bonds to their motherland; the promotion and creation of a positive image of the region; the promotion of the diversity of the Silesian language. The Association is financed by membership fees and donations, grants, inheritance, charity and income from its own activities. Most of its income comes from membership fees.

The political programme of the Association is presented in the form of programmes of the electoral committees that the Association created for the purpose of elections to self-government bodies from 2002 to 2014. More information about the electoral committees created for the purposes of the parliamentary election may be found below.

In 2002 and 2006, electoral campaigns were carried out under the same title "Autonomia to rozwój" ("Autonomy means development"). During the campaigns, the role of self-government and the cooperation of all Silesian circles (including the German minority) was promoted. In 2010, the campaign was titled "Poradzymy" ("We can"). In the campaign, the Association promoted more decentralisation and more competences for regions. It also advocated for regional education (including the creation of a handbook), the promotion of Silesian culture and the betterment of public infrastructure. In 2014, the campaign was titled "Zawsze tutaj, dycki tukej" ("Always here"). The main points of the programme included citizens' activity, their role in the decision-making process and transparency of public offices. A short film titled "Nie daj się zamknąć w skansenie" ("Don't let them close you in a museum") also promoted Silesian culture and traditions, reminding people that diversity and multi-ethnicity is not a historical issue, but a very current one. Two representatives of the *Ruch Autonomii Śląska* gained mandates in the parliamentary elections of 1991. Since 2002, the Association has taken part in elections to self-government bodies. In 2010, it won three mandates in the *Sejmik Województwa Śląskiego* (Council of the Śląskie Voivodeship). From 2011 to 2013, RAŚ became a partner in the regional coalition (with the *Platforma Obywatelska* – the Civic Platform). In 2014, the Association managed to gain four mandates and once again become a member of the coalition in the Sejmik (also with the *Platforma Obywatelska* – the Civic Platform).

Since 2005, the Association has co-organised the *Górnośląskie Dni Dziedzictwa* (Upper Silesian Days of Heritage). The main events take place in September/October every year. Additionally, since 2006, the Ks. August Weltzl award – the *Górnośląski Tacyt* (Upper Silesian Tacyt) prize – has been awarded in two categories: researcher and populariser for people who take part in the development of knowledge about Upper Silesia in a significant way. Since 2007, the best-known event organised by the Association is probably *Marsz Autonomii* (Autonomy March), which takes place around 15 July every year. In 2011, it was transformed into *Dzień Górnośląski* (Upper Silesian Day). Since 2013, the *Dni Samorządności Śląskiej* (Days of Silesian Self-Government) were organised from 15–17 July, and 15 July has become the *Dzień Śląskiej Flagi* (Day of the Silesian Flag) – these days are celebrated on the first weekend after 15 July. A growing awareness of the tragic events that took place in 1945 and in the following years led to the emergence of a new event – the *Marsz na Zgodę* (March to Zgoda) – in 2009, which was later transformed into the *Dzień Pamięci o Tragedii Górnośląskiej* (Day of Commemoration of the Upper Silesian Tragedy). This name for the event has been used since 2013, and it takes place on the last Sunday in January every year. RAŚ is also active in the area of the restoration of Upper Silesian monuments, especially the ones taken from the region and relocated elsewhere. It organises talks, meetings and conferences about history, the present day and the future of the region. It is also engaged in the promotion of the Silesian language, with authors writing in Silesian about Silesia and Silesian symbols. Additionally, it advocates for the restoration of memory about the German-Silesian heritage of the region and the great personalities who are important for the history of the land. For many years, the RAŚ has organised charity events at the beginning of the school year, especially *Tyta dla pierszoka* (sweets for first-year students from disadvantaged families). Today, the Association has more than 10,000 members, according to its own

POLITICAL ORGANISATIONS IN UPPER SILESIA

data.[6] The main periodical of the Association is "Jaskółka Śląska", which has been published since 1990.[7]

4.1.4 Stowarzyszenie Osób Narodowości Śląskiej

The *Stowarzyszenie Osób Narodowości Śląskiej* (Association of Persons of Silesian Nationality) is best known for its long fight for registration. It may be seen as the voice of opposition of the Upper Silesian community towards the centralised ethnic policy of the Republic of Poland. It advocates for the right of belonging, declaring and sharing one's identity.

The Association was created in 2011. After a long process, it was first registered by the District Court on 21 December 2011 (KRS 0000405947). It was formed during the third wave of the creation of Silesian organisations, just after the National Census of 2011, when it was possible to declare Silesian nationality. Its seat was located in Kotórz Mały. The judgement allowing the registration was appealed by the District Attorney (on the basis of the misleading name of the Association) and, on 7 September 2012, the Regional Court decided to sustain the decision of the District Court. This judgement was undermined again, and the case was referred to the Supreme Court, which decided on 5 December 2013 (case III SK 10/13) that the name of the Association could lead to misunderstandings (that a Silesian nationality exists) and therefore was illegal. Accordingly, the case was sent back to the Regional Court, which decided on 7 March 2014 that the Association could not be named as it was, and the Court sent the case back to the District Court to withdraw the Association from the official register or persuade it to change its name and statute. On 12 August 2014, the Association was withdrawn from the register, and on 9 January 2015, it was dissolved by the Court. Since then, it has appeared in the register with the label "in liquidation". The Association contested the last decision but lost its case in the Regional Court on 18 June 2015. Later, it sent an appeal to the Supreme Court, which was refused on 16 October 2015. This decision of the Supreme Court ended the course of the process in Poland and allowed the Association to send its case to the European Court of Human Rights. The application to the ECHR was submitted in March 2017 and was admitted on 23 August 2017.

The *Stowarzyszenie Osób Narodowości Śląskiej* was orientated around the ideology of ethnoregionalism. It promoted the recognition of Silesians as an ethnic group and Silesian as a regional language. The Association wanted to gather people who declared Silesian nationality in order to preserve and

---

6   Ruch Autonomii Śląska. n.d. "Homepage".
7   Jaskółka Śląska. n.d. "Homepage".

cultivate the Silesian language, traditions and culture. It envisioned itself as a place where every Silesian could feel "at home" and meet people who think the same way. It allowed people of different nationalities to become supporting members. The Association decided not to create an electoral committee for the purpose of any elections, and, in 2013, the declaration of the non-political character of the Association was adopted. It took part in the works of the *Rada Górnośląska* (Upper Silesian Council).

The goals of the Association stated in its statute included: the preservation of Silesian identity; the rebirth of Silesian culture; the promotion of knowledge about Silesia; the development of active citizen attitudes among the inhabitants of Silesia; cooperation in the integration of inhabitants in the region; the preservation of bonds between Silesians, regardless of their place of residence and help for returning expatriates; the promotion of a positive image of Silesia and Silesians; the protection of the material and spiritual heritage of Silesia. The funds of the Association came from membership fees, donations, inheritance, charity, grants, subsidies and shares. Most of its income came from membership fees.

The activities of the Association encompassed the organisation of meetings and events. Its flagship project was the *Canon Silesiae* – a library of books written in Silesian or about Silesia. The Association also took part in Silesian celebrations and cooperated with organisations representing minorities in Europe. It also launched the project *Krajoznawcza Odznaka Górnośląsk*a (Upper Silesian Tourist Badge) and participated in charity events. Since the beginning of the process of its liquidation, its members have been closely cooperating with *Pro Loquela Silesiana*, and, since 2016, this cooperation has become an official (agreement).[8]

4.1.5   *Ślōnskŏ Ferajna*

The *Ślōnskŏ Ferajna* (Silesian Band) is an association aimed at promoting Silesian culture, language and traditions. It is concerned with forgotten persons and facts from Silesian history. It promotes using the Silesian language in public and the recognition of the Silesian nationality and language. According to its documents, the Association is non-political (it does not take part in elections and day-to-day politics).

The idea of forming the Association emerged in 2009. The Association has not been registered by the Court but as functioned as an unregistered association listed by the President of the city of Mysłowice under the number 138 since

---

8   Stowarzyszenie Osób Narodowości Śląskiej. n.d. "Homepage".

POLITICAL ORGANISATIONS IN UPPER SILESIA   105

2009. It was re-registered in February 2018 under the number 4. The Association was created during the second wave of the creation of new Silesian organisations, when new ideas concerning the promotion of Silesia and Silesians were being raised. The Association evolved from a local group of the *Ruch Autonomii Śląska*. Its seat is located in Mysłowice.

The *Ślōnskŏ Ferajna* is orientated around the ideology of ethnoregionalism, though it does not take part in elections. Its priority is the activity for the region and its inhabitants. It aims at promoting Silesian culture and its multi-ethnic character. Its goals also include strengthening and promoting Silesian identity. It advocates for the recognition of Silesians as a minority and the recognition of the Silesian nationality and its language. It promotes regional education at all levels of education and the introduction of Silesian symbols (flag, colours, emblem) to public offices in the region. Moreover, it advocates for more self-government in the region and further decentralisation by granting regions more competences based on the modern idea of a Europe of Regions. It takes part in the works of the *Rada Górnośląska* (Upper Silesian Council), and some of its members are also members of the *Śląska Partia Regionalna*.

According to its Statute, the goals of the Association are: awakening and strengthening Silesian identity among the inhabitants of Silesia; activities for the recognition of Silesians as an ethnic minority and *ślōnskŏ gŏdka* as a regional language; acting for the integration of all the inhabitants of Silesia within the region; the promotion of knowledge about Silesia; the rebirth and promotion of Silesian culture; the promotion and development of a positive image of Silesia; supporting the cooperation of all the inhabitants of Silesia – maintaining the cultural diversity of the region; initiating and maintaining cultural and economic contacts with Silesians, regardless of their current place of residence; activities supporting European integration; forming an active civic attitude among the inhabitants of Silesia. The funds come from membership fees.

Since 2009, the Association has organised the Silesian Ball every February. Since 2011, it has co-organised the Day of Remembrance of the Upper Silesian Tragedy. It also organises events on International Children's Day (1 June) and International Mother Tongue Day (21 February). It takes part in Upper Silesian Day (Autonomy March) and other regional celebrations. The Association has also organised conferences, exhibitions and other events aimed at the popularisation of knowledge about the region and at launching a public debate about the region of Silesia.[9]

---

9   Ślōnskŏ Ferajna. n.d. "Homepage".

4.1.6 Związek Górnośląski

The *Związek Górnośląski* (Upper Silesian Union) is one of the biggest and oldest Silesian organisations. It promotes Silesian tradition, customs, culture and speech. Its members have been present in public debate about the region since the 1980s, and many of them have held public offices in the region and the state.

The idea of creating a regional association started in 1989, shortly after the political changes in Poland. Many of the original members of the Association were previously members of the *Klub Inteligencji Katolickiej* in Katowice (Club of Catholic Intelligence in Katowice) and NSZZ *"Solidarność"*. The Association was re-registered by the Court on 25 July 2001 (KRS 0000030109). Its seat is located in Katowice. In 2009, it was given the status of a Public Benefit Organisation. According to the regulations of the *Public Benefit and Volunteer Work Act* from 24 April 2003, non-governmental organisations and other entities operating in the area of public benefit may apply for public benefit status. There are certain benefits and obligations stemming from this status. Pursuant to art. 3, para. 1 of the Act, activities addressing the general public, conducted by NGO s in the area of public tasks defined in the Act, are considered as public benefit activities.

The *Związek Górnośląski* is oriented around the ideology of ethnoregionalism. The main goals of the organisation are the protection and promotion of Silesian traditions. The Union is very moderate in its programme. It advocates for deeper decentralisation and more competences for all the regions in Poland, but its attitude towards Silesian autonomy is rather negative. It also advocates for the protection of Silesian culture and language but has a rather ambivalent stance on the recognition of Silesians as an ethnic minority or Silesian as a regional language. For a long time, it did not take part in any kind of elections as an association, but its members participated in elections as candidates from the lists of other committees and sometimes of state-wide parties. This state of affairs only slightly changed in 2017, when the *Śląska Partia Regionalna* (Silesian Regional Party) was created, and some members of the *Związek Górnośląski* joined it, but the Association itself never supported the initiative. It takes part in the works of the *Rada Górnośląska* (Upper Silesian Council).

After the *Związek Górnośląski* was created in 1989 and further developed in the 1990s, the goals of the Association became less and less demanding. In 1992, the Council of the Association adopted an opinion in which the idea of deep decentralisation involving the creation of autonomous regions with autonomous treasuries was raised. In the same opinion, the Association advocated for the observance of the historical, cultural and social boundaries of

Upper Silesia during the creation of administrative units (Lubina 2009, 65). At the beginning of its existence, the *Związek Górnośląski* had many mayors and members of local councils among its ranks. It also took an active part in the development of policies for the regions. According to one of the founders – Joanna Rostropowicz – in the beginning, the Association promoted many different narrations about the past and present of Upper Silesia. In the end, however, it was the Polish tradition of uprisings and the Polish character of Silesia that prevailed in the programme of the Association (Rostropowicz 2009, 37).

The aims of the Association were included in the *Deklaracja Związku Górnośląskiego* (Declaration of the Upper Silesian Union). There, we can find goals such as: the protection of values of Upper Silesia, which have their cultural roots in Christianity; social integration based on old and new values; the harmonious development of all the inhabitants of Upper Silesia; the representation of the needs and interests of Upper Silesia and its inhabitants; reference to the ancient Piast roots of the Upper Silesian duchies; raising awareness among Upper Silesians about their role in politics and their responsibility for the region, its heritage, dialect and customs, nature and landscape; the promotion of Upper Silesia and its true nature – its multicultural heritage and multi-ethnic reality; the development of the cultural and social bonds within the community; the betterment of the quality of life and protection of the environment; care for monuments of Polish, Czech-Moravian, German and Jewish cultures; cooperation with other similar Associations in Poland; strengthening bonds with Upper Silesians beyond the borders of the region. The Association finances its activities through membership fees, income from economic activities, income from a charity, donations, inheritances and grants and income from real estate and dividends. The main revenues are generated by renting rooms in the building belonging to the Union (the *Dom Śląski*).

The Union organises many cultural events in the region. Since 1993, the event "Śląskie Śpiewanie" ("Silesian Singing") has been organised for children from all over Upper Silesia, including its Czech parts. Since 1995, the Union has also organised a very popular festival of folklore and traditions called the "Śląskie Gody" ("Silesian Celebrations"). Since 1997, it has co-organised the "Konkurs krasnomówczy" ("Speaking Competition"). In 2010, the *Związek Górnośląski* co-organised the "Olimpiada wiedzy o Górnym Śląsku" ("Knowledge contest about Upper Silesia") for the first time. In 2014, the Association founded the "Dom Śląski" ("Silesian House"), which has become a public space for organising meetings and other Silesian events. It is open to anyone interested in the actions and goals of the *Związek Górnośląski*. In 2016, the Association organised events promoting traditional Silesian robes. It was decided that in the future, these events would be held on the first Sunday of August as a Day of

Traditional Silesian Robes. It 2017, the *Związek Górnośląski* took part in the Autonomy March and Upper Silesian Day in July for the first time as an organisation. Once a year, the Union organises a pilgrimage to Piekary Śląskie and meetings of Upper Silesian families in the Sanctuary on St Anne Mountain as well. The Association issues the monthly magazine "Górnoślązak".[10]

4.1.7 *Niemiecka Wspólnota "Pojednanie i Przyszłość"*

The *Niemiecka Wspólnota "Pojednanie i Przyszłość"* (German Community "Reconciliation and Future") is one of the biggest and oldest organisations of the German minority in the Śląskie Voivodeship. The Association cooperates with other Silesian organisations in the Silesian movement and with representatives of the German minority. Its objective is to build bridges between the German minority and society in Poland.

The Association was founded on 1 February 1991 and was registered by the Court on 7 December 2001 (KRS 0000069834). The Association was created as a result of a split within the community of the German minority in the early 1990s. Its seat is located in Katowice.

The Association is a representative of the German national minority living in Upper Silesia. It cooperates with organisations of the Silesian minority and supports their demands for recognition. It also represents Silesians with German roots, which makes it an organisation oriented towards ethnoregionalism in a specific way. Excluding this organisation from the group of Silesian organisations would be a mistake. Still, the specific features and position in the structure of recognised national minorities make it a special case for the purpose of this study. It takes part in the works of the *Rada Górnośląska* (Upper Silesian Council).

According to its Statute, the goals of the Association include: building bridges between the German minority and society in Poland; support for other organisations of the German minority; the protection of German traditions, education and language; achieving equal rights for all national minorities in Poland; the representation of German minority members before the authorities; finding common features in German and Polish cultures; assisting in all the problems of the regions where members of the German minority live; the protection of Upper Silesia from ecological, health, economic, educational, cultural and social degradation; shaping a modern German national awareness that is free from nationalism and has respect for other nations and tolerance for democracy and European ideology. The Association funds its activities

---

10   Związek Górnośląski. n.d. "Homepage".

POLITICAL ORGANISATIONS IN UPPER SILESIA

from membership fees, grants, subsidies, donations and inheritances, charity, economic activity and revenues from ownership.

The Association airs a programme on the Polskie Radio – *Górnośląski Magazyn Mniejszości Niemieckiej Przyszłość i Pojednanie* (Future and Reconciliation, an Upper Silesian programme of the German Minority) – and holds archives in the *Archiwum Państwowe* (State Archives). It co-founded the Polish-German High School in Zabrze (named after Queen Jadwiga) and funds a sports club. It organises help for the homeless through its own Social Care Point and Homeless Shelter. It prepares food for the poor. The organisation conducts German courses, as well as theatrical and other cultural events, such as evenings featuring the poetry of Joseph von Eichendorff. During the summer, it offers camps for children on Rømø Island. It organises lectures and meetings on the history of Upper Silesia and famous Silesians. The Association issues the periodical "Hoffnung".[11]

4.2 Organisations from outside the Upper Silesian Council

4.2.1 *Demokratyczna Unia Regionalistów Śląskich*

The *Demokratyczna Unia Regionalistów Śląskich* (Democratic Union of Silesian Regionalists) is an association promoting Silesian culture and language. It advocates for full and factual regional education and for teaching the Silesian language. It is the youngest organisation within the Silesian movement. The Association was founded in August 2015 and registered by the Court on 3 September 2015 (KRS 0000573047). Its seat is located in Rybnik.

The Association is oriented around the ideology of ethnoregionalism, though it does not take part in elections or day-to-day politics. It was created mostly for teachers interested in regional education and teaching the Silesian language. It also takes part in other initiatives promoting ideas developed outside the organisation. Some of its members also belong to the *Śląska Partia Regionalna*.

According to its Statute, the goals of the Association include: support for the regional community and the bonds within it; the development of regional culture and cultural diversity; the prevention of discrimination based on ethnicity; the protection of the cultural environment and heritage; advocacy for human rights; the promotion of European integration and cooperation with

---

11   Niemiecka Wspólnota "Pojednanie i Przyszłość". n.d. "Homepage".

other societies; the promotion of further decentralisation; support for minorities and the promotion of regional heritage in society.

The Association organises contests about the Silesian language and its orthography (the fifth *Diktand Ślōnskij Godki* took place in 2018). It took an active part in organising Silesian lessons in schools in the city of Rybnik. It takes part in events and actions organised by other Silesian organisations. The Association prepared materials for teaching regional education and the Silesian language. The Association also applied for a place in the *Rada Górnośląska* (Upper Silesian Council) in 2016 but was rejected due to an internal reorganisation within the Council. It issues the quarterly magazine "Rechtōr".[12]

4.2.2   *Nasz Wspólny Śląski Dom*

The *Stowarzyszenie "Nasz Wspólny Śląski Dom"* ("Our Common Silesian Home" Association) focuses on the social situation in the region and the quality of life of its inhabitants. It undertakes activities and projects in many areas of social life in Silesia.

The Association was founded in 2011. It was registered in the National Court Register on 31 May 2012 after many efforts to do so (KRS 0000422603). In order to register, the term "Silesian nationality" was removed from the Statute. Its registration happened during a period of change in the Silesia movement. Conflicts and arguments led to splits in some organisations and to the creation of new ones during the third wave of the creation of Silesian organisations. Also, some organisations became more politically active, and this was contested by others. The Association was registered in the same year as the *Stowarzyszenie Osób Narodowości Śląskiej*. The courts responsible for registering both organisations took their time to determine whether they could be registered in accordance with Polish law. In the end, in 2012, both organisations were registered successfully. The creation of the Association was motivated by the fact that, according to its founders, many social issues present in Silesia had not been solved, and other organisations were not interested in them. Consequently, there was a need for a new association in the region. Its seat is located in Rybnik.

The Association is oriented around the ideology of ethnoregionalism. It promotes the recognition of Silesians as an ethnic group and the Silesian language as a regional language. The Association advocates for the commemoration of Silesians and persons connected to Silesia, e.g., in the naming of streets. The organisation is open to all people who declare themselves as Silesians or live in the region. It advocates for the improvement of the quality

---

12   Demokratyczna Unia Regionalistów Śląskich. n.d. "Homepage".

POLITICAL ORGANISATIONS IN UPPER SILESIA

of life in Silesia. It promotes support for coal mining and other branches of the industry typical for the region. It advocates for self-government and decentralisation but is not attached to the idea of the federalisation of the Republic of Poland (autonomy for other regions). It stresses the need for the creation of a positive image of the region. The Association left the *Rada Górnośląska* (Upper Silesian Council) in 2016 due to the electoral failure of the *Zjednoczeni dla Śląska* Electoral Committee of Voters, organisational problems and a lack of support for its initiatives. Some of its members also belong to the *Ślonzoki Razem* party.

The Statute of the Association lists the following goals: establishing and raising awareness of the Silesian people; the development of Silesian culture; the promotion of knowledge about Silesia; actions aimed at the recognition of Silesian nationality; support for economics and democracy; citizen education; cooperation with regard to integration activities; the promotion of the Silesian language in accordance with ISO-code 693–3 "szl"; working towards achieving a higher level of social justice.

The members of the Association are very active in writing public letters to Polish and Silesian authorities. They have prepared appeals on issues relating to mining and miner strikes, smog, water prices, taxes, amendments to the Garden Plots Act and many others. They organised meetings in Rybnik, during which many social problems were debated. The Association does not publish any periodicals. However, there are some books and leaflets of which its members are authors, e.g., the "Naród Śląski".[13]

4.2.3 *Towarzystwo Społeczno-Kulturalne Niemców Województwa Śląskiego*

The *Towarzystwo Społeczno-Kulturalne Niemców Województwa Śląskiego/ Deutscher Freundschaftskreis in Schlesien* (Social and Cultural Society of Germans of the Śląskie Voivodeship) is one of the oldest organisations of the German minority in the region.

It was founded on 16 September 1990 and re-registered by the Court on 23 March 2011 (KRS 0000001895). Its seat is located in Racibórz. In 2010, it was awarded the status of a Public Benefit Organisation. According to the regulations of the *Public Benefit and Volunteer Work Act* from 24 April 2003, nongovernmental organisations and other entities operating in the area of public benefit may apply for public benefit status. There are certain benefits and obligations stemming from this status. Pursuant to art. 3, para. 1 of the Act,

---

13   Nasz Wspólny Śląski Dom. n.d. "Homepage".

activities addressing the general public, conducted by NGO s in the area of public tasks defined in the Act, are considered as public benefit activities.

It is a representative of the German national minority living in Upper Silesia. It also represents Silesians with German roots, which makes it oriented around ethnoregionalism in a specific way. Thus, this organisation should be included in the group of Silesian organisations. Still, the specific features of the organisation and its position in the structure of recognised national minorities makes it a special case for the purpose of this study. The Association cooperated with the *Ruch Autonomii Śląska* during the creation of the *Zjednoczeni dla Śląska* Electoral Committee of Voters, but it is not a part of the *Rada Górnośląska*.

According to its Statute, the goals of the Association include: promoting activities supporting the German minority; respect for democracy and the rule of law; advocacy for human rights; support for other individuals and organisations respecting the same goals. The Association funds its activities from membership fees, subsidies and grants, donations, inheritance, income from economic activity and others. Most of its revenues come from foreign grants and grants from the Polish budget.

On 17 June, the Association organises a Day of Remembrance for the Victims of the Camp in Zgoda and has done so for more than 20 years. In 2017, it took part in the European Citizens' Initiative for the introduction of regulations by the European Union on the protection of ethnic and national minorities and other groups of indigenous people ("Minority SafePack"). It organises meetings, cultural events and picnics, mostly for the members of the German minority. An important part of its activities is the promotion and preservation of the German language – it organises language courses and contests, one of them being a contest on knowledge about the life and poetry of Joseph von Eichendorff, who lived in Silesia. The Association issues the monthly "Oberschlesische Stimme".[14]

4.2.4   *Związek Ludności Narodowości Śląskiej*

The *Związek Ludności Narodowości Śląskiej* (Union of People of Silesian Nationality) is one of the oldest ethnoregionalist organisations in the region. It is best known for the fight it lost for its registration as an association pursuant to Polish law. It still acts as an organisation, but without legal form.

It was founded on 24 November 1996 by a group of 190 people. On 11 December 1996, its representatives applied to the Katowice Regional Court for the registration of Association. On 24 June 1997, the Katowice Regional

---

14   Deutscher Freundschaftskreis in Schlesien. n.d. "Homepage".

POLITICAL ORGANISATIONS IN UPPER SILESIA

Court granted the application and registered the association under the name "Union of People of Silesian Nationality". On 2 July 1997, the Governor of Katowice lodged an appeal with the Katowice Court of Appeal, asking that the first-instance decision be quashed and that the case be remitted to the Court of the first instance. The Katowice Court of Appeal heard the appeal on 24 September 1997. On the same day, the Court set aside the first-instance decision and rejected the application for the registration of the Association. On 3 November 1997, the applicants submitted an appeal on points of law to the Supreme Court. On 18 March 1998, the Administrative, Labour and Social Security Division of the Supreme Court dismissed it. After that, the case was referred to the European Court of Human Rights (ECHR). The case originated in the application (no. 44158/98) against the Republic of Poland lodged with the ECHR by three Polish nationals, Jerzy Gorzelik, Rudolf Kołodziejczyk and Erwin Sowa, on 18 June 1998. In its Judgement of 20 December 2001, the Chamber found that there had been no breach of Article 11. The Grand Chamber, in its Judgement from 17 February 2004, maintained the decision of the Chamber, with the justification:

> The Court concludes, therefore, that it was not the applicants' freedom of association *per se* that was restricted by the State. The authorities did not prevent them from forming an association to express and promote distinctive features of a minority but from creating a legal entity which, through registration under the Law on associations and the description it gave itself in paragraph 30 of its memorandum of association, would inevitably become entitled to a special status under the 1993 Elections Act. Given that the national authorities were entitled to consider that the contested interference met a "pressing social need" and given that the interference was not disproportionate to the legitimate aims pursued, the refusal to register the applicants' association can be regarded as having been "necessary in a democratic society" within the meaning of Article 11 § 2 of the Convention.[15]

Despite its lack of registration, the organisation still acts within a limited scope. The organisation is oriented around ethnoregionalism. It advocates for the recognition of Silesians as an ethnic minority and Silesian as a regional language. It promotes further decentralisation of the state and also advocates

---

15 Gorzelik and others v. Poland. ECHR. Application No. 44158/98. Judgement 17 February 2004, para. 106.

for the Silesian language and regional education to be taught in schools. One of its goals is the preservation of Silesian culture and heritage. It is interested in Silesian history and in the collective memory of its inhabitants. The organisation cooperates with other Silesian organisations but is not part of the *Rada Górnośląska*.[16]

4.3 Śląska Partia Regionalna

The *Śląska Partia Regionalna* – ŚPR (Silesian Regional Party) was created in October 2017. The documents required for its registration were sent on 13 October to the District Court in Warsaw, which is responsible for the registration of political parties. After that, the support list, which consisted of the signatures of 1,000 citizens, was meticulously checked, specifically in terms of the correctness of the data included (identification number, address and name of the person signing). The district court did not decide on the matter of the party's registration until April 2018, when it was officially registered as a political party. The seat of the party is located in Katowice. Among the founding members were members of *Ruch Autonomii Śląska, Związek Górnośląski, Demokratyczna Unia Regionalistów Śląskich, Niemiecka Wspólnota "Pojednanie i Przyszłość", Pro Loquela Silesiana, Przymierze Śląskie, Ślōnskŏ Ferajna, Związek Ślązaków* and many others – a total of 32 persons, including six women.

The party was created during a time of extraordinary centralisation conducted by the government of *Prawo i Sprawiedliwość* (Law and Justice), which is also known for its efforts in stressing the homogeneity of Polish society and rejection of the lawful recognition of Silesians as an ethnic minority. The party took part as an electoral committee of the *Śląska Parta Regionalna* in the elections to self-government bodies in 2018. As to its ideology, the party can be categorised as ethnoregionalist. During its first convention, which took place on 16 April 2018 in Katowice, the most important points of its programme were presented. The mission of the party includes four issues: self-government, identity, innovation and dialogue. The Association also advocates more specific postulates. The first of them is the need for the activists from within the region, not the parties located in the centre – Warsaw – to take responsibility for the region. Second, it also mentions the need to rebuild the Silesian collective memory and restore awareness and respect for the diverse collective

---

16   Związek Ludności Narodowości Śląskiej. n.d. "News".

POLITICAL ORGANISATIONS IN UPPER SILESIA

memory (and history) of Silesians. The third postulate speaks of the need to create a 'brand' for the region based on post-industrial heritage. One of the most important points of the party's programme includes the City Centre+ project (in response to the governmental Apartment+ project), which aims to revitalise the centres of Silesian cities by creating apartments in old, restored buildings. The public transportation system is an important issue, as well. One of the goals of the party is the development of infrastructure, especially railways and accompanying infrastructure, to ensure intermodality. Furthermore, a new source of financing for self-governments was suggested – the plan for 3x1% VAT, the purpose of which is to share the VAT budgetary income with three levels of self-government bodies. Also, the decentralisation of seats in the central institutions – ministries – to regions was suggested. Lastly, the main task is fighting pollution in the Silesia region.

The goals of the party include: widening and strengthening self-government by handing over a certain extent of legislative power to regions and decentralising public finances; the creation of the necessary conditions for the preservation and development of an identity of the inhabitants in the region; the preservation of the cultural heritage of Silesian lands, including linguistic diversity; the betterment of the quality of life of the residents of the region, especially through the development of public transportation, rational spatial development, the betterment of the state of the environment and the complex revitalisation of city centres and dilapidated neighbourhoods and towns; the betterment of education in the region through focusing education on the development of independent, critical and innovative thinking and support for regional education; the promotion and protection of freedom, human rights and citizens' liberties through the promotion of openness and dialogue. The main sources of financing include membership fees, donations, inheritance and income from assets and revenues as defined by the law on donations and subsidies.[17]

4.4   Ślonzoki Razem

Ślonzoki Razem – ŚR (Silesians Together) was created in August 2017. The documents required for its registration were sent to the District Court in Warsaw, which is responsible for the registration of political parties, in the same month. Upon submission, the District Court investigated whether the Statute of the

---

17   Śląska Partia Regionalna. n.d. "Homepage".

party complied with the law. From time to time, a request for an explanation or additional information was made. The District Court did not decide to register the party until May 2018. The seat of the party is located in Chorzów. The founding members of the party are associated with the *Związek Ludności Narodowości Śląskiej* and *Nasz Wspólny Śląski Dom*.

The idea to create a Silesian party that would cooperate with the German minority was raised as early as 2014. A year later, the Electoral Committee of Voters *Zjednoczeni dla Śląska* was created and took part in the elections to the lower chamber of Parliament. At the same time, the Electoral Committee of Voters, *Ślonzoki Razem*, took part in the elections to the Senate. However, this formula did not work. After this experience, some of the activists decided to register a new political party called *Ślonzoki Razem*. The project started before the *Śląska Partia Regionalna* was created. The party took part as the Electoral Committee of *Ślonzoki Razem* in the elections to self-government bodies in 2018.

As to its ideology, the party is ethnoregionalist, and the most important point in its programme is Silesian identity. Its aims include: the aspiration for the integration of the community of people who declare themselves Silesians, the preservation and teaching of Silesian language – mostly by financing voluntary, open lessons of regional education and Silesian – and support for teaching German and Czech in the region. Moreover, the party plans to support the development and preservation of Silesian culture and tradition. Next, it promotes the idea of further decentralisation of the state through the implementation of autonomous regions with economic autonomy. According to its programme, Poland should be divided into autonomous regions with legislative prerogatives and separate regional treasuries. Moreover, economic autonomy should apply to municipalities (districts should be liquidated). The suggested solution provides that municipalities will collect all public revenues (taxes) produced in their territory and will transfer part of them to the autonomous region and the state. The programme outlines the boundaries of the autonomous regions within their historical borders.

The goal of the party is the well-being and development of Silesia and Silesians. The main sources of financing include membership fees, donations and inheritance and donations regulated by the law.[18]

---

18   Ślonzoki Razem. n.d. "Homepage".

POLITICAL ORGANISATIONS IN UPPER SILESIA 117

4.5 Electoral Committees

In the Polish electoral system, there are at least three ways to register an electoral committee. One of them is through the registration of an electoral committee of voters – a group of people creating a list for particular elections. The second is with an electoral committee of a political party (registered as such by the Court). Until 2018, Silesian ethnoregionalists usually created electoral committees of voters for the purpose of parliamentary elections. Additionally, organisations and associations can have their own electoral committees for the purpose of elections to self-government bodies. The electoral committees of voters created for the purpose of parliamentary elections and electoral committees registered for elections to self-government bodies by ethnoregionalists are presented here.

4.5.1 *Autonomia dla Ziemi Śląskiej*

The *Autonomia dla Ziemi Śląskiej* [AdZS] (Autonomy for the Silesian Land) Electoral Committee of Voters was created for the purpose of the parliamentary elections in 2011. It took part in the elections to the Upper Chamber of Parliament – the Senate.

The Committee was created by the members of the *Ruch Autonomii Śląska* for the purpose of the elections only. The campaign was a continuation of the 2010 electoral campaign for self-government bodies. The main slogan of "Poradzymy" was used by the candidates again.

In the parliamentary elections in 2011, the Electoral Committee of Voters *Autonomia dla Ziemi Śląskiej* supported five candidates to the Senate. The results were as follows: in district 70 – Zenon Lis (14.93%), in district 73 – Paweł Polok (21.92%), in district 74 – Janusz Dubiel (25.30%), in district 75 – Dariusz Dyrda (32.35%), in district 78 – Roman Pająk (7.58%).[19]

4.5.2 *Mniejszość na Śląsku*

The *Mniejszość na Śląsk* [MnŚ] (Minority in Silesia) Electoral Committee of Voters was created for the purpose of the elections to self-government bodies in 2014 and took part in the elections to the Sejmik of the Śląskie Voivodeship. Initially, it was supposed to be named *Narodowości śląskie* (Silesian Nationalities), but the registration of the Committee under this name was refused by the Electoral Commissioner.

---

19   PKW (Państwowa Komisja Wyborcza). 2011. "Wyniki wyborów do Senatu 2011".

The Committee was formed by the initiative of the *Związek Ludności Narodowości Śląskiej, Narodowa Oficyna Śląska* (Silesian National Publishing), *Grupa Standaryzacyjna Języka Śląskiego* (Silesian Language Standardisation Group) and members of the Association *Nasz Wspólny Śląski Dom*.

It used the phrase "Razym Mogymy!" ("Together we can!") as a slogan for the elections. The Committee included its programme in its manifesto issued on 28 September 2014. Its priority was the protection of Silesian culture and language in response to today's threat to Silesian heritage. It demanded special protection for Silesian traditions, heritage and language and for persons of Silesian nationality. The Committee was created for all of the inhabitants of the region and treated its ethnic and national identities inclusively. The protection of the culturally diverse heritage and multi-ethnic character of the modern society of the region gave rise to its name – *Mniejszość na Śląsku* (Minority in Silesia), which aimed at the preservation of diversity. The creators believed that there is a need for a louder voice and stronger representation of the interests of the region and its community.

The Committee declared its close cooperation with the citizens and openness to their needs. It invited its voters and others to debate about the needs of the region and possible solutions to its problems. The main demands of the Committee were presented in its programme. The first involved changing the administrative borders of the Śląskie Voivodeship to reflect the historical borders of the regions (in the case of Silesia, the creation of two: Upper and Lower Silesia). The second discussed fiscal self-determination, which was to be achieved by letting the inhabitants of the region administer their wealth and income through their representatives. This self-determination principle was also to be applied to the natural resources of regions. The third demand was for the Silesian language, heritage, history and culture to be taught in schools. The decentralisation of competences was to include education as well. The fourth demand was for negotiations to be commenced with the central government about the political status of the region in the future.[20]

The Committee took part in elections in the following constituencies:
- Bielsko-Biała, Bielski, Cieszyński, Żywiecki – 854 votes,
- Katowice, Mysłowice, Tychy, Bieruńsko-Lędziński, Pszczyński – 2,091 votes,
- Jastrzębie-Zdrój, Rybnik, Żory, Mikołowski, Raciborski, Rybnicki, Wodzisławski – 2,913 votes,
- Bytom, Gliwice, Gliwicki, Lubliniecki, Tarnogórski – 2,720 votes,

---

20   Mniejszość na Śląsku. n.d. "Homepage".

POLITICAL ORGANISATIONS IN UPPER SILESIA

– Chorzów, Piekary Śląskie, Ruda Śląska, Siemianowice Śląskie, Świętochłowice, Zabrze – 1,516 votes.

They won 10,094 votes (0.8%) in the election to the Sejmik of the Śląskie Voivodeship.

4.5.3   Zjednoczeni dla Śląska

The *Zjednoczeni dla Śląska* [ZdŚ] (United for Silesia) Electoral Committee of Voters was created for the purpose of the parliamentary elections in 2015 and took part in the elections to the Sejm – i.e., the Lower Chamber of the Polish Parliament.

The Committee was formed at the initiative of two minorities living in the region of Upper Silesia. The idea came from the German minority associations *Towarzystwo Społeczno-Kulturalne Niemców Województwa Śląskiego* (Social and Cultural Society of Germans of the Śląskie Voivodeship) and *Niemiecka Wspólnota "Pojednanie i Przyszłość"* (German Community "Reconciliation and Future"). Upper Silesians from these associations, supported by the Upper Silesian Council, became the main force behind the project. *Zjednoczeni dla Śląska* was registered on 13 August 2015 as an Electoral Committee of Voters for the parliamentary elections, which were to take place the same year.

The political programme of the ZdŚ was presented in two documents: "Mission" and "12 points". The former starts by enumerating the problems in the Upper Silesia region: the crisis of black coal mines, social protests, strikes and the degeneration of the natural environment in the region. Then, it states that there is no desire in the central Polish administration to solve the problems that the region Upper Silesia is facing and highlights the lack of commitment towards the region on the part of Silesians elected to Parliament from the state-wide parties. As a result, it goes on to announce the intention for all Silesians (including those with German or Polish national identities) to take responsibility for the region. This goal is to be achieved by forming a Silesian political platform composed of members of diverse Silesian societies who are ready to act as representatives because change can only be made by people with strong connections to the region (Zjednoczeni dla Śląska 2015). The latter document states that people are the greatest asset of Upper Silesia, but its culture and tradition are still undervalued – a situation that can only be changed by regional education, the right to use the minority language and the right to cultivate its own collective memory. Silesians should have real possibilities in education and career development, and the region itself needs a long-term strategy for development. The post-industrial heritage should be considered an asset and be used to decrease unemployment and deepen social integration. The existing industry should thrive and be based on new technologies and a knowledge-based economy. The degradation of the natural and social environment should be stopped. These goals can be achieved by developing a policy tailored to the region in order to promote its economic and social growth. Upper Silesia needs a broad political consensus in order to implement long-term development policies (Jodliński 2015). From these documents stems the conclusion that the ZdŚ was invented to be a regional and ethnic representation, based in the region Upper Silesia. If it was a political party, it could be categorised as ethnoregionalist.

It took part in the elections in two constituencies:

- 30: Jastrzębie Zdrój, Rybnik, Żory, Mikołowski, Raciborski, Rybnicki, Wodzisławski – 7,928 votes;
- 31: Chorzów, Katowice, Mysłowice, Piekary Śląskie, Ruda Śląska, Siemianowice Śląskie, Świętochłowice, Tychy, Bieruńsko-Lędziński – 10,740 votes.

All in all, they gained 18,668 votes in the elections to the Sejm.

4.5.4 *Ślonzoki Razem*

The *"Ślonzoki Razem"* [śr] (Silesians Together) Electoral Committee of Voters was created for the purpose of the parliamentary elections in 2015 and took part in the elections to the Senat – i.e., the Upper Chamber of the Polish Parliament.

It was an initiative of a Silesian organisation – the *Związek Ludności Narodowości Śląskiej* – and took part in the elections in two constituencies:

- 71 – Bytom and Zabrze;
- 74 – Chorzów, Siemianowice Śląskie, Świętochłowice, Ruda Śląska and Piekary Śląskie.

In constituency 71, its candidate, Witold Berus, gained 14.14 % (16,643) votes. In constituency 74, its candidate, Leon Swaczyna, gained 26.22% (42,408) votes.[21]

4.6 Electoral Results in the Region

In the parliamentary elections to the Sejm in 1991, the *Ruch Autonomii Śląska* gained two mandates and received 40,061 votes – 20,261 in the Katowice district (36), which resulted in a mandate for Świtoń Kazimierz, and 19,800 in the Gliwice district (37), which resulted in a mandate for Paweł Musioł.[22]

---

21 PKW (Państwowa Komisja Wyborcza). 2015. "Wyniki wyborów do Senatu 2015".
22 M.P. 1991. 41. 288.

POLITICAL ORGANISATIONS IN UPPER SILESIA

TABLE 1   Elections to Sejmik of Śląskie voivodship 2002. Results RAŚ

District	Votes	Per cent (%)
1	1741	0.9
2	11185	6.1
3	22149	11.1
4	7557	4.1
5	8787	5.9
6	829	0.7
7	870	0.5

DATA FROM PAŃSTWOWA KOMISJA WYBORCZA (STATE ELECTORAL COMMISSION)

In the elections to self-government bodies in 2002, the Electoral Committee of RAŚ won 52,118 (4.2%) votes in the election to the regional council – *Sejmik Województwa Śląskiego* (Sejmik of the Śląskie Voivodeship) (See Table 1). It took part in the elections in the following districts:

– Bielsko-Biała, Bielski, Cieszyński, Żywiecki
– Katowice, Mysłowice, Tychy, Bieruńsko-Lędziński, Pszyczyński.
– Jastrzębie-Zdrój, Rybnik, Żory, Mikołowski, Raciborski, Rybnicki, Wodzisławski.
– Bytom, Gliwice, Gliwicki, Lubliniecki, Tarnogórski.
– Chorzów, Piekary Śląskie, Ruda Śląska, Siemianowice Śląskie, Świętochłowice, Zabrze.
– Częstochowa, Częstochowski, Kłobudzki, Myszkowski.
– Dabrowa Górnicza, Jaworzno, Sosnowiec, Będziński, Zawierciański.

In 2002, the Electoral Committee of RAŚ took part also in the elections to the city council in Katowice, Ruda Śląska and to the district council in Rybnicki (four mandates).[23]

In elections to self-government bodies in 2006, the Electoral Committee of RAŚ won 58,919 (4.35%) votes[24] in the election to the regional council – *Sejmik Województwa Śląskiego* (Sejmik of the Śląskie Voivodeship) (See Table 2).

---

23   PKW (Państwowa Komisja Wyborcza). 2002. "Wyniki wyborów samorządowych – Sejmiki".
24   PKW (Państwowa Komisja Wyborcza). 2006. "Wyniki wyborów samorządowych – Sejmiki".

TABLE 2 Elections to Sejmik of Śląskie voivodship 2006. Results RAŚ

District	Votes	Per cent (%)
1	1815	0.9
2	15805	7.7
3	16778	8.1
4	11700	5.9
5	11139	7
6	662	0.4
7	1020	0.5

DATA FROM PAŃSTWOWA KOMISJA WYBORCZA (STATE ELECTORAL COMMISSION)

The Electoral Committee of RAŚ also took part in the elections to the city council in Ruda Śląska, Rybnik and the district council in Rybnicki (four mandates).

In the elections to self-government bodies in 2010, in the election to the *Sejmik Województwa Śląskiego* (Sejmik of the Śląskie Voivodeship) (See Table 3), the Electoral Committee of RAŚ won 122,781 (8.49%) votes and three mandates: Jerzy Gorzelik, Henryk Mercik and Janusz Wita.

In the elections to city councils, the Electoral Committee of RAŚ ran in Chorzów, Katowice, Ruda Śląska and Rybnik (one mandate) and to district councils in Bieruńsko-Lędziński, Rybnicki (five mandates) and Wodzisławski (one mandate).[25]

In elections to self-government bodies in 2014 – to the *Sejmik Województwa Śląskiego* (Sejmik of the Śląskie Voivodeship) (See Table 4) – the Electoral Committee of RAŚ won 97,131 (7.2%) votes and four mandates: Jerzy Gorzelik, Henryk Mercik, Andrzej Sławik and Janusz Wita.

In the elections to city councils, the Electoral Committee of RAŚ ran in Bytom, Chorzów (two mandates), Jastrzębie Zdrój, Katowice (two mandates), Ruda Śląska, Rybnik, Świętochłowice, Zabrze and to district councils in Bieruńsko-Lędziński, Gliwicki, Rybnicki (one mandate), Tarnogórski (two mandates) and Wodzisławski (one mandate).[26]

---

25   PKW (Państwowa Komisja Wyborcza). 2010. "Wyniki wyborów samorządowych – Sejmiki".
26   PKW (Państwowa Komisja Wyborcza). 2014. "Wyniki wyborów samorządowych – Sejmiki".

POLITICAL ORGANISATIONS IN UPPER SILESIA   123

TABLE 3   Elections to Sejmik of Śląskie voivodship 2010. Results RAŚ

District	Votes	Per cent (%)
1	3570	1.6
2	35265	16
3	32068	14.6
4	17719	8.7
5	29851	17.5
6	1263	0.7
7	3046	1.4

DATA FROM PAŃSTWOWA KOMISJA WYBORCZA (STATE ELECTORAL COMMISSION)

TABLE 4   Elections to Sejmik of Śląskie voivodship 2014. Results RAŚ

District	Votes	Per cent (%)
1	2888	1.1
2	27865	19.2
3	21973	8.8
4	15953	7.3
5	25530	17.6
6	1099	0.5
7	1823	0.7

DATA FROM PAŃSTWOWA KOMISJA WYBORCZA (STATE ELECTORAL COMMISSION)

Another ethnoregionalist committee – the Electoral Committee of *Mniejszości na Śląsku* – took part in the same elections. They won 10,094 votes (0.8%) in the election to the *Sejmik Województwa Śląskiego* (Sejmik of the Śląskie Voivodeship) (See Table 5).

In the elections to self-government bodies in 2018, in the vote to the regional council – the *Sejmik Województwa Śląskiego* (Sejmik of the Śląskie Voivodeship)

124 CHAPTER 4

TABLE 5   Elections to Sejmik of Śląskie voivodship 2014. Results MnŚ

District	Votes	Per cent (%)
1	854	0.3
2	2091	1.4
3	2913	1.2
4	2720	1.3
5	1516	1

DATA FROM PAŃSTWOWA KOMISJA WYBORCZA (STATE ELECTORAL COMMISSION)

TABLE 6   Elections to Sejmik of Śląskie voivodship 2018. Śląska Partia Regionalna

District	Votes	Share (%)
1	2440	0.9
2	13457	5.1
3	9546	3.3
4	13579	5.2
5	11515	5.5
6	1438	0.6
7	2113	0.7

DATA FROM PAŃSTWOWA KOMISJA WYBORCZA (STATE ELECTORAL COMMISSION)

(See Table 6) – the Electoral Committee of the *Śląska Partia Regionalna* achieved 54,092 (3.1%) votes.[27]

The share of votes for ŚPR differs significantly among constituencies. The party achieved the lowest scores (less than 1%) in the northern part of the Śląskie Voivodeship – constituencies 6 and 7 – which encompass the sub-regions of Częstochowa area and Zagłębie Dąbrowskie, and in the southern part – constituency 1 – which encompasses the sub-region of Cieszyn Silesia.

---

27   PKW (Państwowa Komisja Wyborcza). 2018. "Wyniki wyborów samorządowych – Sejmiki".

POLITICAL ORGANISATIONS IN UPPER SILESIA 125

TABLE 7   Elections to Sejmik of Śląskie voivodship 2018. Ślonzoki Razem

District	Votes	Share (%)
1	3119	1.2
2	11672	4.5
3	13090	4.5
4	11870	4.6
5	16637	7.9

DATA FROM PAŃSTWOWA KOMISJA WYBORCZA (STATE ELECTORAL COMMISSION)

The middle score (3.3 %) was achieved in constituency 3. The highest scores (more than 5%) were achieved in constituencies 2, 14 and 5.

In the same elections, in the vote to the regional council – the *Sejmik Województwa Śląskiego* (Sejmik of the Śląskie Voivodeship) (See Table 7) – the Electoral Committee of *Ślonzoki Razem* achieved 56,388 (3.2%) votes.

The share of votes for ŚR differs significantly among constituencies. The party achieved the lowest scores (more than 1%) in the southern part of the Śląskie Voivodeship – constituency 1 – which encompasses the sub-region of Cieszyn Silesia. The middle score (about 4.5 %) was achieved in constituencies 2, 3 and 4. The highest score (almost 8%) was achieved in constituency 5. It did not put forward candidates in constituencies 6 and 7.

The overall electoral result counted *en bloc* is 110,480 (6.3%), but if presented for constituencies, there is a wide range of results (from 0.6% to 13.4%).

In the elections in 2018, due to the division of votes for two ethnoregionalist parties, no mandate was achieved by ethnoregionalists in the *Sejmik Województwa Śląskiego* (Sejmik of Śląskie Voivodeship) (See Table 8).

In the meantime, ethnoregionalists also took part in parliamentary elections. In elections to the Senate, the districts in Upper Silesia are as follows:

– 70 – Gliwice, Gliwicki and Tarnogórski districts;
– 71 – Bytom and Zabrze;
– 73 – Rybnik, Rybnicki and Mikołowski districts;
– 74 – Chorzów, Siemianowice Śląskie, Świętochłowice, Ruda Śląska and Piekary Śląskie;
– 75 – Tychy, Bieruńsko-Lędziński and Mysłowice districts;
– 78 – Bielsko-Biała, Bielski and Pszczyński districts.

TABLE 8   Elections to Sejmik of Śląskie voivodship 2018. En bloc

District	Votes	Share (%)
1	5559	2.1
2	25129	9.6
3	22636	7.8
4	25449	9.8
5	28152	13.4
6	1438	0.6
7	2113	0.7

DATA FROM PAŃSTWOWA KOMISJA WYBORCZA (STATE ELECTORAL COMMISSION), OWN CALCULATIONS

In the parliamentary elections in 2011, the *Autonomia dla Ziemi Śląskiej* Electoral Committee of Voters supported five candidates to the Senate. In district 70 – Zenon Lis (14.93%), in district 73 – Paweł Polok (21.92%), in district 74 – Janusz Dubiel (25.30%), in district 75 – Dariusz Dyrda (32.35%), in district 78 – Roman Pająk (7.58%).[28]

In the parliamentary elections of 2015, the *Ślązoki Razem* Committee took part in the elections to the Senate. In district 71, its candidate Witold Berus won 14.14 % (16,643) of the votes. In district 74, its candidate Leon Swaczyna won 26.22 % (42,408) of the votes.[29]

In the same Elections, the *Zjednoczeni dla Śląska* Committee took part in elections to the Sejm.

It won votes in the following districts:
– 30: Jastrzębie Zdrój, Rybnik, Żory, Mikołowski, Raciborski, Rybnicki, Wodzisławski – 7,928;
– 31: Chorzów, Katowice, Mysłowice, Piekary Śląskie, Ruda Śląska, Siemianowice Śląskie, Świętochłowice, Tychy, Bieruńsko-Lędziński – 10,740 votes.

In parliamentary elections in 2019, ethnoregionalists did not put forward any electoral committees. Instead, they joined state-wide electoral committees. The *Śląska Partia Regionalna* decided to join the *Koalicja Obywatelska* (Civic Coalition), created by the *Platforma Obywatelska* – Civic Platform,

---

28   PKW (Państwowa Komisja Wyborcza). 2011. "Wyniki wyborów do Senatu 2011".
29   PKW (Państwowa Komisja Wyborcza). 2015. "Wyniki wyborów do Senatu 2015".

POLITICAL ORGANISATIONS IN UPPER SILESIA

TABLE 9   Elections to Senate 2019. District 74

Candidate	Kostempski David (Electoral Committe of Voters)	Swaczyna Leon (Ślonzoki Razem)	Tobiaszowska Dorota (Prawo i Sprawiedliwość – Law and Justice)	Henryk Mercik (Koalicja Obywatelska)
Results	20%	14%	38%	28%

DATA FROM PAŃSTWOWA KOMISJA WYBORCZA (STATE ELECTORAL COMMISSION)

Nowoczesna – Modern and other parties. The *Ślonzoki Razem* joined the *Polskie Stronnictwo Ludowe* (Polish Peoples' Party). Results of this decision can be seen in the results of the election to the Senate in district 74 (See Table 9).

Consequently, two representatives of ethnoregionalist parties were fighting against each other for votes, and neither of them won the mandate (single-member district), which was won by the candidate from *Prawo i Sprawiedliwość* – Law and Justice.

Thus far, we have looked only at the election results. The second biggest organisation – the *Związek Górnośląski* – did not take part in elections of any kind as an organisation. Still, its activists ran in the elections on the lists of other committees. The political careers of some of its presidents will be presented as an example.

- Joachim Otte was the president of the *Związek Górnośląski* in 1991–1997. From 1994 to 2014, he was a member of the council of the city of Chorzów, elected from the list of the *Wspólny Chorzów* local committee.
- Jerzy Wuttke was a member of the *Związek Górnośląski* since the beginning of its existence but was chosen as its president in 1997 and acted as such until 2000. In the first semi-democratically elected Sejm (1989–1991), he served as a delegate. Then, in the democratically elected Sejm (1991–1993), he was chosen from the lists of the BBWR *(Bezpartyjny Blok Współpracy z Rządem* – Nonpartisan Block of Cooperation with Government).
- Jerzy Śmiałek was the president of the *Związek Górnośląski* in 2000–2003. From 1990 to 1994, he was president of the city of Katowice on the *Komitet Obywatelski* (Citizens' Committee) and in 1994–2004, he was the head of the board of the KZK GOP (Municipal Transportation Union of the Upper Silesian Industrial District).
- Krzysztof Szyga was the president of the *Związek Górnośląski* in 2003–2006. From 2001 to 2005, he was the head of the structures of the PO *(Platforma Obywatelska* – Civic Platform) in Siemianowice Śląskie. In 2005–2007, he

was a delegate for the Sejm from the PO lists, while in 2010, he was a candidate to the Sejm from the PJN list (*Polska Jest Najważniejsza* – Poland is the Most Important).

- Józef Buszman was the president of the *Związek Górnośląski* from 2008 to 2010. In 1990–1994, he was a member of the city council of Katowice from the *Komitet Obywatelski*, from 1998 to 2002, he was a member of the city council of Katowice from the AWS (*Akcja Wyborcza Solidarność* – Solidarity Electoral Action), in 2001, he was a candidate for the Sejm from the PiS lists (*Prawo i Sprawiedliwość* – Law and Justice), while from 2007 to 2010, he was a member of the Sejmik of the Śląskie Voivodeship from the PO lists (*Platforma Obywatelska* – Civic Platform).
- Andrzej Stania was president of the *Związek Górnośląski* in 2010–2014. From 2000 to 2014, he was president of the Ruda Śląska with the support of the PO (*Platforma Obywatelska* – Civic Platform) and has been a member of the city council in the city from PO lists since 2010.

4.7 Electoral Campaigns in the Region

In 2002 and 2006, campaigns of the Electoral Committee *Ruch Autonomii Śląska* were under the same title – "Autonomia to rozwój" ("Autonomy means development"). During the campaigns, the role of self-government and the cooperation of all Silesian circles (including the German minority) was promoted.

In 2010, the campaign of the Electoral Committee *Ruch Autonomii Śląska* was titled "Poradzymy" ("We can do it"). In the campaign, the Association promoted more decentralisation and more competences for regions. It also advocated for regional education (including a handbook), the promotion of Silesian culture and the betterment of public infrastructure.

In 2014, the campaign was titled "Zawsze tutaj, dycki tukej" ("Always here"). The main points of the programme included citizens' activity and role in the decision-making process and transparency of public offices. Also, a piece titled "Nie daj się zamknąć w skansenie" ("Don't let them close you in a museum") promoted Silesian culture and traditions, reminding people that diversity and multiethnicity are not historical problems but very current ones.

In 2014, the campaign of the *Mniejszości na Śląsku* Electoral Committee of Voters was titled "Razym Mogymy!" ("Together we can!"). Its priority was the protection of Silesian culture and language as a response to today's threat to Silesian heritage. It demanded special protection for Silesian traditions, heritage and language and for persons of Silesian nationality. The creators believed

POLITICAL ORGANISATIONS IN UPPER SILESIA

that there is a need for a louder voice and stronger representation of the interests of the region and its community.

In 2018, the *Śląska Partia Regionalna* presented a complex programme, which was already described in Subchapter 4.3. It is hard to point out one slogan from the campaign, but "Najlepszŏ, bo nasza!" ("The best, because ours!") was probably the most visible. "Pierwszy wybór #dlaŚląska" ("The first choice #forSilesia") was also used during the campaign. The campaign stressed the bottom-up character of the structure of the party and the fact that its members are strongly connected to the region and know its problems.

4.8 Initiatives

Attempt to Register the *Związek Ludności Narodowości Śląskiej* (Union of People of Silesian Nationality)

In 1996, a group of 190 people decided to form an association called the *Związek Ludności Narodowości Śląskiej* (Union of People of Silesian Nationality). On 11 December 1996, their representatives, acting on behalf of the provisional management committee of the ZLNŚ, applied to the Katowice Regional Court for the registration of their association. On 24 June 1997, the Katowice Regional Court, sitting with a single judge *in camera*, granted the applicants' application and registered their association under the name "Union of People of Silesian Nationality". On 2 July 1997, the Governor of Katowice lodged an appeal with the Katowice Court of Appeal, asking that the first-instance decision be quashed and that the case be remitted to the court of the first instance. The Katowice Court of Appeal heard the appeal on 24 September 1997. On the same day, the court set aside the first-instance decision and rejected the applicants' application for the registration of their association. On 3 November 1997, the applicants lodged an appeal on points of law (cassation) with the Supreme Court. On 18 March 1998, the Administrative, Labour and Social Security Division of the Supreme Court, sitting as a panel of three judges, dismissed the applicants' appeal on points of law. Afterwards, the case was referred to the European Court of Human Rights [ECHR]. The case originated in an application (no. 44158/98) against the Republic of Poland lodged with the European Commission of Human Rights under former Article 25 of the Convention for the Protection of Human Rights and Fundamental Freedoms by three Polish nationals, Mr Jerzy Gorzelik, Mr Rudolf Kołodziejczyk and Mr Erwin Sowa, on 18 June 1998. In its Judgement of 20 December 2001, the Chamber found that there had been no breach of Article 11. The Grand Chamber, in its Judgement from 17 February 2004, maintained the decision of the Chamber, with the following justification:

> The Court concludes, therefore, that it was not the applicants' freedom of association *per se* that was restricted by the State. The authorities did not prevent them from forming an association to express and promote distinctive features of a minority but from creating a legal entity which, through registration under the Law on associations and the description it gave itself in paragraph 30 of its memorandum of association, would inevitably become entitled to a special status under the 1993 Elections Act. Given that the national authorities were entitled to consider that the contested interference met a "pressing social need" and given that the interference was not disproportionate to the legitimate aims pursued, the refusal to register the applicants' association can be regarded as having been "necessary in a democratic society" within the meaning of Article 11 § 2 of the Convention.[30]

The initiative did not achieve its goals. However, it did not fail, either. On the contrary: it pointed out the social, political and legal problems of ethnic and national minorities in Poland. Much has changed since the time of the ZNLŚ registration, and the *Act on National and Ethnic Minorities and Regional Language* has been adopted by the Parliament. Still, Silesians are not protected by this legislation. The case of ZNLŚ also served to some extent as the event that led to the consolidation and mobilisation of ethnoregionalists in Upper Silesia.

4.8.1 *Autonomy March*

Every year since 2007, around 15 July, a manifestation called the *Marsz Autonomii* – Autonomy March –takes place in Katowice. It is organised by the *Ruch Autonomii Śląska* in cooperation with other Silesian organisations. In many ways, it promotes the idea of the reintroduction of the autonomy model for the Silesia region, preferably in the form of the asymmetrical decentralisation (regionalisation) of the state. Since the beginning, its participants have highlighted the federal and autonomy arrangements that have been in place throughout Europe. Members of the European Free Alliance also take part in the initiative. In 2011, it was transformed into *Dzień Górnośląski* (Upper

---

30   Gorzelik and others v. Poland. ECHR. Application No. 44158/98. Judgement 17 February 2004.

POLITICAL ORGANISATIONS IN UPPER SILESIA

Silesian Day). Later (since 2013), the days on 15–17 July were called the *Dni Samorządności Śląskiej* (Days of Silesian Self-Governance), and 15 July became the *Dzień Śląskiej Flagi* (Day of Silesian Flag). The days are celebrated on the first weekend after 15 July. About 1,000 participants took part in the eleventh Autonomy March in 2017 and, for the first time in history, members of the *Związek Górnośląski* were also present (Redakcja TVN 24 2017). In 2018, during the March, the Silesian Anthem, written by Michał Wengrzyn and set to music composed by Jacek Glenc, was performed for the first time in five languages: Silesian, Polish, Czech, German and Latin (Redakcja Katowice. Nasze Miasto 2018).

The March goes through Katowice from the Wolności Square to the Sejm Śląski Square, and its participants shout slogans such as "Autonomia to nie skrajność, autonomia to normalność" ("Autonomy is not radical, autonomy is normal") or "Autonomia rzecz wspaniała, bo Śląsk syty, Polska cała" ("Autonomy is a great thing, a win-win situation for Silesia and Poland"). The March ends with stage performances, speeches and a picnic for all. People taking part in the March wear yellow and blue (Silesian colours) and wave Silesian flags. The organisers also speak Silesian.

The Autonomy March is probably the most famous event organised by ethnoregionalists in Upper Silesia. It is also recognised outside the region, and state-wide media usually prepare reports from the event. Its main goal is, obviously, the promotion of autonomy for the region, but also it serves as a platform for the meeting of diverse associations and societies from Upper Silesia. The March is also a commemoration of historical autonomy and the *Constitutional Act that included the Organic Statute for the Śląskie Voivodeship*, which was adopted on 15 July 1920 and provided future Silesian authorities with legislative, administrative and fiscal powers (in force from 1992 to 1945).

4.8.2 *The Day of Commemoration of the Upper Silesian Tragedy*

The growing awareness of the tragic events that took place in 1945 and the following years led to the creation of a new event in 2009: *Marsz na Zgodę* – the March to Zgoda, which was later transformed by the Sejmik of the Śląskie Voivodeship into the *Dzień Pamięci o Tragedii Górnośląskiej* (the Day of Commemoration of the Upper Silesian Tragedy), which takes place every year on the last Sunday of January. Also, after a proposal of the members of the *Ruch Autonomii Śląska*, the year 2015 was named the *Rok Pamięci o Tragedii Górnośląskiej* (Year of Commemoration of the Upper Silesian Tragedy) by the Sejmik of the Śląskie Voivodeship.

During the March to Zgoda, participants walk 10 km from the Wolności Square in Katowice to the entrance of the Świętochłowice-Zgoda Camp. The participants wear the traditional Silesian colours of yellow and blue with black – a symbol of the death of the Silesians who died because of their ethnic and national affiliation. On 9 March 2017, the Silesian organisations called for the creation of a monument in memory of the victims of the Camp in Zgoda in Wolności Square in Katowice.

The victims of Zgoda are also remembered on 17 June – the Day of Remembrance of the Victims of the Camp in Zgoda. The event has been organised by the *Towarzystwo Społeczno-Kulturalne Niemców Województwa Śląskiego* (Social and Cultural Society of Germans of the Śląskie Voivodeship) for more than 20 years.

The March serves as a commemoration of the tragic events, which were forgotten for many years and erased from history by the socialist regime in Poland. The collective memory of Upper Silesians is slowly being reintroduced to the public sphere and public debate by Upper Silesian ethnoregionalists, and the March to Zgoda is one of the activities promoting this.

4.8.3 *National Census 2011 – Campaign*

The National Census took place in 2011. In this census, citizens could declare Silesian nationality (more on the subject can be found in Subchapter 2.7 *Upper Silesians*). Here, it is worth mentioning that Silesian organisations decided to prepare a campaign informing Silesians of this option.

The campaign conducted by the *Ruch Autonomii Śląska* was called: "Masz prawo deklarować narodowość śląską" ("You have the right to declare Silesian nationality"). For the purpose of the campaign, a short film was prepared (Ruch Autonomii Śląska 2011).

Many minorities, not only Silesians, created campaigns to increase the awareness of citizens about the possibility of declaring a minority identity. Because the Silesian nationality was not easy to find in the National Census 2011 form, such campaigns were especially important for unrecognised minorities.

4.8.4 *Regional Education and Teaching Silesian Language*

The latest initiative in the area of promotion of the Silesian language – "Poradzisz? Gŏdej!" ("Can you? Speak up!") aims at promoting the use of the Silesian language in public and in offices. The sign for the campaign is "Gŏdōmy po ślōnsku" ("We speak Silesian"). It has been developed in cooperation with the "Silesia" Foundation and is more and more present in the public sphere. Members of the Association organised and carried out Silesian lessons at different events, including the "Lekcyje ślōnskij gŏdki" ("Silesian lessons") organised in cooperation with the Silesian Muzeum in Katowice or the "Akadymijŏ Ślōnskij Gŏdki" ("Silesian Speech Academy") in cooperation with the Upper

POLITICAL ORGANISATIONS IN UPPER SILESIA

Silesian Ethnographic Park in Chorzów. In schools in Rybnik, an educational programme for regional education was prepared by the *Demokratyczna Unia Regionalistów Śląskich*. Furthermore, thanks to the *Ruch Autonomi Śląska*, in *Biblioteka Śląska*, the *Instytut Badań Regionalnych* (Institute for Regional Studies) was created, led by Ryszard Kaczmarek. The Institute prepared the platform "EDUŚ", with materials for regional education.

It may be that the need for informed and unbiased regional education is the only postulate on which all organisations within the Upper Silesian ethnoregionalist movement agree. This is probably why many small actions and initiatives are taking place in the region in the area of regional education. However, the lack of financial and organisational support from the state has led to a situation in which regional education is not accessible to every student in the region.

4.8.5 *Recognition of Silesians as a Minority and Silesian as a Regional Language*

The citizens' legislation initiative on the modification of the *National and Ethnic Minorities and Regional Language Act* from 6 January 2005 was submitted to the Sejm on 27 August 2014[31] (more on the subject can be found in Sub-chapter 2.7 *Upper Silesians*). It was coordinated by organisations forming the Silesian movement. They collected more than 140,000 signatures required by law. The collecting of signatures started in April 2014 and lasted until August.

The only expert asked to pronounce an opinion on the project – Dr Anna Śliz – gave it a positive assessment. The project was taken into consideration during the existence of the coalition of PO-PSL (Civic Platform-Polish People's Party), but no decision was made before the end of its term in 2015. In the end, the project was rejected by the Lower Chamber of Parliament (by the votes of PiS – Law and Justice – and Kukiz '15) in October 2016. Prior to this, the Sejmik of the Śląskie Voivodeship passed a resolution supporting the initiative.

The great mobilisation of people and resources that led to the success of introducing the citizens' legislation initiative happened during the peak popularity of ethnoregionalists organisations. Still, even this success was not enough to meaningfully influence the outcome, and the Polish Parliament, led by *Prawo i Sprawiedliwość*, rejected the project. One could even say that the relentless fight for the recognition of the Silesian minority and their language started in 2005, and it is still happening 15 years later. In the meantime, once

---

31   Sejm RP. 2014. "Obywatelski projekt ustawy o zmianie ustawy o mniejszościach narodowych i etnicznych oraz o języku regionalnym, a także niektórych innych ustaw".

134   CHAPTER 4

every five years or so, the subject is brought to the Parliament, and it is rejected
every time.

4.9   Protests

4.9.1   *Protest against Further Centralisation of Public Television*
"Regional Forum" was a programme aired on the regional channel of TVP
Katowice, a branch of Polish public television. All of the parties and organisations from the Sejmik of the Śląskie Voivodeship took part in the programme
and had the opportunity to talk about the political and social problems of the
region. It was liquidated in April 2016. Since then, a new programme about
regional politics was introduced, but without the participation of regional
organisations. The *Ruch Autonomii Śląska* organised a protest outside of the
TVP Katowice building on 17 May 2016 (Semik 2016).

4.9.2   *Protest against Rejection of the Citizens' Legislative Initiative*
After the Polish Sejm rejected the Citizens' legislation initiative on modifica-
tion of the *National and Ethnic Minorities and Regional Language Act* from 6
January 2005 (more on the topic in Subchapter 2.6 *Upper Silesians*), the initia-
tors called for the protest. It took place in Katowice on Szewczyka Square on 27
October 2016 and assumed the form of a silent protest (Przybytek 2016).

4.9.3   *Protest against Naming the Square in Katowice after Maria and Lech*
          Kaczyński
In 2016, a group of city councillors made a proposal to call one of the streets
in Katowice after the late Maria and Lech Kaczyński (the presidential couple
who died in a plane crash in Smoleńsk in 2010). It led to opposition from
Silesian organisations, which stated that the streets should be named after
persons who were important for the city and region itself. They decided to
collect signatures in opposition to this proposal. The event started on 27
October 2016.[32]

In 2017, the issue entered the second phase of the conflict. In April 2016,
new legislation was adopted by the Parliament.[33] The new Act aimed at

---

32   Demokratyczna Unia Regionalistów Śląskich. n.d. "Nie dla ulicy/ronda im. Marii i Lecha
      Kaczyńskich".
33   *Ustawa z dnia 1 kwietnia 2016 r. o zakazie propagowania komunizmu lub innego ustroju*
      totalitarnego przez nazwy jednostek organizacyjnych, jednostek pomocniczych gminy,

POLITICAL ORGANISATIONS IN UPPER SILESIA
135

the so-called de-communisation of public space (removing the names of public spaces connected to the socialist regime in Poland in 1944–1989). It is worth noting that de-communisation has been a flagship project of the party *Prawo i Sprawiedliwość* (Law and Justice) for many years. The said Act gave municipalities a year to change the names of their streets and facilities. If they did not, the Voivode was authorised to change the names for them (using the executive power of the representative of the government in the self-government unit). The city council of Katowice changed a few names, conforming with the new law, but did not change the name of the square in the very heart of the city centre, in front of the railway station. Since 1995, the square had been named after Wilhelm Szewczyk – a Silesian poet, writer and literary critique, who wrote in the times of the Polish Peoples' Republic and was a member of the Polish Parliament from 1957 to 1985. This was the reason why on 13 December 2017, the Silesian Voivode used his executive powers and changed the name of the square to the square of Maria and Lech Kaczyński.[34]

This is not a place to debate whether the name of Wilhelm Szewczyk was justly removed from the square. I believe that the story of his life is not black and white, nor is it easy to judge almost thirty years after his death. However, one should note that the square was given his name after its transformation by a democratically chosen self-government and was unchallenged for more than twenty years. The city council of Katowice appealed the decision to the Wojewódzki Sąd Administracyjny (Voivodeship Administrative Court) based on the fact that the decision was made with consulting with the inhabitants of the city, and the President of the city was not given enough time to run such consultations. The Court, in its sentence from 17 May 2018,[35] decided to overrule the decision of the Voivode, and the previous name was upheld. In the justification for the sentence, we can find, among other things, the opinion of experts from the field of literary studies stressing that Wilhem Szewczyk's biography shows he should not be seen as "a symbol of communism" and that his contribution to literature and culture should not be forgotten. The Court based the ruling on the fact that the Voivode did not sufficiently justify his

---

     budowli, obiektów i urządzeń użyteczności publicznej oraz pomniki. Dz. U. 2016 poz. 744 with amendments.

34   Zarządzenie zastępcze nr NPII.4131.4.26.2017. Dziennik Urzędowy Województwa Śląskiego 2017 poz. 7084.

35   Sentence of 17 May 2018. WSA in Gliwice. IV SA/Gl 117/18.

decision to use his extraordinary executive powers in the field, which, as a rule, is in the power of self-government bodies. Later, the case was appealed again (cassation), this time by the Voivode, to the Naczelny Sąd Administracyjny (the Supreme Administrative Court of the Republic of Poland). The Supreme Administrative Court, in its sentence from 20 March 2019, overruled the decision of the Voivodeship Administrative Court and ruled in the Voivode's favour.[36] After the last ruling, the name of the square was that of Maria and Lech Kaczyński.

4.10   Political Organisations in Upper Silesia – Conclusions

Since 1989, the Silesian ethnoregionalist movement has been rapidly evolving. In Chapter 2 – *Political Situation in Upper Silesia* – I presented a model of the activities of the organisations within the movement, in which four groups were distinguished: protagonist, specialised, integration and dissident.

Four organisations within the movement can be categorised as protagonist. Two of them are representatives of the German minority in the Śląskie Voivodeship: *Niemiecka Wspólnota "Przyszłość i Pojednanie"* and *Towarzystwo Społeczno-Kulturalne Niemców Województwa Śląskiego*. A further two are representatives of the Silesian ethnic group: *Ruch Autonomii Śląska* and *Związek Górnośląski*.

Ten organisations can be categorised as specialised. There are five subgroups in this category. Firstly, two organisations concentrate on strengthening the ethnic group: *Stowarzyszenie Osób Narodowości Śląskiej* and *Związek Ludności Narodowości Śląskiej*. Both of the organisations had problems with their registration and are not registered as associations today. Secondly, there are two organisations to develop and promote the Silesian language: *Pro Loquela Silesiana* and *Towarzystwo Piastowania Mowy Śląskiej "DANGA"*. Thirdly, three organisations concentrate on the promotion of the region and its culture: *Fundacja "Silesia"*, *Pomocna Dłoń – Krystyn i Sympatyków* and *Związek Ślązaków*. In general, these organisations have a wider scope of activities. Fourthly, two organisations develop programmes for regional education: *Demokratyczna Unia Regionalistów Śląskich* and *Stowaszyszenie "Silesia Schola"*. Lastly, there is an organisation for the Silesian diaspora in Germany: *Initiative der kulturelle Autonomie Schlesiens*.

---

36   Sentence of 20 March 2019. NSA. II OSK 3455/18.

POLITICAL ORGANISATIONS IN UPPER SILESIA

Two organisations aim mostly at the integration of the organisations and activities within the movement: *Przymierze Śląskie* and *Ślōnskŏ Ferajna*. Another can be categorised as dissident: *Nasz Wspólny Śląski Dom.*

During these years, some organisations started to take part in elections and create electoral committees of voters. RAŚ took part in elections to self-government bodies four times (in 2002, 2006, 2010 and 2014) as the electoral committee of the Association. This is why it is categorised in the study as a proto-party. Its members also created two electoral committees of voters for the purpose of parliamentary elections – *Autonomia dla Ziemi Śląskiej* in 2011 and *Zjednoczeni dla Śląska* in 2015. Two more electoral committees of voters were created by other organisations: *Mniejszość na Śląsku* (for the purpose of elections to self-government bodies in 2014) and *Ślonzoki Razem* (for the purpose of parliamentary elections in 2015). Later, two political parties were created in 2017 but registered in 2018: the *Śląska Partia Regionalna* and party *Ślonzoki Razem.*

The results of elections in the region are presented below (see Tables 10 and 11), counted *en bloc* for all the committees from the Silesian ethnoregionalist movement.

It can be stated that the support for organisations from Upper Silesian ethnoregionalist movements doubled in the 2010s. Still, the results in parliamentary elections are significantly lower (almost by half) than in elections to self-government bodies.

The evolution of the movement is clearly indicating a further politicisation of the Silesian identity. The number of organisations with at least some political goals is growing, as well as the support for electoral committees created

TABLE 10   Parliamentary Elections

Year	Votes
1991	40061
2015 Sejm	18668
2015 Senate	59051

DATA FROM PAŃSTWOWA KOMISJA WYBORCZA (STATE ELECTORAL COMMISSION), OWN ASSESSMENT

TABLE 11   Elections to Sejmik of Śląskie voivodship

Year	Votes
2002	52118
2006	58919
2010	122781
2014	107225
2018	110480

DATA FROM PAŃSTWOWA KOMISJA WYBORCZA (STATE
ELECTORAL COMMISSION), OWN ASSESSMENT

by members of ethnoregionalist organisations. The ethnic and regionalist demands and programmes have become part of the public debate in the region and about the region. Additionally, more and more initiatives and protests can be categorised as having their roots in one of two oppositions: centre-periphery and dominant-non-dominant culture.

CHAPTER 5

Programmes and Postulates of Upper Silesian Organisations

5.1 Introduction

The programmes and postulates of the organisations I have categorised as belonging to the Upper Silesian ethnoregionalist movement differ profusely. Firstly, while some of them are openly political, others aim instead at changing policy from the outside and are focused on social and cultural issues. Secondly, the problem of ethnic identity and its role in their creation is diverse. Thirdly, while in some, the opposition centre-periphery is explicit, in others, it remains implicit or even non-existent.

I have already analysed the written statements that have political goals and are published on the official websites or in other ways in the previous chapter. The FGI results I carried out in 2017–2018[1] are used as the main sources of information here. I have translated the statements, but the original wording is presented in the footnotes. The aim of this chapter is to answer a few research questions based on the qualitative study.

The structure of this chapter is based on specific issues. For each of them, general stances are presented, and common points and exceptions are pointed out. First, the issue of peripheral identity is studied. The auto-identification of respondents, the Silesian identity and its categorisation is elaborated. Then, the political programmes and postulates of the studied organisations are analysed. The chapter ends with an attempt to elaborate on how peripheral identity influences the political programmes of organisations representing the population of that periphery.

---

1 The organisations are anonymised and were given the designations O1, O2, O3, etc. Within the organisations, the interlocutors were also given the designations R1, R2, R3, etc. Consequently, when cited, statements are designated, e.g., O1R3.

© ANNA MUŚ, 2022 | DOI:10.1163/9789004466456_007

5.2 Ethnicity

5.2.1 *Auto-identification*

The role of auto-identification for ethnicity has been confirmed in many studies, but, at the same time, this method of determination of one's identity also has some shortcomings (Babiński 2004). For the purpose of the study, it was necessary to ask the question: "What is your ethnicity?" The respondents were well prepared for the answer (though without a doubt, it is a sensitive and personal question) – the debate about the identity of Silesians is still present in the region and in Poland.

A person can declare Silesian identity as their only identity (in the 2011 census, 45% of Silesian declarations were single declarations).[2] The same is true for the members of the organisations studied here:

O2R1:   Silesian.
O2R2:   Silesian without any other adjectives.
O2R3:   Silesian, no other.
O2R4:   True Silesian.
O2R5:   Silesian
O2R6:   As well.[3]

It is also worth mentioning that all of the interlocutors within O2 declared a single, Silesian identity. This suggests an ideological and ethnic accord within the members of this organisation. The same is true for another organisation – O4.

The second option is a double declaration. In this case, the Silesian (ethnic) identification is one of two, and the second is usually national identification (German or Polish). This is the case in O1, where all of the respondents declared Silesian and Polish or Polish and Silesian identity. The emphasis on the order of these two declarations was strong, which makes it clear that it is important to the respondents which identity is declared first and is (consequently) dominant:

O1R1:   In our Association, all options coexist. For example, I am a Silesian and a Pole. But also, Silesians (without other identification) are present, but not visible. There are no other options.

---

2   GUS (Główny Urząd Statystyczny). 2015. "Tabl. 2.2 Population by a kind and order of national and ethnic identification in 2011".

3   O2R1: Ślązak.
O2R2: Ślązak bez żadnych przymiotników.
O2R3: Ślązak, żodyn inny.
O2R4: Ślązak z krwi i kości.

PROGRAMMES AND POSTULATES OF UPPER SILESIAN ORGANISATIONS 141

O1R2: Poles and Silesians are here as well.

O1R3: In our Association, there are no Silesians and Germans.

O1R1: Our Association is targeted towards people who have their roots among Silesian Insurgents, the thoughts of Wojciech Korfanty, namely Polish Silesia, and this is a wealth for the whole population (...).[4]

In some of the organisations, Silesian-German declarations were also present. In this case, the most important indicator of identity was descent. It is also interesting that a strong local identity became visible in this group:

O3R1: (...) and having in his roots in German and Silesian ancestors. My mother was definitely Silesian. It is common among older Silesians when you ask: who are you? And the answer will always be – Silesian. From my father's side, my ancestors were German (...) and I am an inhabitant of Katowice.[5]

O6R1: I am Silesian-German.[6]

It should also be noted that there is, unsurprisingly, a visible pattern within the organisations. The answers given within one organisation are highly similar, if not identical. The level of cohesion in this field could lead to the conclusion that the identity presented by the organisation and its members is an important factor in deciding membership.

Furthermore, in the case of Silesian identification, the most important point is the distinction between belonging to an ethnic group as opposed to the nation. For example, the problem was raised in relation to the World Cup in football in 2018 and cheering for the Polish national team:

O6R1: How can you say, that 'our' team plays tonight? How is it 'ours'?[7]

O2R5: Ślązak ...

O2R6: Również.

4 O1R1: W naszym Stowarzyszeniu są wszystkie te opcje. Ja na przykład jestem Ślązakiem-Polakiem. Są Ślązacy-Ślązacy, chociaż się za bardzo nie ujawniają. No i właściwie innej opcji nie ma. O1R2: Polacy-Ślązacy też są. O1R3: W naszym Stowarzyszeniu Ślązaków-Niemców raczej nie ma. O1R1: Nasze Stowarzyszenie jest adresowany do tych, którzy mają w korzeniach Powstańców Śląskich, przemyślenia Wojciecha Korfantego, czyli Polski Śląsk i to jest bogactwo dla całej ludności (...).

5 O3R1: (...) I mających w swoich korzeniach przodków niemieckich i śląskich. Mam zdecydowanie Ślązaczka. Jest taki moment, kiedy Pani starszego Ślązaka zapyta o to: kim Ty jesteś? I taki zawsze Pani powie – Ślązak. Z rodziny, z pochodzenia, ze strony ojca to byli Niemcy (...) ja jestem Katowiczaninem.

6 O6R1: Jo jestem Ślonzokiem-Niemcem.

7 O6R1: Jak możesz godać, że grajom „nasi". Jacy „nasi"?

142 CHAPTER 5

This question aims at making a clear statement: if you are 'just' Silesian, you cannot perceive a national team as 'yours' because you declare that you do not belong to this nation. It seems that, from this perspective, Silesian identity can be seen as the only identity and be quasi-national. This is obviously different for persons declaring a double identity, which implies that they belong to both an ethnic group and to the nation. This problem is further elaborated in Subchapter 5.2.5.

5.2.2 Silesianism

The next problem that should be discussed is the various reasons behind auto-identification. What does it mean to be a Silesian? This question has been asked by many, but the answer still seems to be elusive. It may take on different meanings for different people due to the fact that it is a personal choice to belong to any social group. Still, there are at least some indications of how this identity is developed (or, as some would say, created).

The question: "what does it mean to be Silesian?" was posed. One of the answers was very specific, but used general, inclusive terms:

> O2R6: We have a definition, which we have been promoting for years. According to this definition: everyone who was born in Silesia or his/her ancestors come from here, and identifies himself/herself with the culture and, most importantly, declares to be Silesian.[8]

Three elements of this definition are worth highlighting. Silesian identity is, first and foremost, the bond between a person and a territory, which is not necessarily personal (it can be maintained through ancestry). Secondly, it is a connection to the culture as a whole, which does not necessarily mean a blood tie (having ancestors who were Silesian is not a condition *sine qua non* of this identity). Thirdly, an important element is a declaration (auto-identification) that stresses the personal character of the choice of identity.

The concept of a territorial (bound to the land) rather than familial (bound by blood) identity was elaborated further in other answers:

> O2R1: Silesian patriotism is space-related patriotism rather than blood-related patriotism. The patriotism of 'Heimat' [Motherland]. And

---

8 O2R6: My mamy definicję, którą od lat promujemy. I zgodnie z tą definicją albo ktoś jest urodzony na Śląsku albo jego przodkowie i identyfikuje się z kulturą i najbardziej istotne jest to że się poczuwa do bycia Ślązakiem.

PROGRAMMES AND POSTULATES OF UPPER SILESIAN ORGANISATIONS   143

> anyone can, if he or she wants to and identifies himself/herself as
> such, declare him/herself as Silesian, and it is nobody's business.[9]
>
> O4R1:   Bond to the land. It is the land and our bond to it that makes us
> Silesians. Not genes.[10]
>
> O6R1:   Fourth [feature] is knowing your history, your historical iden-
> tity. Automatically, if you know the history of your 'Heimat'
> [Motherland], you develop Silesian patriotism.[11]

The bond to the land should be understood here as an awareness of its history and a connection (or at least acceptance) to the collective memory, which
was developed among the inhabitants of the region of Silesia. This bond also
indicates a connection to the present and the tangible reality of the region. It
is an inclusive category that fits not only people born and raised in the region
but also newcomers who have developed a personal connection to the *genius
loci*. This bond to territory represents not only a real connection to the tangible reality but also a spiritual and allegorical connection based on emotions
and ties.

The term *genius loci* is particularly suitable here. From the statements of
the respondents, it is clear that the space is comprehended as a complex entity
incorporating land, landscape, people and their culture as one, creating an
individual and abstract idea. This idea – at its core – is shared by all Silesians,
but in its particular emanation, it is an individual experience. This Silesian
genius loci is commonplace, seen as singular and individual, but shared with
other Silesians; limited and fixed, but still open to individual experience; an
entity connecting space, time and narration simultaneously. Consequently,
Silesia is imagined – it is a social construct encompassing a community and its
territory. Furthermore, it is imagined as limited (though its boundaries can be
set in various ways and are usually vague) and separate (able to be differentiated from other entities).

In this context, an interesting framework for the study was presented in
Polish scholarly literature by Stanisław Ossowski, who made a distinction
between the private and ideological homeland (1984, 21). In his theory, the

---

9   O2R1: Patriotyzm śląski to patriotyzm miejsca a nie patriotyzm krwi, patriotyzm Heimatu.
I każdy może, jeżeli chce, jeżeli tak się identyfikuje i tak czuje i powie, że jest Ślązakiem,
to nikomu nic do tego.

10   O4R1: Związek z ziemią. To ziemia i przywiązanie od niej czyni nas Ślązakami. A nie geny.

11   O6R1: Czworta to jest poczucie do swojej geszichty. Swojej tożsamości historycznej.
Automatycznie, jak znosz geszichta swojego Hajmatu, wytwarza w Tobie się taki patriotyzm ślonski.

private homeland is seen as a place where a person was born and raised and where intimate ties were forged with other people and with the place. In contrast, the ideological homeland is presented as a delimited structure, a place where a nation (or another kind of compact community) exists. In this theory, the definition of the national and ideological homeland is quite similar to the remarks made by Anderson (1983). Ossowski himself recognised that in the case of some regional communities – his study was conducted in the region of Opole Silesia , the ideological homeland is also a region where a community exists (1967, 251). So, in some cases, the region could be seen as both a private and ideological homeland. The results of my study show that for a part of the Silesian community, the region of Silesia is, indeed, both.

The Silesian landscape also plays a role in developing the Silesian identity. Post-industrial buildings and landscapes are evidence of the industrial past and trigger nostalgic memories of the Silesian 'Golden Age' – the industrial era. This is why the role of industrialisation and recent de-industrialisation in developing modern Silesian identity is crucial. One of the most important values assigned to Silesians by the respondents was hard work, which was historically connected to the large number of mines and ironworks in the region. Therefore, it is no surprise that the coal mine Guido, the miner museum Queen Luise, and the workers' settlements of Giszowiec and Nikiszowiec are among the most cherished monuments of the region. Furthermore, the river Brynica constitutes the most important social border of the region (the border in the north, which separates Silesia from Zagłębie Dąbrowskie). The long-lasting quarrel between Silesians and the inhabitants of Zagłębie Dąbrowskie turned the river into a metaphor for a border between two groups of people. This metaphorical role of the landscape and, consequently, its ability to connect and divide people was recognised by Rainer Guldin (2014) as means to politicise a given geography.

For me, it became clear that there is no single definition of Silesianism shared by all the interviewed organisations. On the contrary, at first glance, the differences in describing and understanding the concept are the most obvious factors. Accordingly, sets of features were elaborated among the groups of organisations.

The first definition of what it meant to be Silesian is based on the interviews conducted within the organisations in which members declared themselves to be 'just' Silesian and, therefore, chose the Silesian ethnic (or national according to some) identity as their only identity. On the grounds of the interview with O2, the following list of determinants of Silesianism can be made:

– First is the specific, very strong bond to the territory of the 'Heimat' – Upper Silesia – understood as a reluctance to make a home elsewhere, a longing

PROGRAMMES AND POSTULATES OF UPPER SILESIAN ORGANISATIONS 145

for homeliness and a deep feeling of responsibility for the land and its people.

- Second is understanding and taking part in Silesian culture and heritage and, above all, understanding its separateness from the dominant culture.
- Third is the usage and understanding (even to a limited extent) of the Silesian language, which has many different dialects, from the urban dialects of the *Górnośląski Okręg Przemysłowy* [GOP] (Upper Silesian Industrial Area) to rural versions from the more southern part of Polish Upper Silesia. This also encompasses an awareness of the rapidly developing literature in the written version of the Silesian language.
- Fourth is an awareness of the collective memory and distinctive history specific to the region. This feature was also stressed in O4. It is especially hard to determine – the respondents were unsure whether it meant an almost scientific level of knowledge about regional history, being raised in families sharing a distinctive collective memory, or simply awareness and acceptance of the existence of a distinctive history and particular collective memory.

Based on the interview with the second organisation forming this group (O4), further features can be added:

- The attitude to work and other people, which was presented in an example by one of the respondents:

O4RI: (…) The first misunderstandings after the incorporation of Silesia to Poland emerged when officials from Małopolska and other parts of Poland had lordly manners and demanded from the Silesian worker to bow before them, just like a peasant from regions they came from would bow. The Silesian worker, on the other hand, was accustomed to the fact that the capitalist (though he exploited him mercilessly) treated him as an equal. He approached him and took hold of his dirty hand with his clean one. And if necessary, he worked with him, for example: August Hegenscheidt [1823–1891, from 1883 owner of the farm in Ornontowice], a great capitalist and creator of the wire factory in Gliwice lost his right hand while starting a wire polishing machine. He was trying to start this machine with his workers. The Polish lord would never have lowered himself to work with his men.[12]

---

12   O4R1: (…) Pierwsze nieporozumienia po inkorporowaniu Śląska do Polski pojawiły się, gdy urzędnicy z Małopolski i innych części Polski mieli wielkopańskie maniery i żądali od

146   CHAPTER 5

- The culture, which incorporates five values: literal observance of the law, tolerance (which came from the multi-ethnic and culturally diversified character of the region), attachment to self-government (the first regional assembly took place in 1402), respect for education (there is a long history of universal education in the region) and culture, including art and literature.
- Another trait connected to the personality of the inhabitants of the region was honesty.

A similar but not identical list was presented by the members of organisation O1, who declared themselves as Silesian-Polish or Polish-Silesian.

- The first element of Silesian identity is an observance of specific customs, mostly connected to celebrations, but also present in everyday life. Here, stable religiosity among the believers from different confessions (Catholics, Protestants of the Augsburg confession and others) can be included as well.
- The second element is understanding the separate history and collective memory, but these are seen in relation to the history of Poland.
- Third is the usage of Silesian. However, this is a more complicated matter, given the language situation. Still, its understanding, at least, is important, even though it is categorised as a dialect. Moreover:

> O1R5:   (...) The Silesian language is not what we hear in Katowice or Bytom. Silesian is an archaic language of the Silesian-Moravian-Czech borderland. And it is not a language which uses Germanisms.[13]

Last but not least:

> O1R5:   (...) Unfortunately, it is what Kazimierz Kutz called 'dupowatość'. Still, we have a problem to cope with many things and situations (...).[14]

śląskiego robotnika czapkowania, tak jak od chłopa pańszczyźnianego. Natomiast śląski robotnik był przyzwyczajony do tego, że kapitalista (choć łupił go niemiłosiernie) traktował go jak równego sobie. Podchodził do niego i brał w swoją czystą dłoń jego brudną. I jak trzeba było, to z nim pracował np. August Hegenscheidt [1823–1891, od 1883 właściciel folwarku w Ornontowicach], wielki kapitalista i twórca fabryki drutu w Gliwicach stracił prawą dłoń w czasie uruchamiania maszyny do polerowania drutu. On tę maszynę uruchamiał wraz ze swymi robotnikami. Polski Pan nigdy by się do tego nie zniżył.

13   O1R5: Jeszcze jedna rzecz – śląski język to nie jest to co słyszymy w Katowicach, Bytomiu. Śląski to jest archaiczny język pogranicza śląsko-morawsko-czeskiego. I nie jest to język ten, który zaopatruje się w germanizmy.

14   O1R5: No i na końcu, to by była piąta cecha. Niestety ta cecha kutzowska – dupowatość. Mimo wszystko, nie radzimy sobie z wieloma rzeczami i wieloma sytuacjami (...).

PROGRAMMES AND POSTULATES OF UPPER SILESIAN ORGANISATIONS 147

The term *dupowatość* is not new to the Polish language. It means more-or-less 'shiftless' or 'helpless'. But the term became popular after it was used in relation to Silesians by the famous Silesian director and senator, Kazimierz Kutz. Public opinion in Silesia started to boil, and sharp opinions were presented, some in agreement with Kutz, some violently against him. Later, the term was defined by Kutz as: "a genetic feature of Silesians, who were for generations forced to submission and docility (...) we are still willing to withdraw, to turn away from reality. It is the effect of Silesians being kept on a short leash for a long time" [by the state and authority Upper Silesia was under][15] (Redakcja DZ 2013).

For the third group of organisations, fragments of interviews with members of O3 and O6 (in which most of the members declared Silesian-German auto-identification) are presented below. The Silesian features in this view are:

– Attachment and respect for order, discipline and modesty. One of the respondents said:

O3R1: Germans were, for indigenous Silesians, similarly as Poles, an example, but in different fields. Surely, Prussian culture fitted Silesians, above all in terms of discipline, modesty, simplicity of life, respect – (using the form 'You' and verbs in the second person of the plural). Knowing one's place, also German culture, organisational and creative skills.[16]

– The next characteristic is understanding and acceptance of the German heritage and place of Silesians speaking German (sometimes even having Silesian-German identification) in the region. This was illustrated by the following situation:

O6R1: We arrive at Moszna [a castle located in Silesia]. And I said: *short test*. I went to one man and said: *nice castle. Who built it?* And he said: *some German*. I asked: *which German?* And he replied: *Winkler*.

---

15   My translation. Original wording: "Dupowatość to genetyczna cecha Ślązaków, których przez pokolenia zmuszano do uległości i potulności – tak o tym specyficznym występku mówi człowiek, który go zdefiniował: Kazimierz Kutz. – Ciągle pokutuje w nas skłonność do zamykania się w sobie, odwracania się od rzeczywistości. To efekt trzymania Ślązaków za twarz przez kilkaset lat – uważa Kutz".

16   O3R1: Niemcy byli dla tych rdzenny Ślązaków, tak jak Polacy, wzorem. Ale w odmiennych dziedzinach. Na pewno Pruskość pasowała do Ślązaków, przede wszystkim dyscyplina, skromność i prostota, szacunek – mówienie per „wy". (...) Znajomość swojego miejsca. Także niemiecka kultura. Też zdolności niemieckie do organizacji, do tworzenia. Przecież tutaj przyjeżdżali głównie fachowcy.

And I continued: *so the Germans came here and built the castle, yes?* So he said: *well, no, he was from here. German from here.* And I asked: *so who was he for you?* And I continued with my questions, but this man could not say that Winkler was a Silesian. And this is what I mean. When I think about Winkler I think – he was one of us, his castle is our heritage. The same is true for Eichendorff. People just can't accept their history. The diverse heritage as a whole.[17]

The lists of features presented above do not create a coherent picture. But how could they? There is no single Silesianism, and the concept itself has many shades. There are Silesians rooted in the Polish perspective, in the Uprisings, in the Piast heritage. There are also those who stress the heritage associated with the industrial period, with the penetration of German culture. And there are those who look for Silesianism somewhere in between, seeing and accepting its different roots, but emphasising that today, it is a separate culture, that Silesianism is separateness. For everyone, however, being a Silesian is an added value – a diverse and individual value.

On the other hand, Silesianism also means multiculturalism, tolerance and the coexistence of diverse nations and ethnic groups in one territory because the concept of Silesianism is always connected to the region, the land and the bond between the region and its inhabitants. Hence, the patriotism of the place is prevalent among all people who declare themselves to be Silesians, regardless of the shades of this identification.

Therefore, one could ask whether Silesian identity is a regional identity, an ethnic identity or something else? The stress on the territorial bond (living in the region) could make it a regional identity, but it is not that simple. From the answers given in the interviews, the question is not just about the territory, but the culture connected to the territory, which creates Silesian identity. Even if descent from Silesians (a familial bond) is not strictly necessary for identification, it is clear that some level of living within the specific culture, namely the observance of its traditions and customs, knowing the language

---

17   O6R1: Podjeżdżamy do Moszny. I jo godom: krótki test. Podchodze do osoby i godom: *fajny ten szlos. Kto to wybudowoł?* A on godo: *no taki Niemiec.* A jo na to: *jaki Niemiec?* I on: *no, taki Winkler.* To jo godom: *a przyjechali tu Niemcy i wybudowali, pra?* A tamten: *no nie, on tu był stond. Taki Niemiec stond.* No to ja pytam dalej: *no to kto to był dla Ciebie?* I tak go pytam, pytam, ale to że był Ślonzok nie padło. I o to się rozłazi. Jo jak godom o Winklerze to godom – nasz, nasz szlos. Ta sama historia jest z Eichendorffem. Ludziom jest cienżko przyjąć swoja geszichta. Tego całego różnorodnego dziedzictwa.

PROGRAMMES AND POSTULATES OF UPPER SILESIAN ORGANISATIONS   149

and understanding the collective memory, are important indicators of belonging to the group. This is the reason why Silesian identity is an ethnic identity instead, but it is strongly linked to the region.

One simple question comes to mind: how can people who have a connection to the same territory, who claim to promote the same ethnicity and to represent the same people, see the nature of what they identify themselves with (*genius loci*) so differently? To answer this question, the relation to Silesia's past (heritage and collective memory) and then to its present and future are studied below.

5.2.3   *Heritage*

The understanding and narration of Silesian heritage are probably the two most controversial subjects in public debate in Upper Silesia. The members of O1 stressed the roots and stable bond of the region to Poland. For example:

> O1R1:   (...) Gaude Mater Polonia [an anthem from XIII century written by Wincenty of Kielcza, performed for the first time in Kraków, in Latin], shall be seen as the oldest anthem of Poland. (...) it was created in Kielcza [a small village between Strzelce Opolskie and Lubliniec]. This is evidence of the Polish roots of this region.[18]

As was already presented in the previous chapter, members of O6, in particular, tell a different story. They stress that the heritage of Silesians speaking German and being connected to German culture is also a part of Silesian heritage. It is not something that was artificially planted there but had its roots in the same land and the same *genius loci*. I also had a long discussion with the members of O3 about Eichendorff, a poet from Łubowice (Lubowitz), who spent a large part of his life in Upper Silesia writing about the land in German. His poetry is an example of the literature of the place and, in this case, of Upper Silesia, to which he made many references. It can be said that the culture of Upper Silesia has its roots in three cultures, namely Czech, German and Polish, thus making it diversified and maybe even multicultural.

On the other hand, a different stance is presented by the interlocutors from group O2:

---

18   O1R1: (...) Gaude Mater Polonia [hymn z XIII w. napisany przez Wincentego z Kielczy, wykonany po raz pierwszy w Krakowie, w całości po łacinie], to jest właściwie najstarszy hymn Polski. (...) ten hymn został stworzony w Kielczy [wieś między Strzelcami Opolskimi a Lublińcem]. To świadczy o tych korzeniach ziemi śląskiej.

O2R1: (...) What does 'multicultural' mean? It is not as if our culture was some kind of a jumble. We have much in common with German and Czech culture, but it does not mean that we have been stirred in a cauldron and made some sort of a cultural-jumble. The same is true for the Polish culture, which has some things in common with Russian culture. We have our own culture, just as they have theirs.[19]

This statement shows us that in the O2 narration, Silesian culture is something separate from others and exists on its own. It is not labelled as 'archaic Polish', 'industrial German' or 'borderland Czech' culture. This does not mean that Silesian culture was resistant to any influence and created out of nothing – on the contrary, every culture is developed and created under the influence of other cultures (mostly Czech, German and Polish, in the case of Silesia). Silesian culture is no different, but it does not make it less individual or worthy. It should be seen as equal, even if it is non-dominant.

The problem of scale is also worth mentioning. If the culture were to be measured by the number of people who live in it, Silesian culture would be relatively small compared to the Polish culture. In a state that claims ethnic homogeneity (Polish homogeneity, obviously), it is definitely non-dominant, seen as an exception and sometimes even as an aberration.

Furthermore, interesting remarks may be drawn from the discussion among the members of O2 about Silesian literature:

O2R1: (...) Silesian literature does not necessarily mean one that is written in Silesian. We have been writing in Silesian a short time. In German and Polish, we can also find books, which are included in the canon of Silesian literature. There are also famous persons who came from Silesia and demonstrated a Silesian identity. To start with, Anzelmach, who said 'Tuus et suus, Anselmus Ephorinus,[20] Silesius non Polonus' and worked at the Jagiellonian University.[21]

---

19   O2R1: (...) Co oznacza ta wielokulturowość? Bo to nie znaczy, że nasza kultura jest jakimś bigosem. To, że nam jest blisko do kultury niemieckiej albo bardzo blisko, czy do czeskiej, to nie znaczy że myśmy zamieszali w kociołku i stworzyli jakiś bigos. Tak samo polskiej kulturze jest blisko do rosyjskiej w wielu aspektach. Także mamy swoją własną kulturę.

20   Anselmus Ephorinus was a XVI-century scholar who came from Mirsk, a village between Lubań and Jelenia Góra (Lower Silesia). It was in his correspondence with Erasmus from Rotterdam where he used the famous phrase.

21   O2R1: (...) literatura śląska, to nie znaczy, że ona jest pisana po śląsku. Po śląsku się pisze od niedawna. Ale po polsku i po niemiecku znaleźlibyśmy takie książki, które w tym kanonie powinny się znaleźć. No i są też postacie historyczne, które gdzieś tam tą

In this view, Silesian literature seems to be something between minor literature and completely separate literature. What makes it even more complicated is that throughout the centuries, this literature was written in Latin, Czech, German, Polish and, recently, in Silesian. Therefore, the key feature that makes a work of literature Silesian is not necessarily its language but rather its relation to the place. The form of communication may be different, the languages diverse (and interchangeable: e.g., Eichendorff's poetry is translated from German to Polish and Silesian), but it is the substance – the contents – which make it a common heritage for Silesians:

> O3R1: Eichendorff was an extraordinary romantic. And a romantic from here: a poet of this landscape.[22]

From the interview with members of O2 stems another important conclusion about Silesian heritage: tolerance. Silesians learned to live among others because it was the 'others' who changed throughout centuries. Different languages, different cultures and religions were a part of the Silesian landscape from the beginning. The principle of peaceful coexistence within a culturally diversified neighbourhood was included (or was even a core principle) in the Silesian tradition for a long time.

5.2.4 Collective Memory

History is the study of facts that originated in the past. What may differ among communities is the collective memory – the narration about these facts. Collective memory is understood here not merely as recollection, but as ways of reproduction and interpretation of the past (Kansteiner 2002). Moreover, the evaluation of events and their impact on the present may also be different. This is why narration about the past is interesting in the case studied here. For this study, some differences between the official German or Polish narration and the narration of the members of Silesian organisations emerge. These differences from the official Polish narration have already been studied by Jaskułowski and Majewski, who distinguished two groups among history teachers in Silesia: the radicals (pushing for a homogeneous Polish narration about the history of this region) and the Silesian discontents (pushing for

---

identyfikację śląską posiadały. Zaczynając od tego słynnego – Anzelmach, który powiedział „Silesius non polonus", a pracował w Krakowie na UJ.

22   O3R1: Eichendorff to był niezwykły romantyk. I to romantyk stąd: romantyk tego krajobrazu.

152   CHAPTER 5

factual and regional narration and a less Warsaw-centred policy of memory)
(2017).

To begin with, two characteristics of Polishness (as they are perceived by
members of the studied organisations), a cult of the state and martyrdom, are
presented:

> O2R2:   For a Silesian, a cult of the state is an alien concept. We do not have
>   it. In comparison to Poland, this is a difference. This is a conse-
>   quence of our history, we have a distance to borders and we know,
>   that they are not necessarily given one once and forever.
>
> O2R6:   On the other hand: a cult of sacrifice for the nation. Martyrdom.
>   Both of my grandfathers survived the Second World War (...) and
>   you could feel that they were proud, that they survived and were
>   able to come back and support their family. It was pride, while
>   in Poland, you would be proud if you had died and bled for your
>   Fatherland. And this is a difference.[23]

From this narration, we can see that members of organisation O2 create a clear
picture of two different kinds of patriotism. They perceive the differences
between the two communities of the Poles and Silesians through these two
frameworks.

The Polish understanding of patriotism is presented as a readiness to sacri-
fice everything for an imagined community – the nation – which is, at the same
time, strongly connected to the state (existing or lost). This picture is certainly
present in Polish literature, e.g., from the period of Romanticism (Mickiewicz,
Słowacki) and was thoroughly studied by Norman Davies (1991(1981), 56–67).

The Silesian understanding of patriotism is a new concept, though not one
without its own history. This patriotism is based on work towards and protection of one's community. It is not the state or nation that is important – it is
family and the local community that deserves protection. Work is another factor, the role of which in Silesian culture was already studied in social science
(Swadźba 2001). As to the ambivalent relation of the indigenous population of

---

23   O2R2: Dla Ślązoka obcy jest kult państwowości, kult Państwa. Tego u nas nie ma. W
     porównaniu z Polską to duża różnica. Z naszej historii to wypływa, że mamy dystans do
     granic i wiemy, że to nie musi być dane raz na zawsze. O2R6: I też, z drugiej strony, kult ofi-
     ary dla narodu. Martyrologia. Obaj moi dziadkowe przeżyli wojnę (...) było słychać dumę
     z tego, że przeżyłem, mogłem wrócić i dzięki temu utrzymać swoją rodzinę. To była taka
     duma. Natomiast w Polsce dumnym byłbyś, gdybyś oddał krew za tą Ojczyznę, a nie z
     tego, że przeżyłeś. I tym się ta mentalność różni.

PROGRAMMES AND POSTULATES OF UPPER SILESIAN ORGANISATIONS 153

Upper Silesia to the nation-state, this was recognised as early as the inter-war period (Szramek 1934, 19–20).

In Polish social science, there is a substantial stance that connects collective memory and space to its buildings, monuments and characteristics (e.g., Malicki 2016). An important and meaningful remark is made in the following quotation: "(...) not a small role in shaping the awareness is played by the historical and symbolic layer of the city"[24] (Malicki 2016, 16). However, in the case of Upper Silesia, the problem of collective memory and space is more complicated. Many of the examples presented below reveal the opposition between the officially erected symbolic places and monuments and the Silesian narration about the events and people to which they refer. In other words, due to the fact that Silesian collective memory was 'concealed' (Hajduk-Nijakowska 2010, 74) for a long time – shared only in the family and among close friends – it is not necessarily consistent with the official narration about history mirrored in the public space. Such examples can be found for many events in the history of the region.

This problem with narration of history goes at least as far as the Napoleonic wars:

> O4R1: Let me give you an example: the Napoleonic wars. In Poland, it is presented in a good light. Napoleon is a hero for Poles. In Silesia, these wars were a hecatomb [especially the invasion of French troops at the turn of 1806/1807 after Prussia's lost battle at Jena]. Total destruction. (...)[25]

Without a doubt, Napoleon and his campaign are seen in Poland as heroic events, when the Polish State, in the form of the Duchy of Warsaw, was restored. There is even evidence of this in the Polish anthem (the third line of the second verse): "Bonaparte has given us an example of how we should prevail". But in Silesia, the time between 1807 and 1813 was a time of destruction, when foreign troops stayed in Silesian cities and plundered them. Still, there is a part of Silesia (referred to at that time as Prussian Silesia or New Silesia – lands mostly belonging to the subregion Zagłębie Dąbrowskie), where the situation was different. During the Napoleonic campaign in 1807, there was an uprising in the districts of Myszków and Siewierz. The insurgents went even to

---

24 My translation.
25 O4R1: Podam na przykładzie wojny napoleońskie. W Polsce są przedstawiane w dobrym świetle. Napoleon to dla Polaków bohater. Na Śląsku te wojny to była hekatomba [zwłaszcza wkroczenie wojsk francuskich na przełomie 1806/1807 roku po przegranej Prus pod Jeną]. Totalne zniszczenie (...).

154   CHAPTER 5

the Upper Silesian city of Tarnowskie Góry to acquire (by force) resources like horses but were stopped by the forces of Andreas Witowski (part of the forces of Duke Eugen von Württemberg, who was born in Lower Silesia himself) (Nawrot 2017). What is even more interesting is that this uprising is almost unknown, even though it is one of the few successful uprisings in Polish history because the lands called New Silesia were incorporated into the Duchy of Warsaw (1807–1815). Additionally, during the campaign of 1812–1813, two battles took place in Silesia: at Bóbr and Kaczawa. To commemorate these events in Lwówek Śląski (Lower Silesia), a statue of Napoleon Bonaparte was erected in 2003 to commemorate the battle at Bóbr and Napoleon's stay in the village in August 1813. All in all, Silesian lands suffered greatly at the beginning of the XIX century due to the constant presence of armies in this territory and the battles that took place there. For some inhabitants of modern Silesia, it was a time of great deeds; for others, it was one of great destruction.

There is also no doubt that in the German collective memory, the national heroes would be the generals who stopped Napoleon – his politics was a threat to Prussian politics and existence. One such example was Gebhard Leberecht von Blücher (1747–1819), who commanded the Silesian Army at Leipzig in 1813 and at Waterloo in 1815. Not surprisingly, one of the markets in Wrocław (Breslau) – today's Salt Market – was called Blücherplatz in 1827–1945. Even today, there are places commemorating the general of the Silesian Army during the Napoleonic wars:

> O6R1:   We travel through Lower Silesia. And there was a man called Gebhard Leberecht von Blücher. He was on the other site, he defeated Napoleon. In Krobielowice (Krieblowitz) [Lower Silesia], he had a castle and a mausoleum. And I spoke to a young person and asked her (and she knew the history, there was an exhibition about von Blücher). And I asked her: *are you a Silesian?* She replied: *Well ... I think so, I was born here.* And I said: *So tell me: Blücher is a hero for you or Napoleon?* And she replied: *I know what you mean ...*[26]

For Silesians, this question will never be simple. The Napoleonic Wars are an example of a conflict between the nations – Prussian on the one side and

---

26   O6R1: Jeździmy po Dolnym Śląsku. Jest taki Gebhard Leberecht von Blücher. Facet co był po drugiej zajcie, co pokonał Napoleona. W Krobielowicach (Krieblowitz) mo zamek, mo mauzoleum. Godom z młodom osobom i zadaje jej pytanie: ona znała tom historie, była tam wystawa von Blüchera. I godom: *jesteś Ślonzoczka?* A ona: *No w sumie chyba tak, tu się urodziłam.* A powiedz mi: *Blücher jest dla Ciebie bohaterem czy Napoleon?* A ona: *wiem o co Panu się rozchodzi.*

PROGRAMMES AND POSTULATES OF UPPER SILESIAN ORGANISATIONS

French, with Polish help, on the other. This is obviously a simplification, but in Silesia, this is how things are perceived. The region itself was only a witness to this conflict, not part of it. In the region, the war was a disaster, as is the case with every military conflict that takes place on the lands where one lives. As to the heroes: one was protecting the *status quo*, the other was trying to change it completely – neither of them fought for Silesians or was interested in their fate.

An even more controversial matter is the narration and evaluation of the so-called 'Silesian Uprisings'. After the Great War, the matter of Polish independence and the borders of the Polish State were debated and caused several conflicts. One of the issues was whether the region of Silesia should remain in Germany (the Weimar Republic) or become part of Poland (the II Republic of Poland). In 1919, 1920 and 1921, three armed conflicts were waged in Upper Silesia. In the Polish narration (which is also presented by some of the Silesian organisations, e.g., O1), the conflicts should be perceived as Polish national uprisings aimed at reconnecting part of the Polish Nation living in Upper Silesia to Poland after five centuries of separate existence within the borders of other states. The monument erected for the participants of the Uprising is an example of such a narration. At first, the monument was erected in 1927 and was located next to Chorzowska Street, but it was destroyed in September 1939. It was rebuilt in 1962 in the same place, but due to the construction of a new road – *Drogowa Trasa Średnicowa* – it was moved (Rzewiczok 2014, 32). Today, it is located in Katowice in the square on Dębowa Street and bears the following dedication :

> Glory for heroic insurgents fallen in the fight for national and
> social freedom
> and
> Glory for the best sons of Dąb [district of Katowice] who paid with
> blood to preserve the Polish character of this land[27]

But this is not the only narration about those events present among the members of the Silesian community:

O2R6:   It was a civil war. We do understand that both sides to the conflict had their reasons and maybe, in some circumstances, we would do the same, but we also know, that there was a great majority of civilians, who saw only fighting for fighting's sake.

---

27   My translation.

O2R3: Since I was a child, I remember my grandfather, who took part in the Third Uprising, and while talking about it he did not use the word 'uprising', he used the word 'war'. This hatred, which was imprinted in the families then was strengthened in the years to come. The glorification of killing your neighbour, your brother is ignominy (...). For us, shooting a neighbour whom you have known for all your life, even within families, there were divisions – this is ignominy.

O2R4: And making heroism out of it. This is incomprehensible. It is not Silesian.[28]

This different narration sees the events not from the perspective of Germany or Poland but from the perspective of the indigenous population of Upper Silesia – a population that was culturally diversified and multi-ethnic. From this perspective, no distinction is made – there are no better or worse Silesians. A diverse cultural background, language or even nationality do not play any role in this narration because the community as a whole was touched by these armed conflicts, and the suffering was a common experience.

Today, there is also a third narration that states that the armed conflicts in 1919, 1920 and especially in 1921 were border-wars between Germany and Poland. This stance is based on the fact that during the wars, both sides representing national interests – the Germans and the Poles – were receiving resources and reinforcements from Berlin and Warsaw, respectively (Szmeja 2017, 179; Kaczmarek 2019, 5–15).

A similar problem with the official narration and Silesian collective memory can be seen in the narration about the Second World War and the post-war period (1945–1950). The differences start with the narration about September 1939. As Maria Szmeja concluded, the official Polish narration about the heroic defendants of Katowice was mostly fiction, and the German Army was greeted with cheers by some (2017, 182). Furthermore, in Polish public debate, the term

---

28   O2R6: To była wojna domowa. My sobie zdajemy sprawę, że obie strony konfliktu miały swoje racje i może w pewnych sytuacjach postąpilibyśmy tak samo, ale zdajemy sobie sprawę, że była ta milcząca większość, która po prostu patrzyła na tych, którzy się tam pierom – robicie haja.

O2R3: Ja pamiętam od bajtla, kiedy mój dziadek, który brał udział w trzecim powstaniu, o tym opowiadał nigdy nie użył określenia „powstanie", a mówił „wojna". Ta nienawiść jaka wrosła w rodziny w tym 1921 roku przez kolejne lata była potęgowana. Gloryfikowanie zabijania swojego sąsiada i brata jest podłością (...). Dla nas strzelanie do sąsiada, którego znam całe życie, bo to nawet w rodzinach się podzielili. To jest podłość.

O2R4: I do tego robienie z tego bohaterstwa. To się w głowie nie mieści. To nie jest śląskie.

PROGRAMMES AND POSTULATES OF UPPER SILESIAN ORGANISATIONS   157

'grandfather from Wehrmacht' became famous after Jacek Kurski (a politician from *Prawo i Sprawiedliwość* [PiS] – Law and Justice) said that the grandfather of the presidential candidate from the opposite party – Donald Tusk from the *Platforma Obywatelska* [PO] (Civic Platform) – was a soldier in the German Army. It was meant as an insult – as evidence of the betrayal of the Polish Nation. But the truth was already well-known to the inhabitants of Silesia and Pomerania-Kashubia: these lands were incorporated into Germany in 1939, and many of its inhabitants were given German citizenship, which inevitably led to enrolment in the army, as in the case of every compulsory recruitment. Many Silesian families had ancestors who served in the Wehrmacht during the Second World War:

> O6R1:   I come to someone's home and I see a portrait of a man in a uniform of the Wehrmacht. And someone may come and say: *why do you have an SS-man here?* [The misinterpretation here was intentional, showing a common mistake]. But for us, this is something that is ours. And we are not ashamed. And I speak to someone and he shows me a picture of his grandfather in the Kriegsmarine. If he would show it to a Pole he would say: *are you proud that your grandfather was in the German Army?* And the answer is: *no*. But they were part of a state and they were citizens of Germany and they had a duty. And understanding this is something we have in common.[29]

For many Silesians, this was simply the reality in which their ancestors lived. It was fundamentally different from the circumstances in other parts of Poland. Still, the official narration makes it somehow shameful or even wrong. Yet, the only crime of many grandfathers of the inhabitants of borderland areas, such as Silesia or Pomerania-Kashubia, was that they were born there, and their fates were bound to the fate of their homelands.

The end of the Second World War brought new differences to the region. The most vivid example of the opposition between the official policy of

---

29   O6R1: Albo przychodza do kogoś do dom i widza portret w mundurze Wehrmachtu. I ktoś by przyszoł i pedział: jak to ty masz tu ss-manów? [Pomyłka celowa, ukazująca często popełniany błąd.] A dla nos to jest coś, co jest nasze. My ani nie mamy gańby. Jo z kimś godom, a on mi pokazuje na telefonie: *patrz, to jest mój Opa w Kriegsmarine.* I jakbyś to Polokowi pokazoł, to on by pedział: *to wy się ciszycie, że wasi dziadkowie byli w niemieckim wojsku?* Nie. Ale byli my w takim a nie inkszym państwie, bylimy obywatelami i mielimy taki a nie inny obowiązek. I to jest coś naszego, wspólnego.

memory and Silesian collective memory was a monument in Wolności Square (Freedom Square) in Katowice. The Monument of Gratitude for the Red Army (the army that took over Silesia in 1945) was erected there in 1945, but for many Silesians, the period 1945–950 was not a time to be grateful for, but rather the time of the Upper Silesian Tragedy, caused partially by the said army. The monument was moved in 2014 to the Russian Military Cemetery in Katowice-Brynów. Since then, there is no monument on Wolności Square. The *Ruch Autonomii Śląska* (Silesian Autonomy Movement) promotes the idea of erecting a monument to the Upper Silesian Tragedy in this place, but they have scant support from the local authorities. Some suggest that a monument of the late US president Ronald Regan should be located there. There is a similar situation in Chorzów, where, in the Hutników Square (Ironmasters' Square) in the city centre, there is a monument commemorating Russian soldiers who took part in overtaking the city of Chorzów in 1945. At the same time, neither city has a monument to the Silesian soldiers who fell in the Second World War or to the victims of the Upper Silesian Tragedy. The consequence of such a state of affairs is simple: the regional collective memory and history of the indigenous population of the region are not seen as worthy of official recognition and still remain in the area of 'concealed' narration, which is accessible only to those belonging to the Silesian community in the narrow (ethnic) sense of the word.

The inclusion of the Silesian-German members of the community in the debate and literature in Poland is a new phenomenon. For decades, Germans remained an alien element in public debate in Poland. They were perceived as occupants. For some time now, there have been strong voices, at least in Silesia, saying that Germans have lived there for centuries and, if they have Silesian identification, they are Silesians as well:

> O1R5: (...) At the same time, a Silesian-German is really someone akin to the countrymen and the Silesian exodus, a concept which we should finally emancipate in some way for our Silesian needs, because they are in fact descendants of this land. Descendants who very often return to Silesia in completely different economic, social and family arrangements, and feel Silesian.[30]

---

30   O1R5: (...) Równocześnie Ślązak-Niemiec to tak naprawdę jest kwestia odwołania się do Ziomkostw i do wychodźctwa śląskiego, które wreszcie powinniśmy w jakiś sposób emancypować dla naszych potrzeb śląskich, ponieważ to są tak naprawdę potomkowie tej ziemi. Potomkowie, którzy bardzo często w zupełnie innych układach gospodarczych, społecznych i nawet rodzinnych wracają na ten Śląsk, czując się Ślązakami (...).

PROGRAMMES AND POSTULATES OF UPPER SILESIAN ORGANISATIONS   159

Not surprisingly, the discussion about the history of Upper Silesia often leads to the topic of self-determination:

> O1R5:   Yes, theoretically, we did not have a separate state, but we were not part of the Polish state either. As Silesia, while we were part of the Bohemian Crown [since XIV century], we were in a similar position as Lithuania with regard to the Kingdom of Poland. (...) Silesian lords were Silesian. And Lithuania found a moment suitable to gain independence after 1921 and create a state [actually the proclamation of independence of Lithuania took place in 1918]. Consequently – we Silesians should have the same right to do so (...).[31]

This is, obviously, a simplification, but it is evidence of a question that has been posed more often lately: why should we not have the right to decide our own fate? This is not meant in terms of separatism or even as a demand – it is just something to remember and ponder, a thought that is evidence of a changing reality.

5.2.5   Categorisation

As was already elaborated, it is not enough to establish individual or collective identity. It is also important to establish how the community is seen. How is the collective categorised? The respondents have given at least three answers to that question.

In organisations O2, O4, O5 and O6, there were two stances. The first claimed that Silesians are an ethnic group and an ethnic minority in Poland. The second claimed that Silesians are a stateless nation within the Polish State. The term 'nationality' was applied to both stances.

In organisation O1, the view was more unified: Silesians are Poles with separate cultures. The term 'cultural minority' was forged for this purpose.

In all of the organisations, the distinction between ethnicity and citizenship was stressed. State and citizenship should not be merged with ethnicity and nationality. In some cases, both states of belonging will be the same, but in

---

31   O1R5: Tak, myśmy teoretycznie swojego państwa nie mieli, ale myśmy też nie byli w Państwie Polskim. Jako Śląsk, w momencie, w którym byliśmy w Koronie Czeskiej [od XIV w.] pełniliśmy taką funkcję jak Litwa. Byliśmy tym, czym Litwa dla Królestwa Polskiego. Natomiast jeśli chodzi o Koronę Czeską, panowie śląscy nie byli panami czeskimi. Byli panami śląskimi. My wtedy byliśmy tym czym Litwa w Rzeczpospolitej. To znaczy, że jeżeli Litwa znalazła moment, w którym dało się wybić na niepodległość, po 1921 roku, i stworzyła swoje państwo [Litwa ogłosiła niepodległość w 1918 roku], to my, Ślązacy, mamy do tego momentu takie same prawo.

some, they will be different. This way, one can be a loyal citizen of the Federal Republic of Germany or the Republic of Poland (citizenship) and a proud Silesian (nationality).

The term 'nationality' was introduced into a public debate about the status of Silesians after the 2002 National Census, in which this term was used. There, the term was understood to mean belonging to a national or ethnic group. Some scholars and politicians strongly contested that it was too broad and encompassed too many different identities with different statuses (e.g. Popieliński 2014; Kijonka 2004; Kornacka 2013). For a time, I was of the same mind as well. However, the present study revealed that, surprisingly, the term not only fit the respondents but also allowed many different stances on the matter to be covered. Further, it did not influence the problem of recognising Silesians as an ethnic minority.

As has already been stated by many scholars, Silesians are categorised as an ethnic group, but some members of the organisations studied here go even further and call them a (stateless) nation. This distinction, obviously, depends on the definition of a nation, which is usually connected to a state in the form of a nation-state (which has no grounds in the present case). The term 'ethnic group' is related to an ethnic minority and provides a more moderate stance in the debate about the status of Silesians. The last term – 'cultural minority' – is not recognised in the scientific literature. In the case of the studied organisations this term was intended to signify the cultural separateness of Silesians and, simultaneously, their belonging to the widely understood Polish Nation.

After the study, it became clear to me that the question about the categorisation of the group resulted in answers that said more about political postulates than anything else. This was unsurprising. In the public debate about the status of Silesians (as in any public debate), words and terms create a reality and construct the way it is seen. This is why the political programmes and postulates of the studied organisations will be elaborated further below.

5.3   Political Programmes and Postulates

5.3.1   *Recognition of the Ethnic Group*
Pursuant to Polish law (especially the *National and Ethnic Minorities and Regional Language Act*), recognition of an ethnic group as an ethnic minority grants the said minority benefits, such as protection and preservation of language and culture, along with funding for these purposes. This is an important step towards introducing solutions to fight discrimination and instruments that can help preserve diversity.

PROGRAMMES AND POSTULATES OF UPPER SILESIAN ORGANISATIONS 161

However, this is just one of the aspects of recognition – the practical one. The other is ideological: recognition is important for any minority because it gives it an assurance of equality and protects it from discrimination, assimilation and the ultimate destruction of its culture and distinctiveness. Lack of recognition by fellow citizens for the members of a minority group may lead to the opposite. Therefore, recognition can be described as the need for the worth, values and distinctiveness of a group of people to be acknowledged. It has a relational character as well and can be seen as a prerequisite to beneficial social interactions between groups and their members (Geis 2018). Members of the Silesian ethnic group understand this, and the situation has led to strong opposition:

O6R1: But how can I cheer for Poland [Polish national team in football]? I went to the Polish parliament, to the Polish government and said: recognise Silesians – the answer was: *no* – give us Silesian language – the answer was: *you can talk as you wish when having a beer* – and whatever we ask for they turn their backs to us. This is the reason for my rebellion, my opposition. (...) We are not against average Poles, but against the ones in power. (...) You cannot say that all Poles are bad and all Silesians are great. But if I attack Poles I attack the ones in government, who do not recognise us and do not give us rights.[32]

Silesians, despite their attempts, are still not recognised as a minority by Polish law, though some organisations still promote it and hope that it will happen:

O2R1: The law is not precise, but pursuant to the relevant Act (which we respect), we want the facts to be recognised. And the fact is that pursuant to the Act, we are an ethnic minority.[33]

---

32   O6R1: Ale jak jo mom kibicować Polsce? Jak jo jada bajszpil do Sejmu Polskiego ida do polskich władz i godom: uznajcie narodowość ślonsko – *nie, nie, nie* – dejcie ślonsko godka – *a wy sie godojcie przy krupniokach* – i wszystko co my ich proszemy, oni się obracajom puklem do nas. I to jest mój bunt, to jest mój sprzeciw. Jak jo wyglondałbych: człowiek, kery domaga się pewnych rechtów dla Ślonska. My nie plujemy na zwykłych Poloków, ale na tych co rzondzom. To jest taka przenośnia – Poloki. Nie możesz powiedzieć, że wszystkie Poloki som be, a wszystkie Hanysy fajne. Jak ja atakuje Poloków, to atakuja tych, kery są dziś przy reskirungu, tych kery nas nie uznawajom i nie dajom nom rechtów.

33   O2R1: Ustawa jest nieprecyzyjna, ale zgodnie z nią (bo szanujemy obowiązujące prawo) chcemy, aby zostały uznane fakty. A fakty są takie, że zgodnie z nią jesteśmy mniejszością etniczną.

162 CHAPTER 5

Members of this organisation link the conditions of recognition of the ethnic minority (guaranteed by law) to the situation of their own group and draw the conclusion that this condition has been met. This stance is shared by members of O3, O4, O5 and O6. They see their own group as an ethnic group that is a minority, and they see this as a fact that should be recognised, in accordance with the legal rules set by the state majority. It is also interesting that they point to the fact that this conclusion originates from respect for law itself. This is clearly a message for the representatives of the majority, who undermine the application of the rule of law in their conduct towards an ethnic group: if the rules are set, they are supposed to be followed. This statement mirrors the comments presented in Subchapter 2.7.

The other organisations have a more practical and ambivalent stance:

> O1R5: (...) Are Silesians a national minority or not? If it was not for the money, it would not be a problem.[34]

Regardless of the fact that pursuant to Polish law, a national minority is a minority that has a kin-state, the question remains: are Silesians a minority? The second part of the statement is more ambivalent. In one interpretation, it could mean that if money did not stand behind the recognition, Silesians would not need the former. The second could mean that authorities and the majority would be more likely to grant recognition if it was not connected to funding from the state budget. Either way, funding is not the only problem in Poland. The principle of the homogeneity of the Polish nation is still accepted and even promoted by many policy-makers (Berdychowska 1998, 16–17). This is done so strongly, in fact, that any attempt to show that diversity exists not only as folklore but also as a separate culture asking for recognition is met by the accusations of being a "concealed German option" (Redakcja Polska the Times. 2011), "volksdeutsch" and "fifth column" (Treter-Sierpińska, n.d.). All of these concepts refer to high treason, to those that invited, welcomed and cooperated with the enemy (Nazis) and to the events of September 1939 in Poland and the occupation during the Second World War.

For some members of the majority group in Poland, there can be no equality for numerous ethnic groups, such as Silesians, because they see any diversity as

---

34   O1R5: (...) Czy Ślązak i śląskość to mniejszość narodowa czy nie? Gdyby nie stały za tym pieniądze, to nie byłoby problemu.

PROGRAMMES AND POSTULATES OF UPPER SILESIAN ORGANISATIONS 163

a threat to the nation. This is probably the main reason why the possibility of recognising Silesians is still questionable.

An interesting argument in the debate about recognition is presented by members of O3, specifically in two aspects. The first is the reason why Silesian organisations were promoted and supported by the Polish elites after 1989:

> O3R1: Polish elites were scared of an increase in the number of declarations of belonging to the German minority and in the electoral success of the German Minority Committee, and decided to support the Silesians. To strengthen Silesians and weaken the Germans.[35]

This interpretation makes it possible to understand why the German minority (and other national and ethnic minorities recognised by law and having representatives in the *Komisja Wspólna Rządu i Mniejszości Narodowych i Etnicznych* – Joint Commission of Government and National and Ethnic Minorities) have a negative opinion about the possible recognition of Silesians by Polish law – the more Silesians are recognised, the fewer Germans we will have. This second aspect is strengthened by the current ethnopolitics of the state. In Poland, funds for supporting recognised minorities are divided into three groups:

– purpose subsidy (art. 18 *National and Ethnic Minorities and Regional Language Act* from 17 January 2005),
– subject subsidy (art. 18 *National and Ethnic Minorities and Regional Language Act* from 17 January 2005),
– additional funds for the education of children belonging to minorities (*Regulation of the Minister of National Education of 15 December 2017 on the manner of dividing the educational part of the general subsidy for self-government units in 2018*).[36]

The recognition of another ethnic group that would be both numerous and represented by the developed structures of active organisations would mean the emergence of competition for funding, and a substantial rise in the state budget for this purpose is very unlikely. In consequence, it is entirely possible that recognised minorities will receive substantially fewer funds. Therefore, such recognition is not in their best interest.

---

35 O3R1: Elity polskie się przestraszyły wzrostu ilości deklaracji przynależności do mniejszości niemieckiej i sukcesu wyborczego komitetu mniejszości niemieckiej. I postanowiły puścić Ślązaków. Wzmocnić śląskość i osłabić niemieckość.

36 Dz. U. 2018. 2395.

5.3.2 *Regional Education*

Regional education, understood as lessons in regional history and traditions, is one of the postulates with which all of the studied organisations agree. The need for regional education comes from the realisation that diversity within the state is something worth cultivating and understanding. The programmes of history, culture and knowledge about society in Polish schools are seen by many as being written for the purpose of unification with the Warsaw-centred point of view. Some teachers – e.g. some of those studied by Jaskułowski and Majewski (2017) – claim that schoolchildren know more about the history of the eastern borderlands and territories, which are no longer part of the Republic of Poland, than about the regions in which they live. This is especially visible in the case of regions in the west and the north that spent centuries under non-Polish domination. This is why the postulate is not limited to the region of Silesia:

> O1R5:   (...) It was then that our work began – as an association – to maintain regional education as one of the elements of the region's identity. And we do not care about Silesian education at all, we only care about regional education for each region. And this should happen.[37]

There are many advantages to teaching regional education. Firstly, it shapes the regional identity of students, along with a feeling of belonging to the community in which they live. Secondly, it gives students the possibility to understand and comprehend the place of their community in the nation-state and in Europe. Thirdly, understanding diversity should lead to the development of tolerance for differences among people (Jarzyńska 2010; Józefowicz 2013). There is, however, one more reason for regional education in the case of Upper Silesia: the collective memory of Silesians was (and, to some extent, still is) a concealed one and in many cases, even Silesian parents may not be able (or willing) to talk to children about the region and its past:

> O2R1:   But I think that our generation [generation of today's parents] had the biggest problems. I came home and I asked some questions and

---

37   O1R5: (...) To wtedy rozpoczęły się nasze prace, jako Stowarzyszenia, żeby podtrzymać edukację regionalną, jako jeden z elementów tożsamości regionu. I nam wcale nie zależy na edukacji śląskiej, tylko nam zależy na edukacji regionalnej dla każdego regionu. I tak się powinno dziać.

PROGRAMMES AND POSTULATES OF UPPER SILESIAN ORGANISATIONS 165

they [parents] would not tell me anything. And then I had a problem: why did my uncle fight on the wrong side? And not in the right formation? And why was he buried so far away? And it was problematic. Throughout the Polish People's Republic time, such topics were avoided in all families.[38]

Members of the studied organisations emphasised that too little is taught about collective memory and the different history of Silesia and famous persons who came from the region, and also its distinctive art and architecture.

Still, teachers, programmes and funds are needed in order to introduce lessons in regional education. There are two models for how regional education can be introduced: as voluntary or obligatory classes. In any case, at least one hour per week in all years of primary school and high school are postulated. There is also no consensus as to whether the Silesian language should be a separate subject or whether it should be taught during regional education classes. As to teachers:

O5R1: It should be taught by people with education in this field (e.g. after post-graduate studies at the University of Silesia). I am not even saying that everyone has to speak Silesian (...).[39]

In 2018, at the Faculty of Philology in the Institute of the Polish Language of the University of Silesia in Katowice, a post-graduate study course was opened, titled *"Wiedza o regionie"* ("Knowledge about the Region"), led by a specialist in Silesian studies – Prof. Jolanta Tambor. It is targeted at teachers and culture animators who wish to acquire knowledge about the region and learn how to share it in the future. Over 50 students enrolled in the course when it started.

Some programmes for regional education have already been created. This includes programmes funded by the Sejmik of the Śląskie Voivodeship, such as the regional education platform "EDUŚ", where materials for lessons in

---

38　O2R1: Ale ja myślę, że to nasze pokolenie miało największe kłopoty. Ja zawsze jak wracałem do domu i o pewne rzeczy pytałem, to mi nic nie chcieli powiedzieć. I potem miałem problem: czemu mój wujek walczył nie po tej stronie? I nie w tej formacji? I czemu tam leży daleko? I to było problematyczne. Przez cały PRL we wszystkich rodzinach unikano takich tematów.

39　O5R1: Powinny prowadzić to osoby z wykształceniem w tym kierunku (np. po studiach podyplomowych na Uniwersytecie Śląskim). Ja już nawet nie mówię, że wszyscy mają godać (...).

regional education are prepared by scholars and available free-of-charge.[40] The platform was created by the *Instytut Badań Regionalnych Biblioteki Śląskiej* (Institute of Regional Studies of the Silesian Library). Furthermore, the *Demokratyczna Unia Regionalistów Śląskich* (DURŚ) created the platform "E-rechtōr", with materials for classes of regional education.[41] Many more such programmes have been prepared.

One more issue regarding funding still exists:

> O2R1: If the government was aware of how to raise young people, it would pay for regional education lessons in each region. An hour [one hour-long class a week] and money should be provided. Now, if this money is to be given by self-government authorities, this would be much more difficult. Some of them cannot afford this, and creating a system is much more difficult. And today, what children receive in the field of education is so incomplete, so short: this is the tragedy of this state.[42]

Local authorities have different approaches to the matter. For example, in Rybnik, grade 4 students in primary school have had one hour a week of regional education since 2016. In the municipality of Studzienice (Pszyczyński district), students have had these classes since the first year of primary school. The city of Katowice planned to introduce regional education starting in the 2018/2019 school year. Regional education is also funded by the cities of Bytom and Czechowice-Dziedzice, and in the city of Chorzów, regional education classes have taken place since the early 2000s. But there are still municipalities where regional education is not taught at all.

The lack of knowledge about the events that took place in Silesia was pointed out by a member of O3. He mentioned that the first people to seek the truth about the history of the region and its population, especially after 1945, were representatives of the German minority and German-Silesians:

---

40   Platform EDUŚ. n.d. "Homepage".

41   Demokratyczna Unia Regionalistów Śląskich. n.d. "Rechtōr. Forum Regionalistów Śląskich".

42   O2R1: Jeżeli rząd byłby świadomy jak wychowywać młodych ludzi, to płaciłby na lekcje edukacji regionalnej w każdym regionie. Powinna być przewidziana godzina i pieniądze. Teraz, jeżeli te pieniądze mają dawać samorządy to jest to o wiele trudniejsze. Jedni mogą dać inni nie, i stworzenie systemu jest o wiele trudniejsze. A dziś to co dzieci otrzymują w zakresie edukacji jest tak dalece niepełne, skrócone, to jest tragedia tego Państwa.

PROGRAMMES AND POSTULATES OF UPPER SILESIAN ORGANISATIONS

O3R1: There are no explorers here. Everything that is being done today and looks to be something new, something discovered, is just a repetition. Like the whole thing related to the Tragedy after 1945. The moment we came to this – in 1989 – nobody was there, we were incredibly alone as we found out about these camps.[43]

The Upper Silesian region is rich in history and traditions and in its many dialects of the Silesian language. To some extent, both its history and traditions differ from the Polish official narration and historical events traditionally taught in Polish educational programmes. Therefore, children and adults know more about distant places and people who lived far away than about their own region. To change this situation, a reliable programme of regional education is needed, a fact that is pointed out by all the studied organisations.

5.3.3 Teaching and Promotion of the Silesian Language

The Silesian language is one of the most crucial and complicated problems that Silesian organisations must deal with (Kamusella 2004). To begin with, since the time of the Polish Peoples' Republic, there have been many stories about problems connected to speaking Silesian. Mirosław Syniawa, in the introduction to his textbook, recollects that a teacher who had come from another part of Poland punished him for using Silesian at school (2010). There are also stories of people who could not apply to public offices because they were rejected as 'incomprehensible'. It is hard to make any general statements. Still, without a doubt, during the era of the Polish Peoples' Republic, using Silesian in the public sphere was a reason for discrimination on the basis of ethnic origin. Later, before the transformation (1989), Silesian became folklore, a language for jokes about workers from Upper Silesia. Therefore, it should come as no surprise that it was used only at home, with friends or with other Silesians. Thus, it has been slowly forgotten, and younger generations can speak it only to a limited extent. These problems of a fading language and collective memory and the need to cultivate the two were brought up during the interviews:

O1R5: (...) This is what we do. We (...) are constantly working on this, not to forget history, not to forget the language. For the next generations

---

43 O3R1: Tu nie ma żadnych odkrywców. To wszystko co się dzisiaj robi i wygląda na odkrycie to jest tylko powtórzenie. Jak cała ta sprawa związana z Tragedią po 1945 roku. W momencie, kiedy myśmy dochodzili do tego, ja też – w 1989, nikogo nie było, myśmy byli niesamowicie osamotnieni, jak te obozy odkrywaliśmy.

168   CHAPTER 5

> to have the material to possibly create their vision of Silesia on the
> basis of what we are doing at the moment (...).[44]

Two organisations that specialise in the problem of the Silesian language were created: *Pro Loquela Silesiana Towarzystwo Kultywowania i Promocji Śląskiej Mowy* (Pro Loquela Silesiana Society for Cultivating and Promoting Silesian Speech) and *Tôwarzistwo Piastowaniô Ślónskij Môwy "DANGA"* (Association for Cultivating Silesian Speech "DANGA"). There are at least two publishers – *Silesia Progress–Ślōnski geszeft* and *Narodowa Oficyna Śląska* – that publish Silesian literature, mostly in Silesian. As was pointed out by one of the interlocutors:

> O2R6:   (...) Now, 20 books in Silesian are published a year.[45]

Modern literature in Silesian is quickly growing. This development leads to challenges in the field of written Silesian language. There are very few historical texts written in some form of Silesian, and the need for codification of the written form has become evident[46]. For some time (and even today), the so-called Steuer orthography was used (with the symbol ů and diphthong 'ou'). As early as 2008, under the leadership of Prof. dr hab. Jolanta Tambor, the Commission of Codification of Silesian Orthography was established and, as a result, the so-called *ślabikŏrzowy szrajbōnek* (with the symbols ã, ŏ, ō, ô and õ), which is the most popular Silesian orthograph today, was created. The Commission still works on other aspects of the written language today, although the personnel structure has changed. Additionally, in 2012, the *Rada Górnośląska* (Upper Silesian Council) promoted the idea of a common Council for the Silesian Language, though this idea was never realised. There are dictionaries of the Silesian language – to name just a few:
- *Ilustrowany słownik gwary śląskiej* – Marek Szołtysek (1998), *Wydawnictwo Śląskie ABC*: Rybnik.
- *Słownik polsko-śląski* t. 1–2 – Andrzej Roczniok (2007), *Narodowa Oficyna Śląska*: Zabrze.

---

44   O1R5: (...) Tym właśnie zajmujemy się. My, wbrew pozorem, cały czas pracujemy nad tym, żeby nie zapomnieć historii, nie zapomnieć języka. Żeby następne pokolenia miały materiał do tego, żeby ewentualnie stworzyć na bazie tego, co my w tej chwili robimy, swoją wizję Śląska (...).

45   O2R6: (...) I teraz 20 książek jest rocznie wydawanych po śląsku.

46   Examples of historical and modern writings in Silesian can be found here: Silling. n.d. „Korpus".

PROGRAMMES AND POSTULATES OF UPPER SILESIAN ORGANISATIONS 169

- *Słownik gōrnoślōnskij gŏdki* – Bogdan Kallus (2015), *Pro Loquela Silesiana*: Chorzów.

There are textbooks as well:

- *Elementarz śląski* – Marek Szołtysek (2001), *Wydawnictwo Śląskie* ABC: Rybnik.
- *Ślabikŏrz niy dlŏ bajtli abo lekcyje ślōnskij gŏdki* – Mirosław Syniawa (2010), *Pro Loquela Sielsiana*: Chorzów.
- *Gōrnoślōnski ślabikŏrz* (2010), *Pro Loquela Sielsiana*: Chorzów.

Teaching Silesian is one of the postulates shared by all the organisations. Still, the approaches to the matter are different. The primary problem is the legal recognition of the Silesian language as a regional language or as a language of the ethnic minority (if the minority is recognised as such). Secondly, the question of whether Silesian should be taught as a mandatory or voluntary subject is disputed:

> O4R5: (...) Therefore, in my opinion, it should be an optional activity for people who are willing to do so. However, due to the fact that people live here, all inhabitants should have a certain level of familiarity. Taught as a separate subject [as voluntary]. It should be also woven into another subject for everyone. All inhabitants should have some elementary knowledge: to understand and to respect diversity. Provided that we will be able to prepare the curricula.[47]

The same problems as those affecting regional education are present here: are there teachers ready to teach Silesian? Can educational programmes be prepared? And how can the funding for it be found? The answers to these questions are similar.

Another interesting matter is lecturing in Silesian. There are two options as to how to preserve a language: teach it as a subject and/or lecture on subjects in the language. As was already mentioned, the number of schoolchildren who speak Silesian fluently is quite small, and there is no single language norm for written Silesian. Hence, the question about lecturing subjects in Silesian was a

---

47   O4R5: (...) Dlatego, moim zdaniem, powinny to być fakultatywne zajęcia dla ludzi chęt-nych. Natomiast ze względu na to, ze ludzie tu mieszkają, jakiś poziom znajomości powinni mieć wszyscy mieszkańcy. Nauczany jako osobny przedmiot. Dla wszystkich powinien być wpleciony w inny przedmiot. Wszyscy mieszkańcy powinni mieć jakąś ele-mentarną znajomość: żeby rozumieć i żeby szanować odmienność. Łącznie z maturą i studiami wyższymi. Pod warunkiem, że będziemy w stanie przygotować programy.

hypothetical one (or, some might rather say, very far-sighted), but still received an answer:

O4R1: All subjects can be lectured in Silesian. We are at a stage where Czechs were after the Spring of Nations, when Czech intellectuals decided to make their own language. And Slovaks even later. They were also laughed at and told that this language is not good for anything. Great literature and movies have been created since then. We are at the beginning of this road and we make similar mistakes as they did at the beginning.[48]

The last statement intended to show that languages in their written, unified form can be developed, and the fact that they do not exist yet does not mean that this is an impossible task. Without a doubt, in the Silesian case, much work will need to be done not only in the creation of a unified written language but also in the preservation of local dialects. The Silesian language has been a spoken language for such a long time that there is substantial diversity within communities. To truly teach it, the language will need to assume a single written version. Still, the growing literature and popularity of the Silesian language are evident. While Silesian organisations should be proud of the work they have done in the matter, they are aware that it is just the beginning of a long road to ensuring the preservation of the Silesian language for future generations.

5.3.4 *Decentralisation and Autonomy*

The problem of decentralisation has been at the centre of public debate about Upper Silesia (Myśliwiec 2013). This is not only true for organisations within the Upper Silesian ethnoregionalist movement but also for state-wide parties and organisations. Indeed, the very existence of this tension based on the allocation of public authority between the centre and this particular periphery is the reason why the ethnoregionalist movement within the region is classified as such. All the organisations within the movement agree on the fact that there is a need for further decentralisation and a fuller introduction of the principle of subsidiarity in Poland as a whole. The principle introducing the idea that

---

48   O4R1: Wszystkie przedmioty można po śląsku wykładać. My jesteśmy na takim etapie, na którym Czesi byli po Wiośnie Ludów. Kiedy intelektualiści czescy postanowili dorobić się własnego języka. A Słowacy nawet później. Też się z nich śmiano i mówiono, ze ten język się do niczego nie nadaje. Od tamtego czasu powstała wspaniała literatura, filmy. My jesteśmy na początku tej drogi i popełniamy podobne błędy, jak oni na początku.

PROGRAMMES AND POSTULATES OF UPPER SILESIAN ORGANISATIONS 171

local affairs should be decided on a local level, regional affairs on a regional level and state-wide affairs on the central level is shared by all of the studied organisations, which also stress the fact that this idea entails the need for representatives of the community to assume responsibility for the locality and the region as well. For this to happen, public authorities within the said communities must be equipped with adequate legal and financial instruments.

This is as far as the agreement goes. Within the movement, there exists a tension between two groups I have categorised as regionalists and autonomists. The first group of activists and organisations opts for further decentralisation of public competences along with public funding to self-government authorities, but without any major changes to the political system of the state. The question about the need for autonomy for the region received the following answer:

> O1R5:   No. I do not know if there is a need. However, there is certainly a need to create a certain part of finances that would be at the disposal of the local and regional government.
>
> O1R11:   (...) More funds for the local and regional government. Greater competences for the Sejmik as the host of the region.[49]

The second group, the autonomists, has a wider and more precise programme for the future of the region:

> O2R4:   (...) We want to convince everyone, both the inhabitants of Silesia, but also to offer proven solutions to Poland. Self-government, based on the principle of subsidiarity, what we call autonomy, that is: deciding on matters wherever this is possible. This is the best solution – for everyone. And money and the ability to decide on their distribution.
>
> O5R1:   A region ruled by the Sejmik with a strong Speaker and Treasury. The Sejmik will be able to create certain things. And the Treasury of Silesia with new taxes, imposed by the Sejmik (...).[50]

---

49   O1R5: Nie. Ja nie wiem czy jest taka potrzeba. Natomiast na pewno jest potrzeba utworzenia pewnej części finansów, który byłby w dyspozycji samorządu.
O1R11: (...) Więcej środków dla samorządu. Większe kompetencje dla Sejmiku jako gospodarza regionu.

50   O2R4: (...) Nam zależy nam tym, żeby przekonywać każdego, zarówno mieszkańców Śląska, ale też proponować całej Polsce sprawdzone rozwiązania. Samorządność, oparcie o zasadę pomocniczości, co my nazywamy autonomią, czyli decydowaniem o swoich sprawach tam gdzie to jest możliwe. To jest najlepsze rozwiązanie – dla każdego. I pieniądze i możliwość decydowania o ich rozdysponowaniu.

172   CHAPTER 5

The introduction of autonomous regions in Poland within the existing *Constitution of the Republic of Poland* from 1997 is believed by some to be impossible. The first doubt is based on article 3: "The Republic of Poland shall be a unitary State". Obviously, the provision states, first and foremost, that the Republic of Poland is not a federation or confederation, but the interpretation differs as to whether the *Constitution* allows for further decentralisation in the form of a system of autonomous regions. Hence, the *Ruch Autonomii Śląska* (Silesian Autonomy Movement), the oldest organisation promoting autonomy for the region (and all the regions in Poland as well), suggested the amendment to some of the constitutional provisions. For example, art. 3:

> Par. 1 The constitution is based on the unbreakable unity of the Republic of Poland, a common and undivided homeland of all its citizens, it also recognizes and ensures the right to territorial autonomy for regions and solidarity among all.
>
> Par. 2 By law, self-government units are also created and participate in the exercise of public authority.[51]

These amendments, while introducing a system of autonomous regions, also ensure the existence of self-government units on the local level. On the other hand, they confirm the unity of the state and a lack of secessionist demands on the side of autonomists. This was confirmed in the interviews:

> O2R1:   We do not have any programme, which aims at creating a state.[52]

Furthermore, Chapter III – "Sources of Law" of the *Constitution of the Republic of Poland* would need to be changed in order to introduce a system of autonomous regions. Two solutions are provided in the suggested amendments:

O5R1: Region rządzony przez Sejmik z silnym Marszałkiem i Skarbem. Sejmik będzie mógł pewne rzeczy kreować. A Skarb Śląski z nowych podatków, nałożonych przez Sejmik (...).

51   Ruch Autonomii Śląska. n.d. "Projekt poprawek do Konstytucji RP". Original wording: "Art. 3 para. 1. Konstytucja opiera się na nierozerwalnej jedności Rzeczypospolitej Polskiej, wspólnej i niepodzielnej ojczyzny wszystkich jej obywateli, a także uznaje i zapewnia prawo do autonomii terytorialnej stanowiących ją regionów oraz solidarności między wszystkimi. Art. 3 para. 2. W drodze ustawy tworzy się także jednostki samorządu terytorialnego, uczestniczące w sprawowaniu władzy publicznej."

52   O2R1: Nie mamy programu, który ma na celu utworzenie Państwa.

PROGRAMMES AND POSTULATES OF UPPER SILESIAN ORGANISATIONS

- art. 85 indicates the inclusion of so-called organic statutes (located in the hierarchy of legal acts just after the *Constitution*) – the statutes regulating the status of autonomous regions;
- art. 93 indicates the inclusion of a provision vesting legislative powers in autonomous regions (the extent of which would be regulated in detail by organic statutes).[53]

Historically, in the *Constitution of the Republic of Poland* from 17 March 1921, art. 3 envisioned that the statute could decentralise legislative power and vest it in self-government units in the field of administration, culture and the economy.[54] The *Constitution* from 1997, in its present form, does not have such provisions, which leads to the need for amendments if a system of autonomous regions is to be introduced.

The most important changes are incorporated in the project within the amendments to Chapter VII – "Territorial Organisation of the State":
- art. 163 foresees the inclusion of autonomous voivodeships in the system of the territorial division of the state;
- art. 164 is an indication that organic statues may shape the scope of the competences of each region differently (so-called asymmetrical decentralisation);
- the provision in art. 174 assures the status of an autonomous region for every voivodeship within the state by the time of entry into force of the amendments;
- art. 176 presents the scope of possible competences executed by the autonomous regions;
- art. 177 presents a list of competences that would lie in the exclusive powers of the central authorities – the Parliament of the Republic of Poland, the Government and the President;
- art. 178 would vest the power of adopting the organic statutes in the Sejm and Senate (Parliament) of the Republic of Poland;
- art. 179 outlines, in general terms, the basis for organising autonomous regions, granting the existence of a legislative body chosen by the inhabitants and an executive, while art. 183 grants financing autonomy, which allows the regions to execute their competences.[55]

The financing of autonomous regions is possible in three ways, as recognised by art. 184 of the project: by allowing authorities of local and regional units to adopt their own fees and taxes, by sharing state-wide taxes and by creating a

---

53 Ruch Autonomii Śląska. n.d. "Projekt poprawek do Konstytucji RP". See: articles 85 and 93.
54 Dz.U. 1921 nr 44 poz. 267.
55 Ruch Autonomii Śląska. n.d. "Projekt poprawek do Konstytucji RP". See: articles 163–185.

174   CHAPTER 5

system of subsidies (in the form of inter-regional funds, which minimise the differences in the incomes of regions).

The project foresees that every voivodeship in Poland would become autonomous and would be able to negotiate its own organic statute and, consequently, the competences it would have in the future. However, the members of autonomist organisations in Silesia are not enthusiastic about the reaction of the inhabitants of other voivodeships:

> O2R4:   However, will others want this? Well, maybe two regions in Poland could be found, but...[56]

As to Upper Silesia, the project of the Organic Statute has already been drafted.[57] The first chapter, "Silesian Autonomous Voivodeship" (art. 1–7), includes a description of the general organisation of authorities in the region: legislative – a Silesian Sejm and Senate, and executive – a government with the President of Ministers at its head, Silesian Ombudsman and Silesian Council of Mass Media. It also foresees the creation of a Silesian Treasury and Silesian Administrative Court. The seats of public institutions are to be located in Katowice, Opole, Bielsko-Biała and Rybnik, but in order to achieve this, the Polish territorial division would have to be changed (today, Opole is in the Opolskie Voivodeship and is not a part of the Śląskie Voivodeship). Chapter II – "Rights and Freedoms" (art. 8–11) incorporates additional rights for citizens living in the voivodeship, encompassing the rights not mentioned *expressis verbis* in the *Constitution of the Republic of Poland*, but lying within the scope of constitutional regulation. Chapter III – "Sources of Law" (art. 12–21) determines the scope of competences of the Silesian Voivodeship and the relation between Polish and Silesian law. Chapter IV – "Administrative System" (art. 22–26) includes provisions about the role and authorities within local self-government units. Chapter V – "Autonomous Institutions" (art. 23–67) regulates in detail the organisation of all the Silesian institutions enumerated in Chapter I. Chapter VI – "Public Order" (art. 68–72) creates the Silesian Guard – regional police with territorially limited competences. Chapter VII – "Public Property" (art. 73–76) indicates that all public property within the territory of the autonomous voivodeship becomes its property and is governed by regional and local authorities by the time the amendments enter into force. Chapter

---

56   O2R4: Natomiast czy inni z tego skorzystają? No jakieś dwa regiony w Polsce pewnie można by znaleźć, ale...

57   Ruch Autonomii Śląska. n.d. "Projekt Statutu Organicznego dla Województwa Śląskiego".

VIII – "Amendments. Transitional Provisions" (art. 77–79) states that amendments in the statute can be adopted by the Silesian Sejm and Senate and are signed by the Speaker of the Silesian Sejm (*Marszałek Sejmu Śląskiego*). The last provisions are inconsistent with the suggested amendments to the *Constitution* (draft of the project of amendments to article 178)[58] because, in general, the same institution that adopts a statute must take part in its changes and, in this case, the Parliament of the Republic of Poland, along with the President, would be required to have the power to approve any amendment to the statute containing the Organic Statute.

This is how the future autonomy for the regions in Poland (especially Upper Silesia) is foreseen by autonomists from the *Ruch Autonomii Śląska*. The suggested model clearly draws from the solutions introduced in the Kingdom of Spain in 1978, and this is not accidental. There are some similarities between Spain and Poland: the states are similar in size; both states are considered to be located on the peripheries of the EU; both have a history of authoritarian systems and a transition to democracy. However, there are still many differences.

Members of another organisation go even further:

O4R3: Poland of regions and Europe of regions.
O4R2: Autonomy for all is understood by many as federalism.
O4R3: The German model would be the best.
O4R1: There would be no problem if all of Europe were federated, as a federation of regions.[59]

The idea of a Europe of Regions goes back as far as the inter-war period (Muś 2016). Today, it has become less popular for many reasons: growing nationalism, the uncertain future of the EU and growing dangers on the global level. Still, what is evident from the statements above is that it was not rejected altogether by the citizens of Europe. Although this idea is very hypothetical, it is extremely difficult to determine whether it is truly the right solution for the regions and its inhabitants, one which would ensure better chances for development. Either way, without a doubt, the process of regionalisation and demands for further decentralisation have become a feature of Poland's

---

58 Ruch Autonomii Śląska. n.d. "Projekt poprawek do Konstytucji RP". See: art. 178.
59 O4R3: Polska regionów i Europa regionów.
    O4R2: Autonomia dla wszystkich przez wielu rozumiana jest jako federalizm.
    O4R3: Model niemiecki byłyby najlepszy.
    O4R1: Nie byłoby tego problemu, gdyby cała Europa była sfederalizowana, jako federacja regionów właśnie.

political landscape, and the centralism-regionalism opposition – based on the debate about the division of public authority between the centre and the periphery – has today been causing growing discontent on a scale greater than ever before.

In the end, it should be mentioned that I could not find any holistic analysis of the costs of the suggested legislation. In short: it is hard to say whether it was evaluated by the autonomists, and it is beyond the scope of this Subchapter. Yet, the following is a relevant question: how much would it cost to introduce suggested changes to the political system in Poland? And on the other hand: how much of an economic value would it have for the region in the long-term perspective? Therefore, I believe that there is still no complete answer to the question: would it be worth it from the perspective of the economy? Although the economy is not the only factor in the decision-making process, it definitely should be taken into consideration.

5.3.5   *Functions and the Role of the Organisation*

One of the goals of the present study was to better understand how organisations within the Silesian ethnoregionalist movement see themselves, their role and their functions within the region. Civic society and models of political participation on many levels were introduced in Poland after 1989 and became quite popular. The ethnoregionalist movements should be seen as part of a wider phenomenon of social mobilisation. Therefore, the place of each organisation within the movement is interesting for the purpose of this study.

Based on the results of the study, I developed a classification of organisations, based on the models of activity they adopted within the Upper Silesian ethnoregionalist movement: sparse, consolidated and observant. Members of the first group are the organisations, which adopted the model of sparse activity, take part in diverse activities and may even be members of different parties and promote their ideas by different means, also beyond the initiatives developed within the movement. This group includes organisations O1 and O6. The second group consists of organisations that prefer consolidated action – their members create their own initiatives within the movement and take part in others to a very limited extent. This group includes O2, O3 and O4. The third group contains organisations that are sceptical about today's development in the ethnoregionalist movement and remain outside the most recent developments but still have a watchful eye on the situation. O5 belongs to this group.

Organisation O1 is an example of an organisation with a sparse model of activity:

PROGRAMMES AND POSTULATES OF UPPER SILESIAN ORGANISATIONS

O1R5: Please note that at the moment, there are people in the association who belong to political parties (...).[60]

For most of the members of this organisation, activity within the Association is just one of the many social and political activities in which they are engaged. This can also be observed in the past political careers of the members of the organisation. The reason for this situation was given in the following interview:

O1R3: It is better to preserve this Silesian identity in the form of respect for diversity.

O1R9: Yes, especially political.[61]

This explanation helps clarify why members of the Association were so reluctant to support any political initiative in Upper Silesia (the Electoral Committee of Voters *Zjednoczeni dla Śląska* or *Śląska Partia Regionalna*). It is the *modus operandi* within the organisation to take part in other projects and promote their ideas in such a way. From the explanation presented above, it can also be deduced that despite common views on Silesian issues, there may be discord regarding other public matters. Nevertheless, this strategy has its shortcomings:

O1R5: (...) We reach to a limited group of people who want to cooperate with us or support our ideas. (...) which, feels like the principle of *dura lex sed lex*, unfortunately. As a result, we are limited and there is only so much we can do. And this is our start – from such a niche and this niche still accompanies us. Nevertheless, we are still an opinion-forming organization. We are still able to speak in a substantive way about Silesia and how we want to understand Silesia. I think that this is one of those features that should accompany the Association until the end of its days. That is to be such a mental compass, a moral compass for residents who identify with us. Because you should notice that the Association is not only addressed to Silesians. The Association is addressed to all who share our position towards Silesia. Since they share

---

60   O1R5: Proszę zauważyć, że w tej chwili w stowarzyszeniu są osoby, które należą do konkretnych partii politycznych (...).

61   O1R3: Że lepiej zachować tą śląskość w postaci szacunku do różnorodności.
     O1R9: Tak jest, zwłaszcza politycznej.

178   CHAPTER 5

> our position, we want to invite them to develop this Silesia as
> we do.[62]

This relatively long quote shows that the organisation is fully aware of the shortcomings of its approach and still accepts it. Firstly, the sparse model creates limited possibilities for the undertakings of the organisation. Secondly, even though the organisation is old and has a stable membership base today, it is not a dynamic one: its activities have not changed much since the 1990s (if anything, they became more limited). Thirdly, this approach leads to the organisation having an inclusive character, which, consequently, means it may not be able to take a consistent stance on important matters.

Organisation O2 is an example of the opposite model of activity – a consolidated one. To begin with, the organisation incorporates an opposite model of political activity and takes part in shaping public policy and politics as a single organisation:

> O2R4:   (...) We take an active part in politics.[63]

Secondly, the programme of the organisation is unified and has a wide scope of issues:

> O2R1:   My vision of my Association is that in the sense of economic issues, our program is a social program in the self-government sense. And we support, for example, civil initiatives. We do not deal with and I hope that we will not deal with such issues as those currently dealt with by the government (e.g., in vitro). We will not speak on such matters.

---

62   O1R5: (...) Docieramy do ograniczonej grupy ludzi, którzy chcą z nami współpracować, bądź popierają nasze idee. (...) które na zasadzie *dura lex sed lex* niestety, ale powodują, że że jesteśmy i możemy robić tylko tyle ile możemy. I to jest to z czego wychodzimy, czyli z takiej niszowości i ta niszowość nadal nam towarzyszy. Niemniej jednak jesteśmy nadal organizacją opiniotwórczą. Nadal jesteśmy w stanie wypowiadać się w sposób rzeczowy na temat Śląska i tego jak chcemy ten Śląsk rozumieć. Myślę, że to jest jedna z tych cech, które powinny towarzyszyć Stowarzyszeniu do końca jego dni. Czyli być takim kompasem mentalnym, kompasem moralnym dla mieszkańców, którzy utożsamiają się z nami. Bo zauważcie państwo, że Stowarzyszenie nie jest adresowany tylko do Ślązaków. Stowarzyszenie jest adresowane dla wszystkich, którzy podzielają nasze stanowisko wobec Śląska. Skoro podzielają nasze stanowisko, chcemy ich zaprosić, żeby rozwijali ten Śląsk tak jak my.

63   O2R4: (...) Bierzemy czynny udział w życiu politycznym.

PROGRAMMES AND POSTULATES OF UPPER SILESIAN ORGANISATIONS 179

O2R4: There is a key in the word autonomy. Autonomy is the most important thing for every human being.[64]

From this quote, it can be concluded that members of the organisation share a common view on the social, political and economic programmes for the region and have fully and consciously decided to avoid matters beyond the scope of their programme. The programme of the organisation leaves its members (and supporters) with autonomy on matters of ideology or consciousness and presents solutions for more pragmatic matters. As to the results of this model of activity in the eyes of the interlocutors:

O2R1: We, however, have some achievements in the area of knowledge, education and public space. And they're quite big (...).

O2R4: We come across the statement: "Silesian awakening". Would it be an awakening without us?

O2R1: Only in the legal sense have we done nothing yet, but we are fighting. And it is also important that we have succeeded as an Association, without public money. Thanks to social activity, we managed to reach such a level (...). We are also trying to promote this regionalism all the time.[65]

This statement shows that, in general, members of the organisation believe that some of its goals have been achieved, and more are within its grasp. The consolidated model of activity has its shortcomings as well, especially limited funding and, consequently, limited success.

The third model of activity of organisations within the movement is best illustrated by O5. This model is based on the particular role of the organisation within the movement – it still takes part in a wide range of activities specific to the movement but assumes the position of an outsider (observer). This

---

64 O2R1: Moja wizja mojego stowarzyszenia jest taka, że w sensie kwestii gospodarczych nasz program jest programem społecznym w sensie samorządowym. I to, co wspieramy np. obywatelskie inicjatywy. My nie zajmujemy się i mam nadzieję, ze nie będziemy się zajmować takimi kwestiami światopoglądowymi, jakimi aktualnie zajmuje się rząd (np. in vitro). Nie będziemy się w takich kwestiach wypowiadać.
O2R4: Jest klucz w słowie autonomia. Autonomia jest najważniejsza i w tym każdego człowieka.

65 O2R1: My jednak mamy pewne dokonania jeśli chodzi o przestrzeń wiedzy, edukacji i przestrzeń publiczną. I to dość duże (...).
O2R4: Spotykamy się z takim stwierdzeniem: „śląskie przebudzenie". Czy takowe by było bez nas?
O2R1: Tylko w sensie prawnym jeszcze nic nie dokonaliśmy, ale walczymy. I ważne jest też to, że nam się udało jako Stowarzyszeniu, bez pieniędzy publicznych. Dzięki aktywności społecznej udało się wejść na taki poziom (...). Też próbujemy ten regionalizm cały czas promować.

180   CHAPTER 5

situation is related to some organisational and personal issues that emerged within the movement, but also to scepticism:

> O5R1:   We are not ready today to debate about how such an autonomous system would look like.[66]

The political programmes promoted by organisations within the Upper Silesian ethnoregionalist movement were presented (and are accessible to the public) and seem well-developed. But they never went beyond the phase of general projects. Based on many interviews with members of the organisations, I also believe that many details of the foreseen political system are vague or non-existent in those projects. Most importantly, there is no economic prognosis as to the costs and benefits of such a transformation of the political system for the region and its inhabitants. Ideology and self-government, as important as they are, cannot be satisfactory reasons for a major change in the political system – it is the economy and the effects on the people that need to be considered in this equation. This is the biggest shortcoming of the policy of the studied organisations within the movement.

The position of observers enabled members of O5 to draw some general conclusions as to the dynamics within the movement:

> O5R1:   What connects us all? Autonomous Silesia, but this is a very distant goal. Regional education, because it connects everyone. And if we start one thing together – one point – then we will continue to act.[67]

Some organisations of the Upper Silesian ethnoregionalist movement were accused of 'going too big' – creating programmes that were too general and lacked solid basics. The last statement is an example of the opposite kind of action: starting with something small and then growing. Moreover, if the movement succeeds in small things, more people will see the need to act together. This suggestion highlights the missing part of the dynamics within the movement: many activists see the things that divide rather than those that connect the organisations within the movement. But a policy of 'baby steps'

---

66   O5R1: My dziś nie jesteśmy gotowi, by rzeczowo podjąć debatę, jak taki system autonomiczny miałby wyglądać.
67   O5R1: Co nas wszystkich łączy? Autonomiczny Śląsk, ale to jest cel bardzo daleki. Edukacja regionalna, bo to wszystkich łączy. I jak zaczniemy jedną rzecz wspólnie robić, jeden punkt, to potem będziemy dalej działać. Potem promocja śląskiej kultury.

PROGRAMMES AND POSTULATES OF UPPER SILESIAN ORGANISATIONS 181

may change this dynamic to the benefit of the movement as a whole. Members of all organisations similarly to O2 declare that:

> O2R3: We are ready to cooperate with anyone who goes in the same direction as we do.[68]

5.3.6 Plans for the Future

Members of the studied organisations were also given a chance to speak about their plans for the future. Two main questions were posed: how do they promote their goals? And what are the foreseeable future goals? Three problems were elaborated on in the answer to the first question: the role of the *Rada Górnośląska* (Upper Silesian Council), the creation of a political party and increasing membership, particularly amongst youths. As to the second question, the answers focused on self-determination, self-government and ethnicity, which came as no surprise.

The issue of the future of the *Rada Górnośląska* (Upper Silesian Council) was brought up by one of the interlocutors:

> O5R1: We no longer take part in the [Upper Silesian] Council's activities for obvious reasons. For us, it was a waste of time. (...) It was a political body in which some wanted to use others. Some people had an appetite to become leaders, while others were supposed to work for their success. And we did not like it much, because we are apolitical (...).[69]

The umbrella organisation gathered associations and foundations with different views on Upper Silesia and diverse political goals, but which demonstrated a set of common interests – interests benefiting Upper Silesia and its inhabitants. Moreover, all of them can be categorised as ethnoregionalist, even if their goals do not encompass everyday politics or if they do not take part in elections. But the most interesting question for me is whether an organisation that promotes decentralisation and the recognition of an ethnic minority

---

68   O2R3: Jesteśmy gotowi do współpracy z każdym, kto idzie w tym kierunku, co my.
69   O5R1: My nie bierzemy już udziału w działalności Rady [Górnośląskiej] z oczywistych dla nas powodów. Dla nas to była strata czasu. (...) To było takie ciało polityczne, w którym jedni chcieli wykorzystać drugich. Jedni mieli apetyt na to aby być przywódcom, a inni mieli na to pracować. I nam się to nie za bardzo podobało, dlatego, że jesteśmy apolityczni (...).

along with language can be apolitical. Is it possible to achieve the goals set by founder-organisations of the Council without politics? Decentralisation demands changes in the political system and, more importantly, the legal system (even without introducing autonomous regions). In the case of ethnicity, this would require a change in the ethnopolitics of the state. In both instances, the goals are highly political, even if they do not require taking part in day-to-day politics. Still, they may be achieved by influencing public policy. Some even say that the mere promotion of an ethnicity that is different from the nationalities recognised by the state is political. This is the reason why political parties were developed within the Upper Silesian ethnoregionalist movement. It is possible, then, that after this development, the situation within the *Rada Górnośląska* will change. The evolution of this umbrella organisation or its dissolution seems to be the probable outcomes.

The *Ruch Autonomii Śląska* (Silesian Autonomy Movement) has participated in elections since 2002 as an Electoral Committee of Voters and has also attempted to create a wider political platform. It achieved limited success, but it was not enough. In 2017, the creation of the *Śląska Partia Regionalna* (Silesian Regional Party) was announced, and a year before that, the party *Ślonzoki Razem* was created (both claiming to be political platforms for many Silesian circles and organisations). With these developments came two questions: how can the roles of parties and other organisations within the movement be divided? And will all the organisations support the creation of political parties and their activities?

The first question was answered in one of the interviews:

> O2R4: Surely, Śląska Partia Regionalna [the Silesian Regional Party] will also be a subject of this political reality, but this is still ahead of us.[70]

It seems possible that no clear-cut divisions will be made as to the activities of the parties and other organisations. Obviously, the parties will take part in elections and become subjects of the day-to-day politics of the region (and maybe even beyond). At the same time, organisations will probably take over social and cultural activities. Still, it may be assumed that the problems of decentralisation and ethnicity will remain the interests of both parties and organisations. This is especially probable because most of the parties' activists

---

70 O2R4: Na pewno Śląska Partia Regionalna siłą rzeczy też będzie podmiotem tej rzeczywistości politycznej, ale to jest dopiero przed nami.

PROGRAMMES AND POSTULATES OF UPPER SILESIAN ORGANISATIONS 183

(or, at least, people who promote them in public) are also members of existing associations.

The second question received varied answers, from open support to caution:

> O1R10: (…) However, when it comes to the attitude towards the party, if the party has such goals in the program as we just said – self-government, as we said – Silesian identity. And if there is a dialogue in the program, openness to others: other Silesian organizations, other regions, etc. and if it has innovation in the program – that Upper Silesia requires innovation in every field: educational, artistic, economic, etc., we will say that it is the same. As was already said here, no stand [of support], but maybe some goals will be common.[71]

This stance makes it clear that there is no common ground as to the political goals within the Upper Silesian ethnoregionalist movement. On the contrary, there are many visions of how to achieve these goals, even if the goals themselves are common. The process of the development of the *Śląska Partia Regionalna* (Silesian Regional Party) revealed that the biggest differences do not lie within the ideologies of the studied organisations (even though they are obvious) but in the model of activity: the split between the founding members of the party was not drawn along the lines of differing visions of the programme but along the issues of day-to-day politics and elections to the self-government bodies emerging in 2018. Some of the founding members decided that their political future should be connected to state-wide parties and not to newly-created initiatives, whose fate is uncertain.

Recruiting new members and attracting people to organised events is one of the goals of every organisation. In the social sciences, it has already been established that the social and political participation of young people is not based on membership in organisations or even taking part in elections, but on new forms of spontaneous participation, which is how young people voice their problems and expectations (*Młodzi 2011* 2011, 280). This is why political

---

71 O1R10: (…) Natomiast, jeżeli chodzi o stosunek do partii, to jeżeli partia będzie miała w programie takie założenia jak właśnie powiedzieliśmy samorządność, jak powiedzieliśmy tożsamość śląska. I jeżeli będzie miała w programie dialog, otwartość na innych, na inne organizacje śląskie, na inne regiony itd. i jeżeli będzie miała w programie innowacyjność, że Górny Śląsk wymaga innowacyjności w każdej dziedzinie: edukacyjnej, artystycznej, gospodarczej itd. to my powiemy, że to jest tożsame. Tak jak Państwo tutaj mówili, żadnego stanowiska nie, ale może niektóre cele będą zbieżne.

184

CHAPTER 5

parties and other organisations need to adjust their programmes and recruitment strategies. An example of such a situation was given in the following interview:

O1R4:   (...) It is our organization that not only goes here from its roots, from its 25-year tradition, but also opens up to new trends. And we cannot forget about that. We have a number of projects that we address to young people. (...) This is us opening to the young generation. So not only do we live our tradition, which is extremely important, but also open to young people.[72]

Decentralisation, self-government and self-determination are still the main goals of all the studied organisations. They are seen especially important today:

O2R6:   These are ideas that are supposed to influence what is happening in politics right now and there will be a solstice. The question is whether in two years or six. This will happen, and this centralization, which now takes place not only will turn back, but will be much lower than the level from before (...). And at this point, since this centralization has reached the size of a pumped-up balloon, it will explode, and it will turn 180 degrees.

O2R3:   For Silesia and for Poland. This is our proposal not limited to Upper Silesia. And in Silesia to all who live here. Because everyone will benefit from it, also the ones who do not agree with us today.[73]

---

72   O1R4: (...) To nasza organizacja nie tylko tutaj idzie od swoich korzeni, od swoich tradycji 25-letniej, ale także otwiera się na nowe nurty. I o tym nie możemy zapomnieć. Mamy szereg projektów, które adresujemy do młodych ludzi. (...) To jest właśnie to otwarcie na młode pokolenie. Więc nie tylko żyjemy tą naszą tradycją, która jest niesamowicie ważna, ale także otwieramy się na ludzi młodych.

73   O2R6: To są pomysły, które mają oddziaływać na to, co się w tej chwili dzieje w polityce i nastąpi pewne przesilenie. Pytanie czy za 2 lata czy za 6. Natomiast to nastąpi, a ta centralizacja która teraz trwa nie tylko proces się odwróci, ale będzie o wiele niżej od tego poziomu sprzed. (...) I w tym momencie skoro ta centralizacja doszła do takich rozmiarów, jak pompowany balon, to wybuchnie, i nastąpi zwrot o 180 stopni.
O2R3: Dla Śląska i dla Polski. To jet nasza propozycja nie ograniczona do Górnego Śląska. A na Śląsku do wszystkich, którzy tu mieszkają. Bo na tym będzie korzystać każdy, też ten, co się z nami dziś nie zgadza.

PROGRAMMES AND POSTULATES OF UPPER SILESIAN ORGANISATIONS 185

The process of centralisation of the public administration and the public authority, along with national unification, is taking place today at a level that has not been seen since 1989. The demands for decentralisation come not only from regional actors but also from state-wide parties and politicians. Not so long ago, the same parties took a stand against any debate about further decentralisation of competences or funding, but today, this view has changed (although it is hard to say whether this is an ideological change or only a tactical change). Furthermore, these demands are becoming more widely accepted in regions with no traditions of ethnoregionalist movements. This change is, without a doubt, a reaction to the encroachment of the central government into almost every area of public (and even private) life. It seems that there is no stronger ally of claims for decentralisation than excessive centralisation and state-control.

As to ethnicity, one response was especially interesting:

> O5R1:   We cannot constantly go for a confrontation. There was a time of struggle and we achieved certain goals. And it was necessary to stabilize this situation. Thinking about regional education, about things that are important for regionalists. To start building a foundation. And we have wasted a good run of luck by not achieving anything. And this is coming to an end. Because this time has been wasted (...) I do not know if it was inspired, but someone really wanted to weaken it all.[74]

Arguing for the recognition of Silesians as an ethnic minority has indeed led to a certain level of confrontation between Polish state-nationalism and the ethnoregionalist movement. This can be observed in the argument around collective memory and the separate character of the Silesian culture. One goal that was achieved was the promotion of awareness about the particular situation of Silesians and gaining some level of sympathy for their cause. But this did not lead to any tangible results, such as legal changes or changes in financing. The

---

74   O5R1: My nie możemy ciągle iść na konfrontację. Był czas walki i osiągnęliśmy pewne cele. I trzeba było ustabilizować tą sytuację. Myśleć o edukacji regionalnej, o tych rzeczach, które są dla regionalistów ważne. Żeby zacząć budować fundament. A myśmy nie osiągając nic zmarnowali dobrą passę. A to się już kończy. Bo ten czas został zmarnowany. I nie osiągnęliśmy w miastach niczego, bo się wszyscy pokłócili. Bo mieliśmy początek i zaczęliśmy się kłócić. (...) Nie wiem czy to było inspirowane, ale komuś bardzo zależało by to wszystko osłabić.

current state of affairs leads us to pose the following question: how can these changes be achieved? Is confrontation the solution? Or should the focus be on working on the basics in the current situation? It seems that this problem is another bone of contention within the movement. We can observe that some argue for building the basics, a policy of 'baby steps', but for many, this is a matter of full recognition of rights, equality and plurality and cannot be accepted any other way.

5.4 Programmes and Postulates of Upper Silesian Organisations – Conclusions

Peripheral identity (Silesian identity) is present among the members of the studied organisations in many shades. Firstly, it can take the form of a single identity, which, in some cases, can be categorised as ethnic identity, while in others, it is a quasi-national identity. Secondly, it can be part of a double identity (as either dominant or supplementary). In these cases, this can usually be categorised as an ethnic identity.

The interviews with the studied organisations made it clear that problems connected to ethnicity, e.g., its cultivation, preservation and recognition, are part of the organisations' programmes. What is also evident is that demands for the recognition of Silesians as a separate ethnic minority are stronger within those organisations whose members declared Silesian identity as their only identity. However, there are some exceptions: members of organisations in which Silesian-German identity was declared also strongly support the demand for recognition. As a result, we can assume that belonging to a minority group or belonging to two minority groups (German and Silesian) leads to a desire for the legal recognition of the group (or both groups). The same is not necessarily true for people who identify themselves with minority and majority groups (Silesian and Polish). Consequently, and as is evident in the interview with O6, the claims for the recognition of a non-dominant group are developed in opposition to the ideology of the dominant group (the thesis about the homogeneity of the Polish Nation). The latter thesis seems to be accepted by persons declaring themselves members of the dominant and non-dominant group (with double identity). This group aims at the preservation of Silesian culture as a regional variation of Polish culture, with a strong emphasis on links between them.

PROGRAMMES AND POSTULATES OF UPPER SILESIAN ORGANISATIONS

Representatives of the Upper Silesian community develop their identity based on elements such as:
– collective memory,
– traditions,
– language and literature,
– territorial-patriotism and relation to 'Heimat',
– auto-stereotypes (tolerance, hard-work, equality) (Muś 2020).

These elements are presented in two ways: as influenced by German or Polish culture or as separate, typically Silesian features. Their presentation and interpretation differ, and they are connected to the ideologies developed by members of organisations.

The ideologies presented in the materials published by the organisations and in the interviews I conducted are based on a series of oppositions:
– the relation to decentralisation: regionalists and autonomists,
– the relation to ethnicity and its description: separate or influenced,
– the chosen model of activity: confrontational or working within the *status quo*,
– the relation to politics: political and apolitical.

Using the model presented above as a combination of these factors, the studied organisations may be categorised as follows:

O1: regionalists, influenced, working within the *status quo*, political;
O2: autonomists, separate, confrontational, political;
O3: autonomists, influenced, working within the *status quo*, political;
O4: autonomists, separate, confrontational, apolitical;
O5: autonomists, separate, working within the *status quo*, apolitical;
O6: autonomists, separate, confrontational, political.

In this study, the centre-periphery opposition was linked to two claims: one for autonomy for regions in Poland (and, consequently, the revision of the allocation of public authority between the centre and the peripheries) and the other for the recognition of the Silesian ethnic group as an ethnic minority in Poland (and, consequently, the recognition of a non-dominant culture as a separate one). In the study, five out of six organisations have autonomist programmes, and four out of six promote the recognition of the Silesian ethnic group as an ethnic minority. Within the Upper Silesian ethnoregionalist movement, programmes that include the centre-periphery opposition are dominant. Furthermore, two out of four organisations that promote both elements categorised as representing opposition are mainly political – they aim at achieving their goals by taking part in the political decision-making process. Further, both base their programmes on active confrontation with the current policy of the state. What is interesting is that the models of their activity differ: one was categorised as consolidated, but the other as sparse.

CHAPTER 6

Political Behaviours and Political Potential

6.1   Introduction

The last chapter includes the results of a quantitative study conducted among the inhabitants of three selected districts within the Śląskie Voivodeship. The study was conducted from June to September 2018. The questions were divided into five groups:
- general information,
- Silesians and auto-identification,
- separateness,
- language and traditions,
- political behaviours.

For most of the questions, the respondents could only make one choice. Where multiple answers were possible, a comment has been made. The results were calculated in SPSS and are presented below.

The first subchapter presents the general information given by the respondents. The second subchapter studies the problem of ethnicity and the most important factors of Silesian identity. The third subchapter deals with the popularity of political postulates of organisations within the Upper Silesian ethnoregionalist movement. The fourth subchapter provides an analysis of the political behaviours of the respondents and the popularity of the studied organisations. The last subchapter studies the relations between chosen, key elements of Silesian identity and political behaviours of the respondents.

The goal of this chapter is to answer the following research questions:
- Based on which elements does the community of Upper Silesia create its own identity?
- How popular are the organisations representing the Upper Silesian community among the members of the said community?
- What is the relationship between peripheral identity and the political behaviours of the community of the periphery?

6.2   General Information about the Respondents

First, the respondents were asked to provide general information about themselves, and the sample met the requirements assumed in the procedure in

---

© ANNA MUŚ, 2022 | DOI:10.1163/9789004466456_008

190 CHAPTER 6

Subchapter 3.5 – *Sampling*. Two additional questions were added in this section about their education and religion.

As to education, more than a third of the respondents held a higher education degree. The second and third groups held vocational and secondary or post-secondary degrees. The smallest group included respondents who held lower junior high school or lower school degrees and consisted of less than a tenth of the respondents. The relations in the study differ from the numbers presented in the analysis of the *Główny Urząd Statystyczny* (Central Statistical Office) for the Śląskie Voivodeship, in which the structure is as follows: higher education degree – 22%, vocational degree – 26%, secondary or post-secondary degree – 36%, lower junior high school or lower school degree – 16% (GUS 2017).

The question about the respondent's religion showed that the vast majority of the respondents – almost 95% – declared Roman Catholicism as their religion. The second and third groups were Protestants and other religions. The 'other' religion category included Buddhism, agnosticism and other answers like 'my own'. Even less (2%) declared themselves to be atheists, while Judaism was declared by 1%. These numbers are similar to the data from the 2011 National Census presented in Subchapter 2.6 – *Upper Silesians*.

Almost half of the respondents described themselves as believers. The second and third groups of respondents described their attitude towards religion as undecided but said they were attached to religious traditions, and deeply religious. The rest of the respondents chose the answers 'neutral' or 'opponent of religion'. The study revealed that religiousness among the respondents was rather moderate, but still, for the majority, religion played an important role in their lives. Nevertheless, the results are different from those of the CBOS 2017 survey conducted nationwide, in which 85% of the respondents declared themselves to be believers and 8% said they were deeply religious (CBOS 2017). While a higher result has only been noted in the number of respondents declaring themselves as deeply religious in the current study, the overall number of those declaring they are deeply religious and believers is 63%. After taking into account those who were undecided, this brings the final overall result to 81%, which is lower than in the CBOS survey.

Among the respondents, two-fifths declared that they go to church every Sunday or Saturday and on holidays. Significantly fewer respondents declared that they go to church only on important holidays and still less only on special occasions. The fourth and fifth answers were once a month and every day or several times a week, and each was given by slightly more than a tenth of the respondents. The fewest respondents chose the answer never. The results are similar to the results achieved, e.g., by CBOS in 2017 in the study conducted nationwide, where 50% of the respondents declared that they go to church at least once a week and 38% said that they go to church at least a few times a year (CBOS 2017).

6.3 Ethnicity – Elements of Silesian Identity

6.3.1 *Auto-identification*

The concept of Silesian identity (also referred to as Silesianism in the previous chapters) was based on elements pointed out by the interlocutors presented in Subchapter 5.2 – *Ethnicity*. As was stressed in Subchapter 3.6 – *Procedure*, the sequential mixed approach design allowed us to explore the research problem and extrapolate its results to the larger population. The questions included in the questionnaire were based on the results of the focus group interviews and stances presented by members of Upper Silesian organisations.

Undoubtedly, in any concept of ethnicity, a major role is played by auto-identification, which was also stressed by the interlocutors in the focus group interviews.

Single identification (German, European, Polish or Silesian) was declared by more than half of the respondents. Double identification (German-Silesian, Polish-Silesian, Silesian-German or Silesian-Polish) was declared by a bit less than half of the respondents. Among the double identifications, Silesian was declared by 55% of the respondents and Polish or German by 45% of the respondents as their first identification. There was no single German declaration. There were two other declarations, although they were not explained. (See Table 12).

TABLE 12   Declared auto-identification

Identification	Share (%)
Silesian	35%
Silesian-Polish	24%
Polish-Silesian	22%
Silesian-German	3%
German-Silesian	1%
Polish	10%
German	0%
European	4%
Other	1%
Total	100%

THE AUTHOR'S STUDY AND ANALYSES; N=383 MISSING VALUE=1

The questionnaire survey was conducted among members of the Silesian community – the inhabitants of constituencies with a high rate of Silesian auto-identifications in accordance with the results of the 2011 National Census. For the selected districts within the constituencies, the numbers are as follows:

- Bieruńsko-Lędziński (36%), Katowice (26%),
- Chorzów (34%), Ruda Śląska (36%),
- Gliwicki (26%), Tarnogórski (33%).

The results of the questionnaire made it possible to achieve a significantly higher rate of respondents who declared themselves as Silesians in either single or double identification, which was important for the book, as it was intended as a study of the relations between ethnic identity and political behaviours.

For the purpose of the study, the association between the studied elements of Silesian identity and auto-identification was researched. The association was studied using the Cramer V association measure. The aim of this part of the study was to determine those elements of Silesian identity that have the strongest ties to auto-identification.

6.3.2   *Territorial and Familial Ties*

The role of ties (territorial and familial) to the territory was stressed as an important factor in Silesian identity. In the quantitative study, almost all of the respondents were born in Silesia, while only 10% were born outside the region. Additionally, 80% of the respondents said their mothers came from Silesia, and 75% said their fathers did. For 69% of the respondents, all three statements – I was born in Silesia, my mother and my father came from Silesia – were true. Consequently, the study revealed that the vast majority of the respondents had strong territorial (place of birth) and familial (origin of mother and father) ties to the region. In terms of association, the strongest association is between the place of birth and auto-identification ($\varphi c=0.35$; $p<0.01$). There is also a strong association between the mother's place of birth and auto-identification ($\varphi c=0.32$; $p<0.01$), and only a moderate association between the father's place of birth and auto-identification ($\varphi c=0.27$; $p<0.01$).

The study revealed that the respondents' answers are contrary to the statement presented in Subchapter 5.2.2 – *Silesianism* that Silesian identity is, first and foremost, a bond between a person and a territory and is not necessarily personal (it can be maintained only through ancestry). Secondly, it is a bond to the culture as a whole, which does not necessarily mean a bond of blood (having ancestors who were Silesian is not a condition *sine qua non* of this identity). Both familial (the origins of respondents' parents) and territorial ties to the region play a significant role in auto-identification. Although the descent from members of an ethnic group may not be a condition *sine qua non*, it also has a significant association with auto-identification. It is also worth noting that in all the cases, this association is a positive one: the more dominant Silesian identification is, the higher the statistical possibility that a respondent was born in Silesia and that the respondents' mother and father come from Silesia, with the exception of respondents declaring themselves Europeans.

The role of descent in defining ethnicity has been lately stressed in scholarly literature to the point, when it is even seen as the only attribute necessary for defining ethnicity, specifically descent-based attributes are seen as nominal elements of ethnic identity (Chandra & Wilkinson 2008). Also, descent is seen broadly not only as group descent but also as a common place of origin or a myth of common ancestry. Other aspects usually evoked in definitions of ethnicity, such as auto-identification or cultural and linguistic features, are by some scholars considered elements of activated ethnic identity. The same study also accepts, that a person has a repertoire of nominal ethnic identities and makes a choice to activate one (or possibly more) of them. My study confirms that without descent it is highly improbable for an individual to categorise herself or himself as belonging to an ethnic group. Consequently, for the purpose of a broad definition of ethnicity as a category, this attribute may be sufficient.

This activated ethnic identity may be relevant in private life and/or in politics. In politics, it may take a form of non-institutionalised activities or institutional ones. Within the category of institutional activities we can distinguish both nonelectoral and electoral behaviour. Arguably, Silesian ethnic identity was meaningful already in the inter-war period in political, institutionalised way (Chapter 2 – *Political Situation in Upper Silesia*). However, the influence of ethnic identity on electoral behaviours of both parties and voters is a phenomenon, which can be observed from early 2000s.

6.3.3   *Categorisation and the Role of the Region*
The role of the categorisation of Silesians as a group, as stated by the respondents in the focus group interviews, was also considered one of the most important elements of Silesian identity. The categories included in the questionnaire were used by the interlocutors in the focus group interviews to categorise Silesians. In the quantitative study, 62% of the respondents categorised Silesians as a part of the Polish Nation. The second most frequent answer, at 44%, was that Silesians are an ethnic group, but the least frequent answer

chosen by the respondents was that Silesians are a nation (22%). Almost 72% of the respondents chose only one categorisation. Two categorisations were chosen by 26%. All three categorisations were chosen by less than 2% of the respondents. Consequently, the study revealed that significantly more respondents categorised Silesians as part of the Polish Nation, as an ethnic group or both than as a separate nation.

Furthermore, there is a strong association between declaring that Silesians are a nation and auto-identification (φc=0.43; p<0.01). There is also a strong association between declaring that Silesians are a part of the Polish Nation and auto-identification (φc=0.49; p<0.01), but there is no association between declaring that Silesians are an ethnic group and auto-identification (p=0.1).

The association between categorisation and auto-identification revealed strong ties between the two categorisation variables: as a separate nation and as a part of the Polish Nation. In case of the categorisation that Silesians are a separate nation, this association is a positive one: the more dominant Silesian identification is, the higher the statistical possibility that a respondent will choose to categorise Silesians as a separate nation, with the exception of respondents declaring themselves as Poles. The latter association is a negative one: the more dominant Silesian identification is, the lower the statistical possibility that a respondent will choose to categorise Silesians as a part of the Polish nation, with the exception of respondents declaring themselves as Poles.

Later, respondents were asked to provide their stance on the role of the region in their lives, a problem that was considered highly important for the interlocutors in the focus group interviews. It should come as no surprise that 90% of respondents agreed that Silesia is important to them, while only 2% disagreed. For more than 70% of the respondents, Silesia is their 'Heimat'. Less than 14% of the respondents disagreed with this statement. Thus, the study revealed the meaningful role of the region in the respondents' life. Still, paradoxically, the most interesting are the missing answers to these questions because almost 10% of the respondents decided not to give any statement about the role of the Silesian region as their 'Heimat'. This could be a result of two factors. Firstly, some respondents may have been unfamiliar with the term. Secondly, some respondents may have associated it with German heritage in Silesian history and refused to answer the question as a sign of opposition.

There is a moderate association between declaring that Silesia is important and auto-identification (φc=0.3; p<0.01) and between declaring that Silesia is a Heimat and auto-identification (φc=0.3; p<0.01). Both variables ('Silesia is important to me' and 'Silesia is my Heimat') proved to have meaningful ties to auto-identification. This association is a positive one: the more dominant Silesian identification is, the higher the statistical possibility that a respondent

POLITICAL BEHAVIOURS AND POLITICAL POTENTIAL

believes that Silesia is important for him/her. Also, Silesia is the 'Heimat' for almost all of the respondents who declared themselves Silesians. For respondents who declared themselves Silesian, Silesian-Polish or Silesian-German, this is true for 96%, 70% and 90%, respectively. For those who chose Polish-Silesian identification, the result was 51%. In the case of respondents who chose only Polish or European identification, it was only about 30%. Consequently, this association is a positive one: the more dominant Silesian identification is, the higher the statistical possibility that a respondent believes that Silesia is his or her 'Heimat'.

6.3.4   Stereotypes and Migration

In Chapter 5, the attitude towards stereotypes about Silesians was discussed, with special emphasis on the so-called 'dupowatość', which was used by the interlocutors in the focus group interviews to describe Silesians. Other words that were used to describe them were the adjectives 'tolerant' and 'neat'. Respondents' views on the matter are presented below (See Table 13).

The study shows that from the three chosen characteristics, the stereotypes most frequently shared by the respondents is that Silesians are neat and tolerant. Simultaneously, only a few of the respondents are ready to characterise Silesians as shiftless or helpless. Still, the association between stereotypes and auto-identification proved to be only moderate in two cases. In the case of the statement that Silesians are shiftless, it was ($\varphi c=0.18$; $p=0.01$), that they were

TABLE 13   Attitude toward stereotypes about the group

	All	Majority	About half	Few	None	It's hard to say	Total
Silesians are *dupowaci* (shiftless/ helpless)	4%	14%	16%	33%	11%	22%	100%
Silesians are tolerant	3%	34%	32%	13%	2%	16%	100%
Silesians are neat	11%	52%	18%	6%	1%	12%	100%

THE AUTHOR'S STUDY AND ANALYSES; N=369 MISSING VALUES=15; N=370 MISSING VALUES=14; N=379 MISSING VALUES=5

neat was (φc=0.19; p<0.01) and there was no association between the statement that Silesians are tolerant and auto-identification (p=0.03). Consequently, the attitude towards stereotypes proved to have only moderate ties to auto-identification and was not studied in depth.

In Chapter 5 – *Programmes and Postulates of Upper Silesian Organisations*, a considerable amount of space was given to stereotypes, and indeed, all of the studied organisations had some idea about what Silesians are like. The association between stereotypes and national identification, in general, has been shown in previous studies. Among them, the study of Smith et al. (2005) allows us to draw two conclusions relevant to this study. Firstly, there is a correlation between national identification and positive stereotypes about one's nation. Secondly, in some cases, other identifications (most notably European or regional) are correlated with negative stereotypes about the nation, and in others, they are independent. Although this study was not designed to discuss their results, two comments stem from this section. Firstly, there are two positive stereotypes:(Silesians are tolerant and neat) and one negative – Silesians are shiftless/helpless, and these diverge significantly from stereotypes about Poles presented in Smith et al. (2005). As a matter of fact, if we take into consideration the full lists of stereotypes from Subchapter 5.2.2 – *Silesianism*, we can see that only one trait overlaps – traditionalism – and it was only mentioned by the organisation openly establishing its Silesian-Polish character. Secondly, taking into consideration that the sample was designed to and did include mostly Silesians, it can be noted that although the association between stereotypes and auto-identification may only be moderate, frequency shows that more respondents are ready to agree with positive stereotypes than negative. Unfortunately, the data collected in this study does not allow us to conclude whether Silesian identity is correlated with negative stereotypes about Poles, but it seems to be a promising field for further study.

Moreover, by the interlocutors from Chapter 5 – *Programmes and Postulates of Upper Silesian Organisations*, Silesians are perceived as attached (or even rooted) to the region and to the locality. This issue was presented to respondents in the questions about their attitude towards migration, which reflects how rooted the inhabitants of the region are to the territory. 61% of the respondents agreed that it would have been a problem for them to move out of Silesia, while only 26% disagreed. At the same time, 61% of respondents believed that they would regret moving out of their region, while less than 18% disagreed. The study proved that most of the respondents are rooted in the Silesian region and do not plan on moving out of it.

POLITICAL BEHAVIOURS AND POLITICAL POTENTIAL   197

Still, there is only a moderate association between declaring that "I would have a problem with moving out from Silesia" (φc=0.24; p<0.01) and auto-identification, and between declaring that "I would regret moving out from Silesia" (φc=0.27; p<0.01) and auto-identification. The attitude towards migration, though seemingly shared by most of the respondents, proved to have only moderate ties to auto-identification and was not studied in depth.

6.3.5   *Diversity and Separateness*
The nature of cultural diversity and the complexity of the history of Upper Silesia was also discussed in Chapter 5 – *Programmes and Postulates of Upper Silesian Organisations*. Interlocutors in the focus group interviews stressed the diverse connections of Silesian history to the history of the states to which it historically belonged.

In this case, most of the respondents agreed that the history of the region is connected to the history of Poland (63%). Fewer respondents saw connections with German (59%) and Czech (53%) history. Simultaneously, more respondents denied connections to the history of Poland (15%) than the number of respondents denying connections to Germany (10%) and Czech (10%) history. Most of the respondents recognised the historical connections of Silesia to all three states to which this region belonged historically, although, in the case of the Czech Republic, the respondents were inclined to choose a neutral answer. In Polish history, the historical disagreement between Poland and Germany about this land is stressed more than any disagreements between Poland and the Czech Republic – this is probably why the answers to the last question were not so final. For many respondents, the historical connections with the Czech Republic (or historically, the Bohemian Crown) are simply either irrelevant or unknown.

Still, there is only a moderate association between auto-identification and recognising connections to the history of any of neighbouring states – Poland (φc=0.24; p<0.01) and Czech (φc=0.18; p<0.01). However, among those associations, the one between auto-identification and declaring that Silesia's connections with the history of Germany are an important element in its history is the weakest (φc=0.17; p<0.01). The attitude towards diversity proved to have only moderate ties to auto-identification and was not studied in depth.

Cultural separateness is one of the most important factors of ethnic identity. This separateness was discussed in length in Chapter 5 – *Programmes and Postulates of Upper Silesian Organisations*. Here, respondents were asked to present their views on the cultural separateness of the region (See Table 14).

Undoubtedly, the most extreme answers were given to the question of whether Silesian culture is separate from Polish culture – 61% of the

TABLE 14   Views on separateness of the Silesian culture

	I absolutely Agree	I agree	I do not agree or disagree	I disagree	I absolutely disagree	Total
Silesian culture is separate from Polish culture	31%	30%	23%	11%	5%	100%
Silesian culture is separate from German culture	17%	36%	33%	13%	1%	100%
Silesian culture is separate from Czech culture	20%	35%	33%	10%	2%	100%

THE AUTHOR'S STUDY AND ANALYSES; N=376 MISSING VALUES=8; N=375 MISSING VALUES=9; N=374 MISSING VALUES=10

respondents answered positively, while 16% answered negatively. In the case of German culture, it was 53% and 14%, respectively, while Czech was 55% and 12%.

Only a few respondents (8%) absolutely agreed with all three statements. Some respondents (10%) absolutely agreed with two statements: that Silesian culture is separate from Polish culture and that Silesian culture is separate from Czech culture. Other respondents (14%) absolutely agreed with two statements: that Silesian culture is separate from German culture and that Silesian culture is separate from Czech culture. A few respondents (10%) absolutely agreed with two statements: that Silesian culture is separate from German culture and that Silesian culture is separate from Polish culture. Only one respondent absolutely disagreed with all three statements.

In the case of the culture of all three nations with which Silesian culture had and continues to have connections, the answers were quite similar. The majority of respondents believe that Silesian culture is separate from all of them. On these grounds, it can be stated that for most of the respondents,

POLITICAL BEHAVIOURS AND POLITICAL POTENTIAL

Silesian culture is indeed seen as separate and Silesians could constitute an ethnic group.

There is a moderate association between declaring that Silesian culture is separate from Polish culture and auto-identification, but it is the only one among the three variables (φc=0.29; p<0.01). There is no association between declaring that Silesian culture is separate from German culture and auto-identification (p=0.2), and there is no association between declaring that Silesian culture is separate from Czech culture and auto-identification (p=0.6).

The attitude towards separateness of Silesian culture from other cultures proved to be meaningful only in the case of Polish culture. As was already stated, ethnicity is relational and situational. The ethnic character of a social relation depends on the situation and context (Eriksen 2010, 69). The ethnic distinctiveness of a minority group becomes important in relation to the majority group within the state in which it lives. As a result, in the case of Upper Silesians today, it is the separateness from the Polish majority that is stressed by persons with a minority auto-identification and undermined by those with a stronger majority identification. This phenomenon can be referred to as 'the rule of the setting'. Consequently, there is a visible tie between auto-identification and perceiving Silesian culture as separate from Polish culture.

6.3.6 *Language and Traditions*
Usage of the Silesian language constituted an extremely important factor of Silesian identity in the view of the interlocutors of the focus group interviews, whose opinions were presented in Chapter 5 – *Programmes and Postulates of Upper Silesian Organisations*. The respondents were also asked how often they use Silesian. Almost 39% of them answered that they use Silesian every day, 18% of the respondents answered that they use Silesian often, and 20% said sometimes. The fourth and fifth groups said rarely (15%) and never (8%). Respondents who chose the answer 'never', were asked to omit the next question. Furthermore, it should be noted that more than three-quarters of respondents declared that they use the Silesian language from 'everyday' to 'sometimes', which is a significantly higher number of declarations than that given in the census in 2011 (63%). This was elaborated further in Sub-chapter 2.6 – *Upper Silesians*.

Moreover, there is a moderate (φc=0.29; p<0.01) association between using the Silesian language and auto-identification. The association between usage of the minority language and auto-identification is visible, but it is not among

TABLE 15   Silesian language. Who do you speak Silesian with?*

Grandparents	39%
Parents	55%
Children	49%
Neighbours	66%
Friends	77%
Colleagues	39%
Strangers (e.g. officials)	16%

THE AUTHOR'S STUDY AND ANALYSES; N=353 MISSING VALUES=31
*Multiple choices were possible

the strongest. Although ties between a language and auto-identification are undoubtedly significant, it seems in the studied case, the relations between the two are more complex, and it is hard to draw further conclusions. Still, the matter deserves scholarly attention in the future.

In the next question concerning who the respondents speak Silesian with, multiple choices were possible (See Table 15).

Answers to this question showed surprising results. Language is generally believed to be transmitted mostly within the closest familial circle. Consequently, it was expected that most of the respondents would use Silesian in communication with family members. However, the study revealed that in the case of Silesian, more respondents use it outside the family to speak with neighbours and friends. There may be a few reasons for such a result. Firstly, as was already mentioned in Subchapter 5.3.3 – *Teaching and promotion of the Silesian language*, using Silesian may have been perceived as a disadvantage in some cases, and, as a result, families tended to teach children Polish and use it at home. Secondly, ties within the neighbourhood and friendship encompass more diverse social circles and may lead to the inclusion in one's life of people more used to speaking Silesian. The fewest respondents use Silesian while talking to strangers. This confirms the assumption that the manifestation of Silesian identity in the public space is rare, and many respondents refrain from such behaviour completely.

The role and observance of Silesian traditions were brought up in Chapter 5 – *Programmes and Postulates of Upper Silesian Organisations*. Specific, separate traditions constitute an important part of Silesian culture as a whole and thus are significant for Silesian ethnic identity. When asked about the role of

Silesian traditions, most of the respondents stated that they are very important or are important to them (79%). The remaining group of respondents chose the following answers: irrelevant, not important and definitely unimportant. Additionally, there is a strong (φc=0.31; p<0.01) association between attitude towards Silesian traditions and auto-identification. Consequently, the variable (attitude towards Silesian traditions) proved to have meaningful ties to auto-identification. This association is a positive one: the stronger the Silesian identification is, the higher the statistical possibility that a respondent believes Silesian traditions to be very or somewhat important.

The observance of typically Silesian traditions that distinguish this ethnic group from others was studied as well. Here, more than nine-tenths of respondents said that they: await gifts from the Baby Jesus at Christmas Eve (in other parts of Poland, the gifts traditionally come from the Angel or 'Gwiazdor'), give children *tyty* (school cones) on their first day of school and make *makówka* (traditional poppy seed bread pudding) for Christmas Eve. Breaking porcelain before a wedding (*Polterabend*) was a less popular tradition, but it was still observed by four-fifths of the respondents. Three-quarters of the respondents still celebrate Saint Barbara Day (patron saint of miners) on 4 December, but this was the least popular tradition among the respondents.

The study showed that most of the respondents still observe typical Silesian traditions and declare them to be important. This led to the conclusion that traditions are the most important factor indicating that this culture is separate from others and constituting grounds for distinguishing separate ethnic identity – an opinion that is widespread among Upper Silesians.

6.4   Political Postulates – Popularity

6.4.1   *Recognition and Education*

Many postulates of organisations within the Upper Silesian ethnoregionalist movement were discussed in Chapter 5 – *Programmes and Postulates of Upper Silesian Organisations*. Their popularity among the respondents is analysed below.

The problem of the recognition of the Silesian language as a regional language and Silesians as an ethnic group was discussed at length in Chapter 2 – *Political Situation in Upper Silesia*. The issue appeared in the public debate more than fifteen years ago and has also gained the attention of scholars. One of the most recent papers by Orlewski (2019) showed that 90% of the respondents agreed that the Silesian language should be recognised as a regional language. My study showed that about 80% of the respondents believed that the language should be recognised, while 10% were neutral. Furthermore, my study also asked about the recognition of Silesians as an ethnic minority. Here, 62% of respondents agreed that Silesians should be recognised by law, while almost 19% chose a neutral answer.

The study revealed that both the recognition of Silesians as an ethnic minority and the Silesian language as a regional language have the support of the majority of respondents. Consequently, the stance promoting legal recognition is more popular among them. But, there are even more supporters for the recognition of the language. However, it can still be stated that the Silesian community supports both demands.

The postulate for teaching regional education seemed to be one of the few points on which all of the studied organisations agreed. Therefore, two problems were analysed here. The first is whether regional education should be taught at schools. Among the respondents, 83% of them agreed that it should. However, less than half of them chose that it should be taught only in Silesia, and more decided that it should be taught at schools in the whole of Poland. The second point raised in the study on many levels was the problem of lack of knowledge among other communities in Poland about Silesia, its specific history and society. This is why the respondents were also asked whether the history and culture of Silesia should be taught beyond the region, although only 23% of them agreed that it should.

Teaching regional education in all of Poland was supported by many respondents (46%) while teaching the history and culture of Silesia beyond the region was supported only by less than a quarter. This leads to the conclusion that for most of the respondents, teaching regional history and culture should be limited to a particular region. Still, teaching regional education remains an important postulate, and the most popular view suggests that programmes and classes should be prepared for all regions in Poland separately.

Thirdly, all of the organisations seemed to agree on a need for teaching the Silesian language and (possibly) also teaching in the Silesian language. The respondents in the quantitative study were also asked about this issue. (See Table 16).

Most of the respondents agreed that Silesian should be taught at school, but 62% of them believed that the Silesian language should be an optional subject. Respondents who chose answers 'it should not be taught at all' and 'it is hard to say' were asked to omit the next two questions. It can be said that this stance is similar to the one supported by the studied organisations, as presented in Subchapter 5.3.3 – *Teaching and promotion of the Silesian language*.

POLITICAL BEHAVIOURS AND POLITICAL POTENTIAL

TABLE 16   Teaching Silesian language at schools

	It should be obligatory for everybody	It should be an optional subject for those who are willing to learn it	It should not be taught at all	It's hard to say	Total
Should Silesian be taught at school?	21%	62%	6%	11%	100%

THE AUTHOR'S STUDY AND ANALYSES; N=381 MISSING VALUES=3

When asked at which level of education the Silesian language should be taught, 84% of the respondents chose in elementary school, 53% in kindergarten and 49% in high school. Most of the respondents seemed to support the view that the earlier the Silesian language is taught, the better. This suggests that the respondents believe the language may become a useful communication tool for future generations and can be perceived as more than a relic of the past or a tool for the preservation of the Silesian culture for its own sake.

Additionally, respondents were asked whether there are subjects that could be taught in the Silesian language. Here, more than 77% of respondents decided that regional education could be taught in Silesian. However, teaching other subjects in the Silesian language gained the support of less than 16% of the respondents. Consequently, for the vast majority of the respondents, regional education should be taught in the Silesian language. While this stance is understandable, it may lead to the strengthening of the belief that Silesian can be used only in certain situations and that it is not a valuable or even acceptable way to communicate in general, a problem that was also recognised in Subchapter 5.3.3. In light of this fact, and keeping in mind that the language is not used in communication with strangers, using Silesian in the public space beyond the close circles of family and friendship seems to be almost excluded. The respondents seem to perceive it as a language that can be used effectively in everyday life, but that is of limited use in public or professional situations.

6.4.2   *Legal Status and Borders of the Śląskie Voivodeship*
Respondents could also state their views on the legal status and boundaries of the Śląskie Voivodeship (See Table 17). Here, the attitude of the respondents

TABLE 17   Legal status of the Silesian voivodship in the future*

A voivodship, as today	47%
A voivodship with broader competences than today (only administrative)	36%
The only autonomous region (legislative competences)	32%
One of more autonomous regions in Poland	47%
A state in a federation (as the Lands in Germany)	35%

THE AUTHOR'S STUDY AND ANALYSES
*Multiple choices were possible

towards the flagship demand of part of the Silesian organisations – autonomy for the region – was especially interesting.

The study revealed that support for a deep decentralisation reform that would transform the status of all regions in Poland into autonomous units is almost as popular as the preservation of the *status quo*. In light of the situation in Poland today, where the dominant political party seems intent on further centralisation, this conclusion may confirm that at least in the Upper Silesian region, an opposition towards a centralised policy exists. All in all, the demand for some form of system with an autonomous status or even the status of a state within a federation was widely supported by the respondents. My findings also support the study by Orlewski (2019), where the support for autonomy was 51%.

The problem of the borders of the Śląskie Voivodeship was not addressed in the focus group interviews. The question was added by the researcher to the quantitative study as part of the analysis of the unity of the Upper Silesian region and the administrative unit – the Śląskie Voivodeship – as perceived by the respondents (See Table 18). The research problem behind the question was: are the boundaries of today's Śląskie Voivodeship adequate for the respondents, and, in particular, do the vast majority of them have strong ties to the region of Upper Silesia, understood as a historical and cultural unit?

The answers given by the respondents indicate that for many, the borders of the voivodeship today do not meet their expectations. The administrative unit should encompass the cultural unit, i.e., the region of Upper Silesia, which is not the case at present. It should be mentioned that the administrative units in Poland do not encompass the exclusively historical Upper Silesian ones: the Opolskie Voivodeship encompasses also territories of Lower Silesia, and the Śląskie Voivodeship encompasses also territories of Małopolska (Lesser Poland), part of Wyżyna Krakowsko-Częstochowska (part of Polish

POLITICAL BEHAVIOURS AND POLITICAL POTENTIAL 205

TABLE 18 Possible changes to the borders of the Śląskie voivodship*

Yes, by excluding historically non-Silesian areas (e.g. Częstochowa district)	45%
Yes, by including part of the Opolskie voivodship	45%
Yes, by excluding other areas	9%
Yes, by including other areas	3%
No	22%
It's hard to say	18%

THE AUTHOR'S STUDY AND ANALYSES; N=368 MISSING VALUES=16
*Multiple choices were possible

Jura, called Częstochowa Upland), Zagłębie Dąbrowskie (Dąbrowa Basin) and Żywiecczyzna (Żywiec Area). Consequently, the Śląskie Voivodeship stretches too far to the north and too little to the west. A significant group of respondents recognised this fact and supported the changes that could be made in this matter in the future.

6.4.3 *Priorities for Newly Registered Silesian Parties*
Lastly, respondents were able to state their views on the priorities for newly registered Silesian parties (See Table 19). This question was based on an analysis of the political programmes presented by both parties for the purpose of elections to decentralised bodies in 2018 (described in Subchapter 4.3 – *Śląska Partia Regionalna* and Subchapter 4.4 – *Ślonzoki Razem*).

Apparently, for the vast majority of respondents, degradation of the natural environment and air pollution are the most important problems in Upper Silesia today. Economic and cultural problems followed. This leads to the conclusion that while the economic situation is a meaningful problem, the attachment to Silesian culture and culture, in general, should also play an important role in regional policy.

6.5 Political Behaviours – Popularity of Studied Organisations

6.5.1 *Voting Behaviours*
Voting behaviours were one of the studied political behaviours. They were analysed as voting behaviours in the past and near future. Furthermore, some

TABLE 19   Priorities for the newly registered Silesian parties (Śląska Partia Regionalna and Ślonzoki Razem)*

Ecological	65%
Economical	51%
Social	20%
Cultural	46%
Ethnic	38%
Infrastructural	40%
Political	24%

THE AUTHOR'S STUDY AND ANALYSES
*Multiple choices were possible

TABLE 20   Attitude toward voting on ethnoregionalist party

	I absolutely agree	I agree	I do not agree or disagree	I disagree	I absolutely disagree	Total
I would vote for a Silesian party if I could	33%	29%	25%	7%	6%	100%
I would vote for a regional party if I could	27%	27%	31%	9%	6%	100%

THE AUTHOR'S STUDY AND ANALYSES; N=373 MISSING VALUES=11; N=368 MISSING VALUES=16

general questions about voting behaviours were posed in order to study the popularity of organisations belonging to the Upper Silesian ethnoregionalist movement. Accordingly, the questions were posed in the questionnaire. (See Table 20).

More than half of the respondents agreed that they would vote for a Silesian party if they could. More than half of the respondents also agreed that they would vote for some regional party if they could. The study shows that the majority of respondents would like to vote for a Silesian ethnoregionalist party and that this group is even bigger than the potential electorate of

POLITICAL BEHAVIOURS AND POLITICAL POTENTIAL 207

some regional party. However, this potential did not translate into actual voters' support in previous elections, the results of which are presented in Subchapter 4.6 – *Electoral Results in the Region*. There may be a few reasons for such a state of affairs. Firstly, the ethnoregionalist committees were not widely recognised (Muś 2017a). Secondly, hypothetical support for ethnoregionalist parties does not necessarily transform into real support for particular candidates and programmes.

When asked about their voting behaviours in the past, almost half of the respondents (46%) stated that they did not vote for the *Ruch Autonomii Śląska* Electoral Committee of Voters in the past. The second group (32%) declared that they did vote for the Committee, while the fewest respondents (22%) declared that they did not vote, but they would. Moreover, 61% of the respondents stated that they did not vote for the *Mniejszość na Śląsku* Electoral Committee of Voters. The second group (23%) declared that they did not vote for the Committee, but they would, while the fewest (16%) respondents declared that they did vote. Almost 64% of the respondents stated that they did not vote for the *Zjednoczeni dla Śląska* Electoral Committee of Voters. The second group (almost 23%) declared that they did not vote for the Committee, but they would, while the fewest respondents (13%) declared that they did vote. Additionally, 65% of the respondents stated that they did not vote for the *Ślonzoki Razem* Electoral Committee of Voters. The second group (20%) declared that they did not vote for the Committee, but they would, while the fewest (15%) respondents declared that they did vote.

The declared support for ethnoregionalist committees in previous elections only partially overlaps with the potential support presented in the table above (Table 20). Furthermore, the results of the study are by far higher than the results presented in Subchapter 4.6 – *Electoral Results in the Region*. The most interesting results are from the analysis of the elections in 2018 and 2019 (See Table 21). The survey was conducted in the summer of 2018, months before elections to self-government bodies. Respondents were then asked for whom they would vote.

When asked about their voting plans in the elections to self-government bodies in 2018, most of the respondents stated that they did not know yet if they would vote for any of the studied committees. Some (about 30%) declared that they would vote for the ŚPR, and only 15% said that they would vote for *Ślonzoki Razem*. Still, as was presented in Subchapter 4.6 – *Electoral results in the region*, both parties only got 6.3% of the votes in the elections to self-government bodies. The overall electoral result counted *en bloc* was 110,480 (6.3%), but when presented for constituencies, there is a wide range of results (from 0.6% to 13.4%). (See Table 22).

208 CHAPTER 6

TABLE 21 Voting in the upcoming elections in 2018 and 2019

	Yes	I don't know yet	No	Total
In the elections to self-government bodies in 2018 I will vote for Śląska Partia Regionalna	33%	50%	17%	100%
In the elections to self-government bodies in 2018 I will vote for Ślonzoki Razem	15%	55%	30%	100%
In the elections to Parliament in 2019 I will vote for Śląska Partia Regionalna	29%	56%	15%	100%
In the elections to Parliament in 2019 I will vote for Ślonzoki Razem	14%	58%	28%	100%

THE AUTHOR'S STUDY AND ANALYSES; N=376 MISSING VALUES=8; N=371 MISSING VALUES=13; N=376 MISSING VALUES=8; N=372 MISSING VALUES=12

TABLE 22 Elections to Sejmik of Ślaskie voivodeship 2018. En bloc

District	Votes	Share of Silesian declarations (%)
1	5559	2.1
2	25129	9.6
3	22636	7.8
4	25449	9.8
5	28152	13.4
6	1438	0.6
7	2113	0.7

DATA FROM THE PAŃSTWOWA KOMISJA WYBORCZA (STATE ELECTORAL COMMISSION), AUTHOR'S CALCULATIONS

Thus, in the study, a highly interesting phenomenon emerged, which I called the 'voting gap'. The voting gap can be defined as the difference between the support for ethnoregionalist parties, declared in the questionnaire survey I conducted in 2018, and the real support studied committees achieved in the elections to self-government bodies in 2018. To analyse the problem, two extremely useful indexes must be defined: the Index of Regional Mobilization [IRM] and the Index of Ethnic Mobilization [IEM], both are slightly modifiedmeasures introduced by Oliver Strijbis and Michał Kotnarowski (2015, 460).

The first index, IRM, is ascribed as 'r'.

$$r = \frac{a}{b * f}$$

In the equation, 'a' signifies the number of votes given to ethnoregionalist parties (counted *en bloc*), 'b' signifies the total population of the studied territory (administrative unit) and 'f' is the voter turnout expressed in decimal form.

The second index, IEM, is ascribed as 'e'.

$$e = \frac{a * IPE}{c * f}$$

In the equation, 'a' signifies the number of votes given to ethnoregionalist parties (counted *en bloc*), IPE is the *Index of Party Ethnicity* (Strijbis & Kotnarowski 2015, 460), 'c' signifies the population of the ethnic group in the studied territory (administrative unit) and 'f' is the voter turnout expressed in decimal form.

Based on a previous study (Muś 2017b, 371), the IPE in the elections to decentralised bodies was assessed to be 0.96, which means that 96% of voters who gave their votes to one of ethnoregionalist committees were Silesians. While for the Parliamentary elections it was 0.92. The level of party ethnicity leads to a conclusion, that voting behaviour of Silesians is atypical. Previous studies in other multi-ethnic regions led rather to the conclusion, that the effect of ethnicity on voting is higher in elections on the state-level than local level (Zamfira 2015, 170–171). Here, we can see in Table 21, that even hypothetically (in questions about future voting behaviour), the support for ethnoregionalist parties is lower in case of state-wide elections than regional ones.

The results of the *Śląska Partia Regionalna* and *Ślonzoki Razem* calculated *en bloc* in elections to self-government bodies (to the *Sejmik Województwa Śląskiego*) in 2018 were used to calculate the IRM and IEM. Furthermore, the share of people declaring themselves as Silesians/Upper Silesians was also presented in the table below (Table 23). The indexes and shares are calculated for both the whole Śląskie Voivodeship and for the lands that were historically seen as the Upper Silesian region and where the Silesian ethnic group is concentrated (districts 2, 3, 4 and 5).

The share of votes for both ethnoregionalist parties calculated *en bloc* for the voivodeship is 6.3%, but for the historical region Upper Silesia, it is 10%. This difference is confirmed by the IRM, which is 4% for the whole voivodeship, while for the Upper Silesia region, it is 7%. The second index, the IEM, confirms the fact that statistically, Upper Silesians mostly vote for ethnoregionalist parties, and they are heavily concentrated in the Upper Silesian region (Orlewski 2019, 78) because the IEM for both the voivodeship and the Upper Silesia region is 28%. In the Upper Silesia region, 26% of the population declare themselves to be Silesian, while in the whole Śląskie Voivodeship, this share is 16%.

With only a few calculations, it can be easily stated that there is a considerable difference in the numbers presented above. Firstly, Table 20 suggests that 62% of the respondents would like to vote for a Silesian party in general. However, Table 21 shows that only some of them declare that they would vote for the existing ethnoregionalist parties: 33% for ŚPR and 15% for ŚR. During the analysis of the results of the questionnaire survey, one fundamental question emerged: did respondents treat the choice between the parties as an alternative, so that choosing one of them excluded the possibility to choose

TABLE 23   Votes, IRM, IEM and the share of Silesians (all presented in %)

Territory	Votes	IRM	IEM	Share of Silesian declarations
Śląskie voivodship	6.3	4	28	16
Upper Silesia	10	7	28	26

AUTHOR'S CALCULATIONS

POLITICAL BEHAVIOURS AND POLITICAL POTENTIAL

the other? If this were true, we would be able to draw the conclusion that the results show the support of respondents at 48% (calculated *en bloc* for both parties). If it were not true and at least one of the respondents chose both parties, the support would be lower and impossible to determine exactly – it would be somewhere in the range from 33% to less than 48%. Either way, without a doubt, the support for specific ethnoregionalist parties in Polish Upper Silesia is lower than for the general idea of supporting some ethnoregionalist party.

Further, even the lowest level of support presented above – 33% – is six times higher than the electoral results in the voivodeship and three times higher than the results calculated for the Upper Silesian region. This difference is significant and far beyond any reasonable margin of error. Consequently, one is obliged to look for further explanations, which I have divided into two groups: general and particular.

To begin with the general explanations, firstly, both ŚPR and ŚR financed their electoral campaigns on their own, mostly from donations and self-funding provided by candidates, and received no public funding. The *Act on Political Parties* from 1997[1] foresaw subventions for parties that achieved 3% of votes in the state-wide elections to the Sejm. This situation inevitably leads to disproportional funding and, consequently, the visibility of electoral campaigns of ethnoregionalist parties. In short: it is possible that many voters were not aware that ethnoregionalist parties exist and take part in the elections. Obviously, respondents in the questionnaire survey had the knowledge from the questionnaire, so the support for ethnoregionalist parties in the study may have been artificially increased by the research itself.

Secondly, the voting system in Poland during elections to decentralised bodies in elections to the *Sejmiki* (regional councils) pursuant to the *Electoral Code* from 2011[2] is proportional, which means that representatives are elected by proportional representation, where the distribution of seats is effected on the basis of the d'Hondt method. Parties win seats according to the aggregate vote for their candidates in a constituency and then allocate them to those with the highest totals. As with any highest average method, the d'Hondt method results in a relative bias towards big parties at the expense of smaller parties. Voters, being aware of this bias, tend to vote for bigger (in the Polish case,

---

1 Dz.U. 1997 Nr 98 poz. 604.
2 Dz.U. 2011 nr 21 poz. 112.

almost always state-wide) parties due to fear of casting a 'wasted' vote that will not influence the final division of seats in any given assembly (Myśliwiec 2019, 33).

Thirdly, the electoral result of ethnoregionalist parties in Upper Silesia should be seen in relation to the state-wide campaigns of Polish (state-wide) political parties. Already in 2018, many Polish journalists have used the term 'Polish-Polish war' for the fierce political conflict on the Polish political scene (Bartkiewicz 2018). Some say that it is a conflict between democratic, liberal and pro-European Poles and those who are close-to-authoritarian, conservative and nationalist. Others say that it is simply a political conflict between two camps: liberal (represented by the *Platforma Obywatelska* – Civic Platform, *Nowoczesna* – Modern and the left, including the *Sojusz Lewicy Demokratycznej* – Democratic Left Alliance, *Razem* – Together, *Wiosna* – Spring) and conservative (represented by *Prawo i Sprawiedliwość* – Law and Justice and smaller associated parties). However, regardless of the true nature of the conflict, which is not a part of this study, it truly seems to influence every area of public life in Poland and leads to the polarisation of debates based on an axis other than the centre-periphery opposition.The conflict is undoubtedly state-wide and is mostly related to state-wide politics and political decisions made at the Parliamentary level, so it could be argued that in the elections to self-government bodies, it should have little to no influence. But was this the case? An interesting case study is the election of the *Prezydent* (mayor) of the city of Katowice – the main city of the Śląskie Voivodeship. In September, the regional newspaper conducted a survey[3]. (See Table 24).

The support declared in the survey was as follows. Marcin Krupa (37%) represented a local committee, *KW Wyborców Forum Samorządowe i Marcin Krupa*, but received public political support from *Prawo i Sprawiedliwość*. Jarosław Markowski (23%) represented a coalition of the *Platforma Obywatelska* and *Nowoczesna*, Jarosław Gwizdak (19%) represented the local committee *KW Prawo do Katowic* and Ilona Kanclerz (15%) represented the *Śląska Partia Regionalna*. Others received the support of 6% of respondents who took part in the survey. But what happened during the elections in October[4]? (See Table 25)

---

3 Redakcja DZ. 2018. *Wybory samorządowe 2018: Sondaż DZ: Katowice, Sosnowiec, Rybnik, Bytom, Zabrze, Częstochowa, Bielsko-Biała. Kto wygra wybory?*

4 PKW (Państwowa Komisja Wyborcza). 2018. "Wyniki wyborów samorządowych – Prezydent Miasta Katowice".

POLITICAL BEHAVIOURS AND POLITICAL POTENTIAL 213

TABLE 24 Survey. Election of the mayor (Prezydent) of the city of Katowice. September 2018

Candidate	Marcin Krupa	Jarosław Makowski	Jarosław Gwizdak	Ilona Kanclerz	Others
Support	37%	23%	19%	15%	6%

DATA FROM DZIENNIK ZACHODNI

TABLE 25 Results. Election of the mayor (Prezydent) of the city of Katowice. October 2018

Candidate	Marcin Krupa	Jarosław Makowski	Jarosław Gwizdak	Ilona Kanclerz	Others
Support	55%	24%	11%	6%	4%

DATA FROM PAŃSTWOWA KOMISJA WYBORCZA (STATE ELECTORAL COMMISSION)

The support in the elections was as follows: Marcin Krupa (55%), Jarosław Markowski (24%), Jarosław Gwizdak (11%), Ilona Kanclerz (6%), and others (4%). Looking at the results, it is hard to avoid the conclusion that the victor (with the support of the state-wide party) gained votes at the expense of local and regional committees. Regardless of whether this was the effect of positive or negative voting, the polarisation of state-wide politics and emergence of two opposite camps led to the situation in which this conflict is the main reason for voting and the opposition centre-periphery or dominant-non-dominant culture has become secondary for voters.

This conclusion supports findings based on study in Central Europe within the framework of Lipset-Rokkan theory of cleavages, recently summarised among others by Fernando Bértoa (2013). This study suggests, that in Poland the main two axis of voter alignment are religious-secular and interventionist-liberal. From those two axis four cross-cutting fields emerge, from which today the most important are populist (religious and interventionist) and liberal democratic (secular and economically liberal). The centre-periphery cleavage (with ethnic component) exists, but plays only limited role and for most voters is secondary.

As to particular explanations, both parties representing the Silesian ethnoregionalist movement appealed to the regional and ethnic identity of their voters not only through their names but also with their programs. One could argue that the main target group of voters for both parties were people who categorise themselves as Silesians. Silesians are an ethnic group living mostly in the urban area of Upper Silesia. The IEM, created to measure the support of an ethnic group for a party and in the elections to self-government bodies in 2018, if the support for both ethnoregionalist parties is taken into consideration, turned out to be 28% (Table 23). This means that statistically, 28% of Silesians voted for one of the ethnoregionalist parties, and the number has decreased since the last elections to self-government bodies in 2014 when it was 33% (Muś 2017b). However, the number of votes actually increased from 107,225 in 2014 to 110,480 in 2018. The decrease in the value of the IEM may be due to a higher turnout in the studied elections in the Śląskie Voivodeship in 2018, which was 52.4%, whereas in 2014, it was only 43.3%. Either way, the target group for ethnoregionalist programs seems to be rather stable (about 100,000 voters). Still, in the elections in 2018, it was almost equally divided into two groups voting for two ethnoregionalist parties. This, in turn, led to a loss of seats in regional the Sejmik of the Śląskie Voivodeship (regional council), which were previously held by ethnoregionalists.

Also, results of the study into the voting plans in the upcoming elections confirm a phenomenon that has already been observed: that the support for ethnoregionalist parties in Upper Silesia is significantly higher in the elections to self-government bodies than in the elections to Parliament, however atypical it may be (e.g., Janusz 2018, 17; Muś 2017a, 169).

Relatively low level of regional support for ethnoregionalist parties (IRM) can be explained by the hypothesis already suggested in scholarly literature, that ethnicity (and in our case ethnoregionalism) plays more important role in poorer regions, when identity can be reinforced by other socio-economic factors (Zamfira 2015, 170–171). In the case of Upper Silesia, the relative good economic situation of the region and its inhabitants creates a situation, when economic factors can not be so easily used. However, respondents' replies to the question about priorities for newly registered ethnoregionalist parties suggests, that economical issues should be considered by those parties and included in their programmes (Table 19).

Additionally, there is almost no change in the support for the ethnoregionalist committees over a decade, what may support the hypothesis suggested in literature, that the electorate of ethnoregionalist parties is loyal (Aha 2019). In studied case, support for the RAŚ Electoral Committee in the previous elections transformed into support for ŚPR in 2018, while support for MnŚ

POLITICAL BEHAVIOURS AND POLITICAL POTENTIAL 215

transformed into support for śR in 2018. Similarly, support for the śR Electoral Committee in previous parliamentary elections transformed into support for śR in 2019. The only change is the rise in the declared support for śPR in the upcoming elections in 2019 in relation to the support for ZdŚ. The declared support was obviously different in the actual elections. Additionally, neither śPR nor *Ślonzoki Razem* created electoral committees in 2019. In parliamentary elections in 2019, ethnoregionalists did not put forward any electoral committees. Instead, they joined state-wide electoral committees. The *Śląska Partia Regionalna* decided to join the *Koalicja Obywatelska* (Civic Coalition), created by the *Platforma Obywatelska* – Civic Platform, *Nowoczesna* – Modern and other parties. *Ślonzoki Razem* joined the *Polskie Stronnictwo Ludowe* (Polish Peoples' Party).

Finally, a general question strongly connected to the aim of the study was posed directly to the respondents. Their stance on the topic is presented below (See Table 26).

The majority of respondents confirmed that their ethnicity (not specified here) influenced their voting behaviour. Consequently, it should be considered one of the factors voters consider in their voting decisions.

In scholarly literature has been presented a hypothesis, that there is a direct link between power and pride. Specifically, members of minorities tend to be less proud of being citizens of a nation when members of their group are not represented in the government (Wimmer 2017). This is one of the reasons for ethnic voting. However, my findings show, that only about one thirds of Silesians actually vote for ethnoregionalist parties, even if more than two thirds of the respondents stated, that their ethnicity influences their voting behaviours. Further in this study (Subchapter 6.6 – *Relation Between Silesian*

TABLE 26 Voting behaviour and ethnicity

	I absolutely agree	I agree	I do not agree or disagree	I disagree	I absolutely disagree	Total
My ethnic/ national identity influences my voting behaviour	35%	27%	23%	8%	7%	100%

THE AUTHOR'S STUDY AND ANALYSES; N=378 MISSING VALUES=6

Identity and Political Behaviours) it is proven, that the more dominant Silesian auto-identification is (either as single identification or as the first from complex identification) the higher is the probability, that a person engages in political behaviours related to ethnoregionalist movement (including voting behaviour). Consequently, many people declaring dominant Silesian identity vote for Upper Silesian ethnoregionalist parties. However, they are only a bit more than half all of the people, who declared Silesian identity. The rest declared this identity as secondary to Polish (or in much fewer cases) German. This group assumes, that their national group is already represented in the government, so their voting decisions are based on other factors and their voter alignment can be explained in the same way as it is for the whole population of Poland.

6.5.2 *Participation in Electoral Campaigns, Membership and Participation in Events*

Another suggested factor in political behaviours is participation in the electoral campaigns of ethnoregionalist committees. The respondents were asked a few questions about their participation in campaigns in different roles in the past and their plans for the future, as well as hypothetical questions.

In general, only 44% of respondents stated that they would support the electoral campaign of a regional party (Silesian) in any way. At the same time, 27% said that they would not. Even fewer (33%) decided that they would provide financial support for the electoral campaign of a regional party (Silesian), and in this case, more respondents (39%) stated that they would not.

Similar questions were asked about supporting electoral campaigns in the past (See Table 27).

As to the support for electoral campaigns in the past, most of the respondents – 61.0% – declared that they did not support the campaigns of any of the studied electoral committees of voters and only 17% stated otherwise. Simultaneously, 69% of the respondents did not provide financial support for campaigns of one of the studied electoral committees, while 10% did so.

The study revealed that only a minority of the respondents is willing to support the electoral campaigns of ethnoregionalist organisations in any way, while even fewer actually did so in the past. What is worth noting is that the number of respondents who were ready to provide financial support for such a campaign is significantly lower than the number of respondents who voted or were ready to vote for ethnoregionalist committees. Still, 10% of the respondents were ready to support the campaigns of one or more ethnoregionalist committees financially (this support is one of their few incomes, as they do not receive any budgetary support). This leads to the conclusion

POLITICAL BEHAVIOURS AND POLITICAL POTENTIAL 217

TABLE 27   Supporting electoral campaigns in the past

	YES	NO, but I would like to	NO	Total
I supported the campaign of Ruch Autonomii Śląska or Mniejszość na Śląsku or Zjednoczeni dla Śląska or Ślonzoki Razem	17%	22%	61%	100%
I provided financial support for the campaign of Ruch Autonomii Śląska or Mniejszość na Śląsku or Zjednoczeni dla Śląska or Ślonzoki Razem	10%	21%	69%	100%

THE AUTHOR'S STUDY AND ANALYSES; N=358 MISSING VALUES=26; N=355 MISSING VALUES=29

that there is a significant bond between the electorate and ethnoregionalist parties.

Furthermore, membership in ethnoregionalist organisations was also recognised as a form of political behaviour. The engagement of the respondents was studied by means of two questions. Their answers are presented below (See Table 28).

In the case of membership in an organisation that belongs to the *Rada Górnośląska* (Upper Silesian Council), the vast majority of the respondents declared that they did not hold a membership (68%). The second group (21%) declared that they would like to change that, while 11% of the respondents declared that they are members.

The results concerning membership in ethnoregionalist organisations are similar to the results of financial support given to the campaigns of ethnoregionalist committees. This suggests that the same group of people who first belonged to the ethnoregionalist organisations later become active supporters of electoral committees created by organisations within the movement. However, this also leads to the conclusion that it is likely there is little support from outside this group (those who are not members of some ethnoregionalist organisation) for the electoral efforts.

Last but not least, participation in initiatives and protests organised by ethnoregionalist organisations was taken into consideration as a form of political behaviour. The vast majority of respondents had never taken part in protests

TABLE 28   Membership in ethnoregionalist organisations

	YES	NO, but I would like to	NO	Total
I am a member of an organisation belonging to Rada Górnośląska	11%	21%	68%	100%

THE AUTHOR'S STUDY AND ANALYSES; N=364 MISSING VALUES=20

organised by organisations belonging to the *Rada Górnośląska* or similar organisations (78%). Only slightly fewer of the respondents (76%) had never taken part in the Autonomy March, the March to Zgoda or other initiatives with political goals organised by organisations belonging to the *Rada Górnośląska* or similar initiatives. It also seems probable that the same group of 5% of the respondents declared that they took part in both protests and initiatives more than 10 times. The participation rate in the case of protests is 22%, and in the case of initiatives, 24%.

The study revealed that the participation rate in events organised by ethnoregionalists is higher than membership, support for campaigns and even electoral results. This may suggest that there is still the actual, measurable potential for better results in the elections in the foreseeable future. A question that needs to be answered is how to translate the interest of the population in political events organized by ethnoregionalists into the support of voters in the elections.

6.5.3   *Political Behaviours Index*

Indexes in social sciences are useful but not easy to create. In the case of multidimensional problems, such as the political behaviours studied in this work, the first problem to be addressed is which variables should and can be included in the index. Secondly, the chosen variables must be at the same level of measurement and have the same scales (Mayntz, Holm, Hübner 1985, 59). In the case of this study, the index of political behaviours was created on the grounds of the theoretical assumptions based on the definition of the term,the particular behaviours and their aspects studied in this chapter. The index was constructed as a sum of points in the 1 (no) to 3 (yes) scale from answers concerning the following statements:
- I voted for *Ruch Autonomii Śląska.*
- I voted for *Mniejszość na Śląsku.*

- I voted for *Zjednoczeni dla Śląska*.
- I voted for *Ślonzoki Razem*.
- In elections to decentralised bodies in 2018, I will vote for *Śląska Partia Regionalna*.
- In elections to decentralised bodies in 2018, I will vote for *Ślonzoki Razem*.
- In elections to Parliament in 2019, I will vote for *Śląska Partia Regionalna*.
- In elections to Parliament in 2019, I will vote for *Ślonzoki Razem*.
- I supported the campaign of *Ruch Autonomii Śląska* or *Mniejszość na Śląsku* or *Zjednoczeni dla Śląska* or *Ślonzoki Razem*.
- I financed the campaign of *Ruch Autonomii Śląska* or *Mniejszość na Śląsku* or *Zjednoczeni dla Śląska* or *Ślonzoki Razem*.
- I am a member of a Silesian organisation.
- I am a member of an organisation belonging to the *Rada Górnośląska*.

The Political Behaviours Index [PBI] in studied case can be characterised by the following basic statistics (See Table 29):

TABLE 29   Basic statistics

N	Mode	Median	Range	Min	Max
334	16	18.5	23	12	35

Below, a histogram of the studied index is displayed as a visualisation of the distribution of the scores in the index.

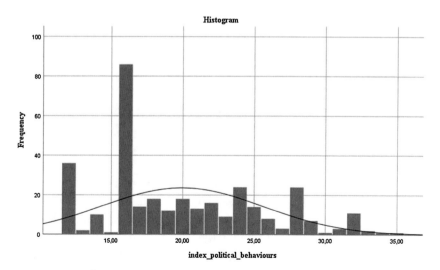

THE AUTHOR'S STUDY AND ANALYSIS

TABLE 30   Distribution

Kołmogorow-Smirnow test

Statistics	Df	Significance
0.16	334	0

THE AUTHOR'S STUDY AND ANALYSES
Z(334)=0.16; p<0.001

The PBI can be characterised by a positively skewed, platykurtic distribution. The distribution indicates that the largest group of respondents does not engage in any or in only a few of the studied political behaviours (groups with 12 and 16 points). The distribution of values from 17 to 28 is low and similar. There were very few respondents whose scores were 29 and above.

The distribution of the PBI differs from the normal distribution (See Table 30). Only non-parametric tests may be used in further analysis.

The correlation between the PBI and four general pieces of information given by the respondents – district, gender, age and education – was measured using the rho-Spearman and tau-b Kendall correlation. The study revealed that there are no correlations between the selected variables.

6.6   Relation between Silesian Identity and Political Behaviours

Relations between six of the most important factors of Silesian identity (presented in Subchapter 6.3 – *Ethnicity – Elements of Silesian Identity*) and the political behaviours represented by the PBI (presented in Subchapter 6.5.4) was studied here.

Firstly, the following question was posed: does categorising Silesians as a separate nation differ the scores in the PBI? This was studied using the non-parametric Mann-Whitney U test (See Tables 31 and 32).

There is a difference in the score of the PBI between respondents who categorised Silesians as a separate nation and those that did not. The former tended to have a higher score than the latter. This leads to the conclusion that statistically, the respondents who categorise Silesians as a separate nation are more ready to support different political behaviours promoted by the studied organisations supporting ethnoregionalist movements in Upper Silesia.

POLITICAL BEHAVIOURS AND POLITICAL POTENTIAL

TABLE 31   Differentiation. Categorisation as a separate nation and PBI – ranks

	N	Mean	Sum
Yes	66	231.8	15300.5
No	263	148.23	38984.5

THE AUTHOR'S STUDY AND ANALYSES

TABLE 32   Differentiation. Categorisation as a separate nation and PBI – test

Mann-Whitney U	4268.5
Wilcoxon	38984.5
Z	-6.5
Significance	0

THE AUTHOR'S STUDY AND ANALYSES
U=4268.5; p<0.001

This is probably because in the programmes of many organisations and electoral committees categorised as ethnoregionalist, the cultural separateness of Silesians is stressed and promoted, and the committees call for real action in the matter of preserving and strengthening a non-dominant, Silesian culture.

Secondly, the following question was posed: does being born in Silesia change the scores in the PBI? This was studied using the non-parametric Mann-Whitney U test (Tables 33 and 34).

There is no difference in the score of the Political Behaviours Index [PBI] between respondents who were born in Silesia and those who were not. This leads to the conclusion that statistically, the respondents who were born in Silesia and those who did not have the same attitude towards supporting different political behaviours promoted by the studied organisations supporting ethnoregionalist movements in Upper Silesia. But, we should keep in mind, that the vast majority of respondents in this study was born in the region.

Thirdly, the following question was posed: does the fact that a respondent's mother comes from Silesia differentiate the scores in the PBI? This was studied using the non-parametric Mann-Whitney U test (Tables 35 and 36).

There is a difference in the score of the PBI between respondents whose mothers come from Silesia and respondents whose mothers do not. The former tended to have a slightly higher score than the latter . This leads to the conclusion that statistically, the respondents whose mothers' place of origin is

222 CHAPTER 6

TABLE 33   Differentiation. Being born in Silesia and the PBI – ranks

	N	Mean	Sum
Yes	302	166.83	5563
No	32	173.84	50382

THE AUTHOR'S STUDY AND ANALYSES

TABLE 34   Differentiation. Being born in Silesia and the PBI – test

Mann-Whitney U	4629
Wilcoxon	50382
Z	-0.4
Significance	0.7

THE AUTHOR'S STUDY AND ANALYSES
U=4629; p=0.7

TABLE 35   Differentiation. Mother comes from Silesia and PBI – ranks

	N	Mean	Sum
Yes	264	172.2	45460
No	68	144.4	9818

THE AUTHOR'S STUDY AND ANALYSES

TABLE 36   Differentiation. Mother comes from Silesia and PBI – test

Mann-Whitney U	7472
Wilcoxon	9818
Z	-2.2
Significance	0.03

THE AUTHOR'S STUDY AND ANALYSES
U=7472; p=0,03

POLITICAL BEHAVIOURS AND POLITICAL POTENTIAL 223

TABLE 37   Correlation. *Silesia is important* for me and the PBI – test

N	331
Tau-b Kendall	0.3
Rho-Spearman	0.4
Significance	0

THE AUTHOR'S STUDY AND ANALYSES
T=0.3; ρ=0.4; p<0.001

in Silesia are more ready to support different political behaviours promoted by the studied organisations supporting an ethnoregionalist movement in Upper Silesia. Consequently, it seems possible that convictions and ideological ties to the region are transmitted within families by mothers.

Fourthly, the following question was posed: is there is a correlation between declaring that Silesia is important to a respondent and the PBI? (Table 37) This was studied using non-parametric tau-b Kendall and rho-Spearman correlations.

There is a moderate, positive correlation between statements given by respondents that Silesia is important to them and the PBI. This statement leads to the conclusion that statistically, the more important the role of the region as declared by the respondents, the higher the support for different political behaviours promoted by the studied organisations supporting ethnoregionalist movements in Upper Silesia. This may be linked to the fact that organisations and committees within the ethnoregionalist movement claim to represent the community of Upper Silesia and its interests. Consequently, the larger the role of the region in a respondent's life, the better he or she fits within the target group of ethnoregionalist programmes. This leads to higher engagement in the studied political behaviours.

Fifthly, the following question was posed: is there is a correlation between declaring that Silesia is one's 'Heimat' and the PBI? (Table 38) This was studied using the non-parametric tau-b Kendall and rho-Spearman correlations.

There is a moderate, positive correlation between statements given by the respondents that Silesia is their 'Heimat' and the PBI. The consequence is similar to the one presented as a comment on the correlation between the variable 'Silesia is important to me' and the PBI. The correlation here is even stronger because the declaration of a region being someone's 'Heimat' implies stronger emotional and ideological ties to it. Therefore, the consequences observed in relation to the PBI are also more significant.

TABLE 38   Correlation. *Silesia is my Heimat* and PBI – test

N	313
Tau-b Kendall	0.4
Rho-Spearman	0.5
Significance	0

THE AUTHOR'S STUDY AND ANALYSES
T=0.4; ρ=0.5; p<0.001

TABLE 39   Correlation. Silesian traditions and the PBI – test

Correlation. Silesian traditions and PBI – test

N	332
Tau-b Kendall	0.2
Rho-Spearman	0.3
Significance	0

THE AUTHOR'S STUDY AND ANALYSES
T=0.2; ρ=0.3; p<0.001

Sixthly, the following question was posed: is there a correlation between declaring that Silesian traditions are important to the respondent and the PBI? (Table 39) This was studied using the non-parametric tau-b Kendall and rho-Spearman correlations.

There is a weak, positive correlation between statements given by the respondents that Silesian traditions are important to them and the PBI. The test revealed that statistically, the declared role of traditions in a respondent's life – which may indicate an ethnic group origin – is only loosely correlated to the support for different political behaviours promoted by the studied organisations supporting ethnoregionalist movements in Upper Silesia. This statement seems to prove that conscious declarations of the attitude towards the region and its community as a social and political entity are more important for the political behaviours of respondents than mere ties with ritual behaviours based on traditions transferred within families. The ideological tie to the entity is more strongly correlated to political behaviours than ethnic origin, although the second is still correlated.

POLITICAL BEHAVIOURS AND POLITICAL POTENTIAL 225

TABLE 40   Correlation. Auto-identification and PBI – test

N	333
Tau-b Kendall	0.4
Rho-Spearman	0.4
Significance	0

THE AUTHOR'S STUDY AND ANALYSES
T=0.4; ρ=0.4; p<0.001

Lastly, the following question was posed: is there is a correlation between declared auto-identification and the PBI? (Table 40) This was studied using non-parametric tau-b Kendall and rho-Spearman correlations.

There is a moderate, positive correlation between auto-identification and the PBI. The study revealed that statistically, auto-identification and the PBI are correlated: the more dominant the Silesian declaration is, the higher the statistical probability that the respondent achieved a higher score in the PBI.

6.7   Political Behaviours and Political Potential – Conclusions

In order to determine which of the studied elements of Silesian identity are the most important, two factors were taken into consideration: how many respondents chose positive answers for the question and whether there is a strong positive relationship between two variables: auto-identification and the studied element of Silesian ethnic identity.

On the basis of an analysis of frequencies, associations and their nature (only positive ones are taken into consideration at this point), the most important elements of Silesian identity include:
– categorisation of Silesians as a separate nation,
– being born in Silesia,
– if a respondent's mother comes from Silesia,
– positive attitude towards Silesian traditions,
– declaration that Silesia is important to them, and
– declaration that Silesia is their 'Heimat' (Muś 2020).

These elements can be divided into two groups: elements of consciously chosen ethnoregionalist ideology and elements based purely on ethnic origin. Among the former are auto-identification, the categorisation of Silesians as a separate nation, the declaration that Silesia is important to them and the declaration that Silesia is their 'Heimat'. The latter include being born in Silesia, the fact that a respondent's mother comes from Silesia and their attitude towards Silesian traditions.

Among the studied variables, the variable that differentiates the most scores in the PBI is the categorisation of Silesians as a nation. The second is whether a respondent's mother comes from Silesia. As to correlations, the strongest correlation is between declaring that Silesia is a respondent's 'Heimat' and the PBI. A weaker correlation is observed between declaring that Silesia is important for the respondent and the PBI. The weakest is between declaring that Silesian traditions have an important role in a respondent's life and the PBI. Furthermore, there is a moderate, positive correlation between auto-identification and the PBI.

Based on the suggested categorisation of elements into two groups – ideological and based purely on ethnic origin – further conclusions may be drawn. The elements that are more prone to lead to a differentiation of scores in the PBI and show a statistically stronger correlation to the index are ideological factors.

Moreover, the political potential of the Upper Silesian ethnoregionalist movement was studied on the grounds of support for ethnoregionalist committees and hypothetical voting declarations.

Firstly, as to voting in the past, 32% of the respondents voted for the Electoral Committee of the *Ruch Autonomii Śląska*, 16% voted for the Electoral Committee of Voters *Mniejszość na Śląsku*, 13% voted for the Electoral Committee of Voters *Zjednoczeni dla Śląska* and 15% for the Electoral Committee of Voters *Ślonzoki Razem*.

Secondly, as to voting in the elections to decentralised bodies in 2018, 33% of the respondents declared that they would vote for the Electoral Committee of the *Śląska Partia Regionalna* (Silesian Regional Party), and 15% declared that they would vote for the Electoral Committee of *Ślonzoki Razem* (Silesians Together). In the elections to Parliament in 2019, 29% of the respondents declared that they would vote for the Electoral Committee of the *Śląska Partia Regionalna* (Silesian Regional Party), and 14% declared that they would vote for the Electoral Committee of *Ślonzoki Razem* (Silesians Together).

Voting for a hypothetical Silesian ethnoregionalist party was also studied. In this case, 62% of the respondents definitely agreed or agreed that they would like to vote for such a party. Similarly, 54% of the respondents definitely agreed or agreed that they would vote for some regional party if they could. The results indicate that there is still a gap between potential support for parties representing the Silesian ethnoregionalist movement and the real voting behaviours of respondents.

Concluding Remarks

The territorial axis in the Lipset-Rokkan theory assumes the existence of an opposition between the centre of the state and its peripheries, which leads to voter alignment based on this cleavage. The existence of this opposition and its political potential constituted the main research problems of the study. In the studied case, the political potential was understood not only as voting behaviours and voter support but also in terms of office and policy success. The centre-periphery opposition in the Upper Silesian case is a historical, modern-day and (probably) future phenomenon. Evidence of its existence includes the presence of an ethnoregionalist movement in the Upper Silesian region since the beginning of the xx century and an ethnoregionalist ideology in the region that was strong enough to cause its rebirth at the end of the same century.

The centre-periphery opposition during the inter-war period was most visible after the Piłsudski *coup d'etat*, when the policy of further centralisation in Poland was introduced. After 1926, Silesian parties, politicians and organisations began paying closer attention to the separate powers vested in the Silesian autonomous authorities by the *Constitutional Act including Organic Statute for the Śląskie Voivodeship* from 15 July 1920 and to the separate laws introduced in the region. Moreover, the political argument between *Sanacja* (Sanation) and Michał Grażyński – representing Polish centralism – and Christian Democrats and Wojciech Korfanty – representing Upper Silesian autonomists – led to the failure of the work on a new and full Constitutional Act for the Śląskie Voivodeship (the Organic Statute was foreseen as a provisional measure). Furthermore, historical conflicts in the region on the scope of autonomy, the political system and national belonging were and still are present in public debate and in the awareness of its inhabitants, laying the groundwork for argument about the continuity of ethnoregionalist movements, albeit a mostly symbolic one. The hypothesis assuming that the centre-periphery opposition was already present in Upper Silesia during the inter-war period was confirmed.

The peripheral identity in the case of Upper Silesians is present in many shades. As established in the study, there are differences in political goals, the understanding of Silesianism and even in the language used by persons (and organisations) declaring themselves as Silesians, Silesian-Germans or German-Silesians and Silesian-Polish or Polish-Silesians. Usually, the more dominant the Silesian identity is, the wider and deeper the political demands. The understanding of Silesianism also differs – the more dominant a Silesian identity is, the bigger the role given to separate elements of Silesian culture,

© ANNA MUŚ, 2022 | DOI:10.1163/9789004466456_009

CONCLUDING REMARKS

history and heritage, and the less they are seen as connected with Poland and the neighbouring states. Furthermore, the more dominant the Silesian identity is, the more popular the usage of the Silesian language. This pattern was present in the qualitative but also in the quantitative study, so it can be related to ethnoregionalist organisations as entities and to individual Silesians. The hypothesis assuming that peripheral identity influences the aims, scope and language of the programmes of ethnoregionalist organisations was confirmed.

The most important elements of Silesian identity are presented differently by ethnoregionalist organisations and respondents in the quantitative study. The members of ethnoregionalist organisations stressed the role of:
- language,
- a territorial bond to the territory,
- customs and traditions,
- separateness from the dominant culture,
- collective memory distinct from the narration about history known to the dominant culture.

For the respondents, the most important elements were:
- categorisation of Silesians as a group,
- familial bond to the region,
- declared role of the region in respondents' life,
- positive attitude to Silesian traditions.

These elements differ slightly from the elements I assumed in the hypothesis.

The qualitative study confirmed the hypothesis assuming that the ideologies of organisations representing the community of Upper Silesia are created in one of two ways: in opposition to the dominant culture or by promoting the specific variation of the dominant culture. This difference is especially present in the intra-group conflict between Upper Silesian ethnoregionalist organisations: some of them can be categorised as autonomist, also aimed at the recognition of Silesians as a separate ethnic group, while others may be categorised as regionalist, also aimed at the preservation of the Silesian version of Polish culture, without claims for recognition.

The study revealed that three models of activity are present among Upper Silesian ethnoregionalist organisations, but these were slightly different ones than assumed by the hypothesis. These models are: sparse, consolidated and observant. The first group includes organisations that adopted the model of sparse activity: their members take part in diverse activities, and they may even be members of different parties and promote their ideas by different means, sometimes remaining beyond the initiatives developed within the movement. The second group consists of organisations that prefer consolidated action, create their own initiatives within the movement and take part in others to a very limited extent. The third group contains organisations that are sceptical about today's developments in the ethnoregionalist movement and remain outside the most recent developments but still have a watchful eye on the situation.

One of the claims encompassing the centre-periphery opposition is the demand for the autonomy of the territory and the recognition of the non-dominant culture. Both claims are present in the programmes of some of the organisations representing the Upper Silesian community. Moreover, in many cases, opposition towards centralisation and assimilation was raised by members of the interviewed organisations. The hypothesis assuming that the centre-periphery opposition is present in the political programmes of some of the organisations representing the Upper Silesian community was confirmed.

In the quantitative study, more than half of the respondents agreed that their ethnic or national identity influences their political behaviours. Additionally, some of the most important elements of Silesian identity were factors that differentiated political behaviours, while others were correlated with the political behaviours of respondents. The hypothesis assuming that peripheral identity is one of the determinants of the political behaviours of the Upper Silesian population was confirmed.

The quantitative study also proved that there is a correlation between declared auto-identification and engaging in political behaviours connected to the ethnoregionalist movement. Consequently, the hypothesis assuming that support for ethnoregionalist organisations is closely related to the ethnic identity of a person was confirmed. It was also shown, that the more dominant Silesian identity is (declared as a single identity or as the first in complex identity) the more it is possible that a person voted for ethnoregionalist party.

The political potential of the ethnoregionalist movement was studied on three levels. Firstly, it can be stated that the modern political situation of the Upper Silesian region leaves room for the ethnoregionalist movement. The economic and political importance of a region with limited administrative competences drives political demands for change in the allocation of power between the centre and periphery and between the dominant and non-dominant ethnic groups within the state.

Secondly, today's Upper Silesian movement emerged after 1989 and was created at a time when society believed in great changes and in the betterment of everyday life. The political transformation in Poland provided the opportunity for many voices to be heard and movements to be created, including in the area of ethnic and regional policy. This movement was (and is) dynamic and evolves rapidly, playing an increasingly important political role in the region. The role of ethnic and regional identity in the popularity of the movement is

CONCLUDING REMARKS

unquestionable. The increasing popularity of Silesianism and everything connected to Silesian culture leads to more support for the movement.

Furthermore, it was revealed in the quantitative study that ethnoregionalist committees enjoy a stable level of support of about 30% of the respondents. But from the results of previous elections to self-government bodies, the support for the committees is no more than 15% (in districts), which leaves a gap between declared support and real voting behaviours. Voting for a hypothetical Silesian ethnoregionalist party was also studied. In this case, more than 60% of respondents agreed that they would like to vote for such a party. The results indicate that there is still a gap between the potential support for parties representing the ethnoregionalist movement and the real voting behaviours of the respondents.

To conclude, the increasing role of Silesian identity among the population of Upper Silesia, together with the political, social and economic situation of the region, constituted the factors that led to the emergence and stabilisation of support for a political ethnoregionalist movement. As demonstrated, one of the determinants of the popularity of the movement is the existence of the centre-periphery opposition in many dimensions and levels of the awareness of Upper Silesians as a group. This opposition is embodied in the ethnoregionalist ideology shared not only by Silesian organisations, but also by at least a part of the population of Upper Silesia. Consequently, the territorial axis in the classic Lipset-Rokkan hypothesis can be applied to studies on voter alignment and the party system in Poland, especially in the studied region.

However, this study also supports more recent findings based on study in Central Europe within the framework of Lipset-Rokkan theory, that in Poland the main two axis of voters alignment are religious-secular and interventionist-liberal. From those two axis four cross-cutting fields emerge, from which today the most important are populist (religious and interventionist) and liberal democratic (secular and economically liberal). The centre-periphery cleavage axis (with ethnic component) exists, but plays only limited role and for most voters even in Upper Silesia is only secondary.

After the study was finalised, some conclusions as to the research process were also considered, and the study itself was found to have some shortcomings. During the qualitative study, it was revealed that conducting focus group interviews with some of the organisations within the ethnoregionalist movement would be impossible (mostly due to change in their structures or dissolution). Furthermore, some problems were not discussed during FGI due to the limited time the organisations were ready to spend on the study – one such problem included demands for changes in the boundaries of the Śląskie Voivodeship. Therefore, it was impossible to compare the results of the qualitative study with the quantitative study in this field. The nature of the problems studied led to doubts during the creation of a questionnaire for the questionnaire surveys. The researcher needed to choose between in-depth questions, thorough study into selected issues, and unified questions encompassing a wide range of problems. As a result, the questionnaire itself became a kind of hybrid – offering in-depth insight into some issues and aiming at unification in others. The nature of the problems and the possible methods of analysis used in social sciences led to leaving some questions open for further study and did not provide final answers.

Additionally, the exploratory nature of the study, not only as to its main hypothesis, research problems and its application to the case of the region of Upper Silesia in Poland but also as to methods chosen for the purpose of the study, proved to have some effect. The least surprising one was the lack of previous direct studies for comparison. Another was that during the study, some interesting minor research problems were discovered, but there was no place (and tools) for their analysis (e.g., the relationship between knowledge and usage of the Silesian language and auto-identification).

This study contributes to a scholarly discussion about the possibility of applying the cleavage based on the territorial axis (as suggested by Lipset and Rokkan) in the study of voter behaviours and its (eventual) need for modification. It is clear that at least in the territory studied, the regularities observed by these two researchers are still valid for the study of voter behaviours and do not need further modifications. Still, the conclusions of the study are regionally limited, and it is doubtful whether they can be applied elsewhere in Poland. The goal of the study was, above all, to research and analyse within a valid theoretical framework the phenomenon of the ethnoregionalist movement in Upper Silesia, which has become heavily politicised in recent years, and this goal was achieved.

As was already stated, the evolution of the Upper Silesian ethnoregionalist movement is dynamic. Without a doubt, it will be useful to conduct comparative studies in the future to determine the nature of the changes of the studied phenomenon more precisely over time and to analyse the regularities observed in this study. Some interesting results may also come from the study into the Upper Silesian ethnoregionalist movement, which evolved from a social to a political phenomenon in light of numerous social movements with political goals that emerged in Poland after 2016: the *Komitet Obrony Demokracji* (Committee for the Defence of Democracy) and the *Czarny Protest* (Black Protest). Furthermore, the study revealed that there is very little scholarly literature on the history of Silesian ethnoregionalist movements in general, especially on the problem of whether we can observe a continuation (or even

CONCLUDING REMARKS

continuity) or, instead, a symbolic rebirth of the ethnoregionalist ideology in Upper Silesia throughout the xx century.

Finally, general issues connected to the situation of unrecognised minorities were raised in the study. In light of the hypothesis, the general problem of political representation of unrecognised minorities and the strategies of representation of their political interests were researched to some extent in the case of Silesians. Moreover, the nature and popularity of political postulates voiced by members of unrecognised minorities were studied, but both problems demand a wider and more in-depth study, placing them in a state-wide and European context.

Annex

Sampling – Questionnaire

The research was conducted on a group of 384 persons in three constituencies created for the purpose of elections to self-government bodies on regional level in 2014: (1) constituency with the highest rate of support for *Ruch Autonomii Śląska*, (2) constituency with the second highest rate, (3) constituency with the medium rate:
- Bieruńsko-Lędziński, Pszczyński, Katowice, Mysłowice, Tychy – 135;
- Chorzów, Piekary Śląskie, Ruda Śląska, Siemianowice Śląskie, Świętochłowice, Zabrze – 112;
- Gliwicki, Lubiniecki, Tarnogórski, Bytom, Gliwice – 137.

The quotas were created in accordance with population rate within the chosen population.

As to gender, two categories were created: man and woman, the rate will be 50% man and 50% woman.

As to age, six groups were created: 18–29, 30–39, 40–49, 50–59, 60–69, 70< with the respective rate of: 17%, 18%, 17%, 17%, 17% and 14%.

What is especially interesting for the study is the percentage rate of persons identifying themselves as Silesians (also in double declarations). For the districts within the constituencies, the numbers are as follows:
- Bieruńsko-Lędziński (36%), Pszczyński (30%), Katowice (26%), Mysłowice (26%), Tychy (17%) – average: 27%;
- Chorzów (34%), Piekary Śląskie (37%), Ruda Śląska (36%), Siemianowice Śląskie (30%), Świętochłowice (33%), Zabrze (15%) – average: 31%;
- Gliwicki (26%), Lubiniecki (27%), Tarnogórski (33%), Bytom (18%), Gliwice (10%) – average: 23%.

References

Legislation, Judgements and *Soft Law*

Charter of Fundamental Rights of the European Union, Official Journal of European Communities. OJ 2012/C 326/02.

Charter of United Nations 1945.

Convention on the Prevention and Punishment of the Crime of Genocide 1948. UNTS, vol. 78, p. 277.

Convention on the Reduction of Statelessness 1961. UNTS. vol. 989, p. 175.

European Charter for Regional or Minority Languages 1992. ETS No. 148.

Framework Convention for the Protection of National Minorities 1995. ETS No. 157.

International Convention on Elimination of All Forms of Racial Discrimination 1965. UNTS, vol. 660, p. 195.

International Covenant on Civil and Political Rights 1966. UNTS, vol. 999, p. 171.

International Covenant on Economic, Social and Cultural Rights 1966. UNTS, vol. 993, p. 3.

UNESCO Convention from 1960 against Discrimination in Education, UNTS. vol. 429, p. 93.

UNESCO Convention from 2003 for the Safeguarding of the Intangible Cultural Heritage. UNTS, vol. 2368, p. 3.

UNESCO Convention from 2005 on the Protection and Promotion of the Diversity of Cultural Expressions. UNTS, vol. 2440, p. 311.

Council Directive 2000/43/EC of 29 June 2000 implementing the principle of equal treatment between persons irrespective of racial or ethnic origin. OJ L 185, 24.7. 1996, p. 5.

Konstytucja Rzeczpospolitej Polskiej z dnia 17 marca 1921 roku. Dz.U. 1921 nr 44 poz. 267.

Konstytucja Rzeczypospolitej Polskiej z dnia 2 kwietnia 1997 r. uchwalona przez Zgromadzenie Narodowe w dniu 2 kwietnia 1997 r., przyjęta przez Naród w referendum konstytucyjnym w dniu 25 maja 1997 r., podpisana przez Prezydenta Rzeczypospolitej Polskiej w dniu 16 lipca 1997 r. Dz.U. 1997 nr 78 poz. 483.

Ustawa Konstytucyjna z dnia 23 kwietnia 1935 r. Dz.U. 1935 nr 30 poz. 227.

Ustawa Konstytucyjna z dnia 6 maja 1945 r. o zniesieniu statutu organicznego województwa śląskiego. Dz.U. 1945 nr 17 poz. 92.

Ustawa Konstytucyjna zawierająca statut organiczny Województwa Śląskiego, z dnia 15 lipca 1920 r. Dz.U. 1920 nr 73 poz. 497.

Ustawa z dnia 1 kwietnia 2016 r. o zakazie propagowania komunizmu lub innego ustroju totalitarnego przez nazwy jednostek organizacyjnych, jednostek pomocniczych gminy, budowli, obiektów i urządzeń użyteczności publicznej oraz pomniki. Dz. U. 2016 poz. 744.

Ustawa z dnia 13 listopada 2003 r. o dochodach jednostek samorządu terytorialnego. Dz.U. 2003 nr 203 poz. 1966.

REFERENCES

237

Ustawa z dnia 23 stycznia 2009 r. o wojewodzie i administracji rządowej w województwie. Dz.U. 2009 nr 31 poz. 206.

Ustawa z dnia 24 kwietnia 2003 r. o działalności pożytku publicznego i o wolontariacie. Dz.U. 2003 nr 96 poz. 873.

Ustawa z dnia 24 lipca 1998 r. o wprowadzeniu zasadniczego trójstopniowego podziału terytorialnego państwa. Dz.U. 1998 nr 96 poz. 603.

Ustawa z dnia 27 czerwca 1997 r. o partiach politycznych. Dz.U. 1997 nr 98 poz. 604.

Ustawa z dnia 29 grudnia 1992 r. o radiofonii i telewizji. Dz. U. 1993 nr 7 poz. 34.

Ustawa z dnia 4 marca 2010 r. o narodowym spisie powszechnym ludności i mieszkań w 2011 r. Dz.U. 2010 nr 47 poz. 277.

Ustawa z dnia 5 czerwca 1998 r. o samorządzie powiatowym. Dz.U. 1998 nr 91 poz. 578.

Ustawa z dnia 5 czerwca 1998 r. o samorządzie województwa. Dz.U. 1998 nr 91 poz. 576.

Ustawa z dnia 5 stycznia 2011 r. – Kodeks wyborczy. Dz.U. 2011 nr 21 poz. 112.

Ustawa z dnia 6 stycznia 2005 r. o mniejszościach narodowych i etnicznych oraz o języku regionalnym. Dz.U. 2005 nr 17 poz. 141.

Ustawa z dnia 7 kwietnia 1989 r. Prawo o stowarzyszeniach. Dz.U. 1989 nr 20 poz. 104.

Ustawa z dnia 7 września 1991 r. o systemie oświaty. Dz.U. 1991 nr 95 poz. 425.

Ustawa z dnia 8 marca 1990 r. o samorządzie gminnym. Dz.U. 1990 nr 16 poz. 95.

Rozporządzenie Ministra Edukacji Narodowej z dnia 15 grudnia 2017 r. w sprawie sposobu podziału części oświatowej subwencji ogólnej dla jednostek samorządu terytorialnego w roku 2018. Dz. U. 2018 poz. 2395.

Ogłoszenie Państwowej Komisji Wyborczej z dnia 31 października 1991 o wynikach wyborów do Sejmu Rzeczpospolitej Polskiej, przeprowadzonych 27 października 1991. M.P. 1991 nr 41 poz. 288.

Accordance with International Law of the Unilateral Declaration of Independence in Respect of Kosovo. Advisory Opinion ICJ. Reports 2010.

Gorzelik and others v. Poland. ECHR. Application No. 44158/98. Judgement 17 February 2004.

Legal Consequences for States of the Continued Presence of South Africa in Namibia (South West Africa) notwithstanding Security Council Resolution 276 (1970). Advisory Opinion ICJ. Reports 1971.

Legal Consequences of the Construction of a Wall in the Occupied Palestinian Territory. Advisory Opinion ICJ. Reports 2004.

Western Sahara. Advisory Opinion ICJ. Reports 1975.

A/RES/1514(XV) *Declaration on the granting of independence to colonial countries and peoples.*

A/RES/2649 (XXV) *The Importance of the Universal Realization of the Right of Peoples to Self-Determination and of Speedy Granting Independence to Colonial Countries and Peoples for the Guarantee and Observation of Human Rights.*

A/RES/2625 (XXV) *Declaration on Principles of International Law concerning Friendly Relations and Co-operation among States in accordance with the Charter of the United Nations.*

A/RES/47/135 *Declaration on the Rights of Persons Belonging to National or Ethnic, Religious and Linguistic Minorities.*

CCPR. 1994. *General Comment no. 23 (50).* CCPR/C/21/Rev.1/Add.5.

CERD. 1996. *General Recommendation No 21: Right to Self-Determination.* UN Doc. A/51/18.

Advisory Committee on the Framework Convention for the Protection of National Minorities. 2013. *Third Opinion on Poland.* Council of Europe. ACFC/OP/III(2013)004. Accessed 22.08.2020. https://rm.coe.int/CoERMPublicCommonSearchServices/DisplayDCTMContent?documentId=090000168008c6a1.

Advisory Committee on the Framework Convention for the Protection of National Minorities. 2019. *Fourth Opinion on Poland.* Council of Europe. ACFC/OP/IV(2019)003. Accessed 22.08.2020. https://rm.coe.int/4th-op-poland-en/1680993391.

Capotorti Francesco 1977. *Study on the Rights of Persons Belonging to Ethnic, Religious and Linguistic Minorities.* UN Commission on Human Rights working paper. E/CN.4/Sub.2/384 (20 June 1977).

CEI. 1994. *CEI Instrument for the protection of minority rights.*

Chernichenko, Stanislav Velentinovich. 1997. *Definition of Minorities: 2nd Working paper.* UN Commission on Human Rights working paper. E/CN.4/Sub.2/AC.5/1997/WP.1 annex: Minorities – working definition (2 April 1997).

Commentary of the Working Group on Minorities to the United Nation Declaration of Rights of Persons Belonging to National or Ethnic, Religious and Linguistic Minorities, UN 2005. E/CN.4/Sub.2/AC.5/2005/2.

E.U. Network of Independent Experts on Fundamental Rights. 2005. *Thematic Comment no. 3. The Protection of Minorities in European Union.* CFR-CDF.ThemComm2005.en.

OSCE. 1990. *Charter of Paris for the New Europe.*

OSCE. 1990. *Document form Copenhagen.* Copenhagen.

OSCE. 1992. *The Challenges of the Change.* Helsinki.

OSCE. 1994. *Towards the Genuine Partnership in the New Era.* Budapest.

Parliamentary Assembly of the Council of Europe. 1993. *Text of the proposal for an additional protocol to the Convention for the Protection of Human Rights and Fundamental Freedoms, concerning persons belonging to national minorities.* Recommendation 1201.

UN Office of the High Commissioner for Human Rights (OHCHR). 2010. *Minority Rights International Standards and Guidance for Implementation.* HR/PUB/10/3.

UNESCO. 1989. *Meeting of Experts on further study of the concept of the rights of the people.*

Yearbook of International Law Commission I session 1949, UN 1956.

REFERENCES   239

Sejm RP. 2011. "Druki Sejmowe VI kadencja – druk 3835". Official website. Accessed
   29.07.2020. http://orka.sejm.gov.pl/Druki6ka.nsf/0/07E763D118244637C125785E00
   4136FD?OpenDocument; http://orka.sejm.gov.pl/rexdomk6.nsf/Opdodr?OpenPage
   &nr=3835.
Sejm RP. 2014. "Obywatelski projekt ustawy o zmianie ustawy o mniejszościach narodowych i etnicznych oraz o języku regionalnym, a także niektórych innych
   ustaw". Official Website. Accessed 29.07.2020. http://www.sejm.gov.pl/Sejm7.nsf/
   PrzebiegProc.xsp?nr=2699.
Sejm RP. 2020. "Projekt Ustawy No: EW-020-98/20". Offical Website. Accessed
   28.07.2020. http://orka.sejm.gov.pl/Druki9ka.nsf/Projekty/9-020-98-2020/$file/9
   -020-98-2020.pdf.
Sejm RP. n.d. "The Constitution". Official Website. Accessed 28.08.2020. https://
   www.sejm.gov.pl/prawo/konst/angielski/kon1.htm.

Documents of Local and Regional Self-Government Bodies and Related Judgements

Sprawozdanie roczne z wykonania budżetu województwa opolskiego w 2015 roku,
   załącznik do uchwały nr 1887/2016 Zarządu Województwa Opolskiego z dn. 28
   marca 2016 roku.
Sprawozdanie roczne z wykonania budżetu województwa śląskiego w 2015 roku, załącznik
   1 do uchwały nr 541/103/V/2016 Zarządu Województwa Śląskiego z dnia 23 marca
   2016 roku.
Sentence of 17 May 2018. WSA in Gliwice. IV SA/Gl 117/18.
Sentence of 20 March 2019. NSA. II OSK 3455/18.
Zarządzenie zastępcze nr NPII.4131.4.26.2017. Dziennik Urzędowy Województwa
   Śląskiego 2017 poz. 7084.

Official Statistics, Electoral Results and Polls

CBOS (Centrum Badania Opinii Publicznej). 2017. *Przynależność Polaków do ruchów i
   wspólnot religijnych*. No 84/2017.
ČSÚ (Český Statistický Úřad). 2014. "Náboženská víra obyvatel podle výsledků sčítání
   lidu". Praha. Accessed: 14.06.2020. https://www.czso.cz/documents/10180/20551795/
   17022014.pdf/c533e33c-79c4-4a1b-8494-e45e41c5da18?version=1.0.
ČSÚ (Český Statistický Úřad). 2016. "1-17 Obyvatelstvo podle národnosti a mateřského
   jazyka podle výsledků sčítání lidu v letech 1970, 1991, 2001 a 2011". In: *Demografická*

příručka – 2015. Praha: ČSÚ. Accessed 20.08.2020. https://www.czso.cz/documents/ 10180/32846217/130055160116.pdf/15ef6512-9714-4a15-81a2-0e680482e945?version=1.0.

ČSÚ (Český Statistický Úřad). 2016. "Tabl. 1-16 Obyvatelstvo podle národnosti podle výsledků sčítání lidu v letech 1921–2011". In: *Demografická příručka – 2015.* Praha: ČSÚ. Accessed 20.08.2020. https://www.czso.cz/documents/10180/32846217/ 130055160116.pdf/15ef6512-9714-4a15-81a2-0e680482e945?version=1.0.

GUS (Główny Urząd Statystyczny). 2004. *Raport z wyników Narodowego Spisu Powszechnego Ludności i Mieszkań 2002.* Warszawa: GUS.

GUS (Główny Urząd Statystyczny). 2013. "Tabl. 3 Ludność według płci i gęstości zaludnienia oraz województw w 2011 roku". In: *Ludność. Stan i struktura demograficzna.* Warszawa: GUS.

GUS (Główny Urząd Statystyczny). 2015. "Produkt Krajowy Brutto". Atlas Regionów. Accessed 10.06.2020. http://swaid.stat.gov.pl/AtlasRegionow/AtlasRegionowMapa .aspx.

GUS (Główny Urząd Statystyczny). 2015. "Tabl. 2.2 Population by a kind and order of national and ethnic identification in 2011". In: *Struktura narodowo-etniczna, językowa i wyznaniowa* Polski. Narodowy Spis Powszechny 2011. Warszawa: GUS.

GUS (Główny Urząd Statystyczny). 2015. "Tabl. 54 Ludność województw według identyfikacji narodowo-etnicznych w 2011 roku". In: *Struktura narodowo-etniczna, językowa i wyznaniowa* Polski. Narodowy Spis Powszechny 2011. Warszawa: GUS. Accessed 03.08.2020. https://stat.gov.pl/spisy-powszechne/nsp-2011/nsp-2011 -wyniki/struktura-narodowo-etniczna-jezykowa-i-wyznaniowa-ludnosci-polski-nsp -2011,22,1.html.

GUS (Główny Urząd Statystyczny). 2015. "Tabl. 9. Wpływy z podatków PIT i CIT w dochodach jst" In: *Financial Economy of Local Government Units 2015.* Warszawa: GUS.

GUS (Główny Urząd Statystyczny). 2015. "Tabl. 20 Ludność według rodzaju i liczby języków używanych w domu w 2011 roku". In: *Struktura narodowo-etniczna, językowa i wyznaniowa* Polski. Narodowy Spis Powszechny 2011. Warszawa: GUS.

GUS (Główny Urząd Statystyczny). 2015. "Tabl. 45 Ludność według identyfikacji narodowo-etnicznych oraz przynależności wyznaniowej w 2011 roku". In: *Struktura narodowo-etniczna, językowa i wyznaniowa* Polski. Narodowy Spis Powszechny 2011. Warszawa: GUS.

GUS (Główny Urząd Statystyczny). 2015. "Tabl. 74 Ludność województw według przynależności do wyznania religijnego w 2011 roku". In: *Struktura narodowo-etniczna, językowa i wyznaniowa Polski. Narodowy Spis Powszechny 2011.* Warszawa: GUS. Accessed 03.08.2020. https://stat.gov.pl/spisy-powszechne/nsp-2011/nsp-2011 -wyniki/struktura-narodowo-etniczna-jezykowa-i-wyznaniowa-ludnosci-polski -nsp-2011,22,1.html.

GUS (Główny Urząd Statystyczny). 2015. "Tabl. 75 Ludność powiatów według przynależności do wyznania religijnego". In: *Struktura narodowo-etniczna, językowa*

REFERENCES

i wyznaniowa Polski. Narodowy Spis Powszechny 2011. Warszawa: GUS. Accessed 03.08.2020.https://stat.gov.pl/spisy-powszechne/nsp-2011/nsp-2011-wyniki/struktura -narodowo-etniczna-jezykowa-i-wyznaniowa-ludnosci-polski-nsp-2011,22,1.html.

GUS (Główny Urząd Statystyczny). 2017. *Województwo śląskie. Vademecum samorządowca 2017.* Katowice: GUS.

GUS (Główny Urząd Statystyczny). 2018. "Ludność w miastach i na wsi". Atlas Regionów. Accessed 10.06.2020. http://swaid.stat.gov.pl/AtlasRegionow/AtlasRegionowMapa .aspx.

GUS (Główny Urząd Statystyczny). 2018. "Ludność w miastach i na wsi". Atlas Regionów. Accessed 10.06.2020. http://swaid.stat.gov.pl/AtlasRegionow/AtlasRegionowMapa .aspx.

GUS (Główny Urząd Statystyczny). n.d. "The NUTS Classification in Poland". Official Website. Accessed 29.07.2020. https://stat.gov.pl/en/regional-statistics/ classification-of-territorial-units/classification-of-territorial-units-for-statistics -nuts/the-nuts-classification-in-poland/.

https://wybory2018.pkw.gov.pl/pl/geografia/246900#results_vote_elect_mayor _round_1.

PKW (Państwowa Komisja Wyborcza). 2018. "Wyniki wyborów samorządowych - Prezydent miasta Katowice". Official Website. Accessed: 10.06.2020.

PKW (Państwowa Komisja Wyborcza). 2002. "Wyniki wyborów samorządowych – Sejmiki". Official Website. Accessed: 10.06.2020. http://wybory2002.pkw.gov.pl/.

PKW (Państwowa Komisja Wyborcza). 2006. "Wyniki wyborów samorządowych – Sejmiki". Official Website. Accessed: 10.06.2020. http://wybory2006.pkw.gov.pl/ kbw/geoWojewodztwo21aa.html?id=240000&.

PKW (Państwowa Komisja Wyborcza). 2010. "Wyniki wyborów samorządowych – Sejmiki". Official Website. Accessed: 10.06.2020. http://wybory2010.pkw.gov.pl/geo/ pl/240000/240000.html.

PKW (Państwowa Komisja Wyborcza). 2011. "Wyniki wyborów do Senatu 2011". Official Website. Accessed: 10.06.2020. http://wybory2011.pkw.gov.pl/wyn/pl/000000 .html#tabs-1.

PKW (Państwowa Komisja Wyborcza). 2014. "Wyniki wyborów samorządowych – Sejmiki". Official Website. Accessed: 10.06.2020. http://samorzad2014.pkw.gov.pl/ 357_Sejmiki_wojewodztw.

PKW (Państwowa Komisja Wyborcza). 2015. "Wyniki wyborów do Senatu 2015". Official Website. Accessed: 10.06.2020. http://parlament2015.pkw.gov.pl/351_Wyniki_Senat.

PKW (Państwowa Komisja Wyborcza). 2015. "Wyniki wyborów do Sejmu RP 2015". Official Website. Accessed: 10.06.2020. http://parlament2015.pkw.gov.pl/349_wyniki_sejm/0/0.

PKW (Państwowa Komisja Wyborcza). 2018. "Wyniki wyborów samorządowych – Prezydent Miasta Katowice". Official Website. Accessed: 10.06.2020.

PKW (Państwowa Komisja Wyborcza). 2018. "Wyniki wyborów samorządowych – Sejmiki". Official Website. Accessed: 10.06.2020. https://wybory2018.pkw.gov.pl/pl/geografia/240000#results_vote_council.

Political Documents and Official Websites

Demokratyczna Unia Regionalistów Śląskich. n.d. "Nie dla ulicy/ronda im. Marii i Lecha Kaczyńskich". Accessed 15.08.2020. https://www.dursmlodzi.org.pl/?p=542.

Demokratyczna Unia Regionalistów Śląskich. n.d. "Rechtōr. Forum Regionalistów Śląskich". Accessed 15.08.2020. https://www.dursmlodzi.org.pl/?page_id=604.

Demokratyczna Unia Regionalistów Śląskich. n.d. "Homepage". Accessed 15.06.2020. http://www.dursmlodzi.org/.

Deutscher Freundschaftskreis in Schlesien. n.d. "Homepage". Accessed 15.06.2020. https://www.dfkschlesien.pl/pl/.

Fundacja "Silesia". n.d. "Ogólne". Accessed 15.06.2020. https://www.facebook.com/pg/fundacjasilesia.chorzow/about/?ref=page_internal.

Jodliński, Leszek. 2015. *12 punktów dla Śląska*.

Mniejszość na Śląsku. n.d. "Homepage". Accessed 15.06.2020. https://www.facebook.com/permalink.phpstory_fbid=1488435151434923&id=1488434304768341.

Nasz Wspólny Śląski Dom. n.d. "Homepage". Accessed 15.06.2020. http://www.nwsd.pl/index.php.

Niemiecka Wspólnota "Pojednanie i Przyszłość". n.d. "Homepage". Accessed 15.06.2020. http://www.deutschegem.eu/pl-10.php.

Pro Loquela Silesiana. 2017. "Stanowisko". Accessed 15.06.2020. http://silesiana.org/stanowisko-pro-loquela-silesiana-towarzystwa-kultywowania-i-promowania-slaskiej-mowy-ruchu-autonomii-slaska-i-zwiazku-gornoslaskiego-w-sprawie-aktov-dyskryminacji-slazakow-ze-wzgledu-n/.

Pro Loquela Silesiana. n.d. "O nas". Accessed 15.06.2020. http://silesiana.org/o-nas/.

Ruch Autonomii Śląska. 2011. Masz prawo zadeklarować narodowość śląską. "YouTube channel of RAŚ". Accessed 21.08.2020. https://www.youtube.com/watch?time_continue=2&v=YbT7mES-FCc.

Ruch Autonomii Śląska. n.d. "Homepage". Accessed 15.06.2020. http://autonomia.pl/.

Ruch Autonomii Śląska. n.d. "Projekt poprawek do Konstytucji RP". Accessed 21.08.2020. https://autonomia.pl/projekt-konstytucji-rp/.

Ruch Autonomii Śląska. n.d. "Projekt Statutu Organicznego dla Województwa Śląskiego". Accessed 21.08.2020. http://autonomia.pl/statut-organiczny/.

Stowarzyszenie Osób Narodowości Śląskiej. 2012. "Powołano Radę Górnośląską". Accessed 15.06.2020. http://slonzoki.org/tag/rada-gornoslaska.

REFERENCES

Stowarzyszenie Osób Narodowości Śląskiej. n.d. "Homepage". Accessed 15.06.2020. http://slonzoki.org/.

Śląska Partia Regionalna. n.d. "Homepage". Accessed 15.06.2020. http://partiaslaska.pl/.

Ślōnskŏ Ferajna. n.d. "Homepage". Accessed 15.06.2020. http://www.ferajna.eu/.

Ślonzoki Razem. n.d. "Homepage". Accessed 15.06.2020. https://slonzokirazem.com/.

Zjednoczeni dla Śląska. 2015. *Misja*.

Związek Górnośląski. n.d. "Homepage". Accessed 15.06.2020. https://www.zg.org.pl/.

Związek Ludności Narodowości Śląskiej. n.d. "News". Accessed 15.06.2020. http://zlns.ubf.pl/news.php.

Compact Publications

Anderson, Benedict. 1983. *Imagined Communities. Reflection on the Origin and Spread of Nationalism*. London-New York: VERSO.

Arystoteles. 2003. *Dzieła wszystkie I*. Translated by Paweł Siwek. Warszawa: Wydawnictwo Naukowe PWN.

Babbie, Earl. 2008. *Podstawy badań społecznych*. Translated by Witold Betkiewicz, Marta Bucholc. Warszawa: Wydawnictwo Naukowe PWN.

Babiński, Grzegorz. 2004. *Metodologia a rzeczywistość społeczna. Dylematy badań etnicznych*. Kraków: Zakład Wydawniczy "NOMOS".

Bartolini, Stefano, and Peter Mair. 1990. *Identity, Competition, and Electoral Availability: The Stabilisation of European Electorates 1885–1985*. Cambridge: Cambridge University Press.

Berdychowska, Bogumiła. 1998. *Mniejszości narodowe w Polsce. Praktyka po 1989 roku*. Warszawa: Wydawnictwo Sejmowe.

Billig, Michael. 1995. *Banal Nationalism*. London-Thousand Oaks-New Delhi: Sage.

Blaschke, Jochen. 1980. *Handbuch der westeuropäischen Regionalbewegungen*. Frankfurt am Main: Syndikat.

Błaszczak-Wacławik, Mirosława, Wojciech Błasiak, and Tomasz Nawrocki. 1990. *Górny Śląsk szczególny przypadek kulturowy*. Warszawa: Wydawnictwo Naukowe Jan Szumacher.

Bokszański, Zbigniew. 2005. *Tożsamości zbiorowe*. Warszawa: Wydawnictwo Naukowe PWN.

Ciągwa, Józef. 1988. *Autonomia Śląska 1922–39*. Katowice: Wydawnictwo Muzeum Śląskiego.

Creswell, John W. 2013. *Projektowanie badań naukowych*. Translated by Joanna Gilewicz. Kraków: Wydawnictwo UJ.

Davies, Norman. 1991. *Boże Igrzysko. Historia Polski*. Vol. 2. Translated by Elżbieta Tabakowska. Kraków: Wydawnictwo Znak.

244 REFERENCES

Deleuze, Gilles, and Felix Guattari. 2003. *Kafka: Toward a Minor Literature.* Mineapolis-London: University of Minnesota Press.

Dobrowolski, Piotr. 1972. *Ugrupowania i kierunki separatystyczne na Górnym Śląsku i w Cieszyńskim w latach 1918–1939.* Kraków: Wydawnictwo Naukowe PWN.

Eagelton, Terry. 1991. *Ideology. An Introduction.* London-New York: Verso.

Edensor, Tim. 2002. *National Identity, Popular Culture and Everyday Life.* Oxford-New York: Berg.

Eriksen, Thomas H. 2010. *Ethnicity and Nationalism.* London-New York: Pluto Press.

Faulks, Keith. 1999. *Political Sociology. A Critical Introduction.* Edinburgh: Edinburgh University Press.

Fouéré, Yann. 1980. *Towards a Federal Europe.* Swansea: Christopher Davies Publishers Ltd. Reprint of: Fouéré, Yann. 1968. *L'Europe aux Cents Drapeaux.* Paris: Presses D'Europe.

Gerlich, Marian G. 2010. *"My prawdziwi Górnoślązacy ...". Studium etnologiczne.* Warszawa: Wydawnictwo DiG.

Gulczyński, Marian. 2010. *Politologia. Podręcznik akademicki.* Warszawa: AlmaMer.

Guldin, Rainer. 2014. *Politische Landschaften. Zum Verhältnis von Raum und nationaler Identität.* Bielefeld: Transcript Verlag.

Héraud, Guy. 1990. *L'Europe des ethnies.* Paris: L.G.D.J.

Heywood, Andrew. 2010. *Politologia.* Translated by Natalia Orłowska, Barbara Maliszewska. Warszawa: Wydawnictwo PWN.

Janusz, Grzegorz. 2011. *Ochrona praw mniejszości narodowych w Europie.* Lublin: Wydawnictwo UMCS.

Johnson, Janet B., H.T. Reynolds, and Jason D. Mycoff. 2010. *Metody badawcze w naukach politycznych.* Translated by Agnieszka Kloskowska-Dudzińska. Warszawa: PWN.

Kaczmarek, Ryszard. 2019. *Powstania Śląskie 1919–1920-1921: Nieznana wojna polsko-niemiecka.* Kraków: Wydawnictwo Literackie.

Kamusella, Tomasz. 2007. *Silesia and Central European Nationalisms: The Emergence of National and Ethnic Groups in Prussian Silesia and Austrian Silesia, 1848–1918* West Lafayette: Prude University Press.

Karch, Brendan. 2018. *Nation and Loyalty in a German-Polish Borderland. Upper Silesia 1848–1960.* Cambridge: Cambridge University Press.

Kijonka, Justyna. 2016. *Tożsamość współczesnych Górnoślązaków. Studium socjologiczne.* Katowice: Stowarzyszenie Thesaurus Silesiae – Skarb Śląski.

Knutsen, Oddbjørn. 2018. *Social Structure, Value Orientation and Party Choice in Western Europe.* London: Palgrave.

Kunce, Aleksandra, and Zbigniew Kadłubek. 2007. *Myśleć Śląsk – wybór esejów.* Katowice: Wydawnictwo Uniwersytetu Śląskiego.

Lasswell, Harold D. 1936. *Politics: Who Gets What, When, How.* New York-London: Whittlesey House, McGraw-Hill Book Co.

REFERENCES

Lijphart, Arend. 1977. *Democracy in plural societies: A comparative exploration.* New Haven: Yale University Press.

Lublin, David. 2014. *Minority Rules: Electoral Systems, Decentralization, and Ethnoregional Party Success.* Oxford: Oxford University Press.

MacIntyre, Alasdair. 2007. *After Virtue. A Study in Moral Theory.* Notre Dame: University of Notre Dame Press.

Malicki, Krzysztof. 2016. *70 lat po Zagładzie. Przeszłość Żydów w pamięci zbiorowej mieszkańców Rzeszowa.* Wydawnictwo Uniwersytetu Rzeszowskiego: Rzeszów.

Marcoń, Witold. 2009. *Autonomia Śląska 1922–1939. Wybrane Zagadnienia.* Toruń: Wydawnictwo Adam Marszałek.

Markowski, Radosław. 2009. *Rozwój rozłamów socjopolitycznych: determinanty i konsekwencje.* Warszawa: Wydawnictwo IFiS PAN.

Mayntz, Renate, Kurt Holm, and Peter Hübner. 1985. *Wprowadzenie do metod socjologii empirycznej.* Translated by Wanda Lipnik. Warszawa: PWN.

Mik, Cezary. 1992. *Zbiorowe prawa człowieka.* Toruń: Wydawnictwo Naukowe UMK.

Mucha, Janusz. 2005. *Oblicza etniczności. Studia teoretyczne i empiryczne.* Kraków: Zakład Wydawniczy "NOMOS".

Nijakowski, Lech M. 2006. *Domeny symboliczne. Konflikty narodowe i etniczne w wymiarze symbolicznym.* Warszawa: Wydawnictwo Scholar.

Novikov, Anna. 2015. *Shades of Nation: The Dynamics of Belonging among Silesian and Jewish Populations in Eastern Upper Silesia (1922–1934).* Osnabrück: Fibre.

Nowak, Stefan. 2012. *Metodologia badań społecznych.* Warszawa: Wydawnictwo Naukowe PWN.

Ossowski, Stanisałw. 1967. *Dzieła III.* Warszawa: Wydawnictwo Naukowe PWN.

Ossowski, Stanisałw. 1984. *O ojczyźnie i narodzie.* Warszawa: Wydawnictwo Naukowe PWN.

Popiołek, Kazimierz. 1972. *Historia Śląska. Od Pradziejów do 1945 roku.* Katowice: Wydawnictwo "Śląsk".

Potulski, Jakub. 2007. *Socjologia polityki.* Gdańsk: Wydawnictwo Uniwersytetu Gdańskiego.

Preece, Jennifer J. 1998. *National Minorities and the European Nation-States System.* Oxford: Clarendon Press.

Przewłoka, Agnieszka. 2016. *Kluby Inteligencji Katolickiej w województwie katowickim 1956–1989.* Katowice: IPN.

Riedel, Sabine. 2006. *Regionaler Nationalismus. Aktuelle Gefahren für die Europäische Integration.* Berlin: SWP.

Rokkan, Stein, and Derek W. Urwin. 1982. *The Politics of Territorial Identity: Stides in European Regionalism.* London-Beverly Hills-New Dehli: Sage Publications.

Rothschild, Joseph. 1981. *Ethnopolitics: A Conceptual Framework.* New York: Columbia University Press.

Rougemont de, Denis. 1970. *Lettre ouverte aux Européens.* Paris: Albin Michel.

Rougemont de, Denis. 1977. *L'Avenir est notre affaire*. Paris: Albin Michel.

Rzewiczok, Urszula. 2014. *Dąb. Dzieje dzielnicy Katowic*. Katowice: Muzeum Historii Katowic.

Sekuła, Elżbieta A. 2009. *Po co Ślązakom potrzebny jest naród? Niebezpieczne związki między autonomią i nacjonalizmem*. Warszawa: Oficyna Wydawnicza ŁOŚGRAF.

Shively, Phillips. 2001. *Sztuka prowadzenia badań politologicznych*. Translated by: Elżbieta Hornowska. Poznań: Zysk i S-ka.

Silverman, David. 2012. *Prowadzenie badań jakościowych*. Translated by Elżbieta Hornowska. Warszawa: PWN.

Skorowski, Henryk. 1999. *Europa Regionu. Regionalizm jako kategoria aksjologiczna*. Warszawa: Wyd. Fundacji AKT.

Smith, Anthony D. 2010. *Nationalism*. Cambridge: Polity Press.

Smolorz, Michał. 2013. *Śląsk wymyślony*. Katowice: Antena Górnośląska.

Sokół, Wojciech, and Marek Żmigrodzki. 2005. *Współczesne partie i systemy partyjne. Zagadnienia teorii i praktyki politycznej*. Lublin: Wydawnictwo UMSC.

Sołdra-Gwiżdż, Teresa. 2010. *Socjologia wobec Śląska – jedność czy wielość?* Opole: Wydawnictwo Instytut Śląski.

Stjepanovic, Dejan. 2018. *Multiethnic Regionalisms in Southeastern Europe. Statehood Alternatives*. London: Palgrave Macmillan UK.

Strauss, Levi. 2012. *Jerozolima i Ateny oraz inne eseje z filozofii politycznej*. Kęty: Marek Derewiecki.

Swadźba, Urszula. 2001. *Śląski etos pracy*. Katowice: Wydawnictwo Uniwersytetu Śląskiego.

Syniawa, Mirosław. 2010. *Ślabikŏrz niy dlŏ bajtli abo lekcyje ślŏnskij gŏdki*. Chorzów: Pro Loquela Sielsiana.

Szmeja, Maria. 2008. *Etniczność – o przemianach społeczeństw narodowych*, Kraków: Zakład Wydawniczy Nomos.

Szmeja, Maria. 2017. *Śląsk – bez zmian (?): ludzie, kultura i społeczność Śląska w perspektywie postkolonialnej*. Kraków: Zakład Wydawniczy "Nomos".

Szpotański, Stanisław. 1922. *Sprawa Górnego Śląska na Konferencji Pokojowej w Paryżu*. Warszawa: Księgarnia Perzyński, Niklewicz i Ska.

Szramek, Emil. 1934. *Śląsk jako problem socjologiczny. Próba analizy*. Katowice: K. Miarka sp. Wyd.

Trosiak, Cezary. 2016. *Górny Śląsk. Między regionalizmem-autonomią-separatyzmem*. Poznań: Wydawnictwo Naukowe WNPiD UAM.

Wanatowicz, Maria W. 2004. *Od indyferentnej ludności do śląskiej narodowości? Postawy narodowe ludności autochtonicznej Górnego Śląska w latach 1945–2003 w świadomości społecznej*. Katowice: Wydawnictwo Uniwersytetu Śląskiego.

Weber, Max. 1926. *Politik als Beruf*. München-Leipzig: Verlag von Dunckler & Humbolt.

REFERENCES 247

Wojtasik, Waldemar. 2012. *Funkcje wyborów w III Rzeczypospolitej: teoria i praktyka.* Katowice: Wydawnictwo Uniwersytetu Śląskiego.

Wolff, Stefan. 2006. *Ethnic Conflict: A Global Perspective.* Oxford: Oxford University Press.

Wolny, Konstanty. 1920. *Autonomja Śląska.* Mikołów: K. Miarka.

Yang, Phillip. 2000. *Ethnic Studies: Issues and Approaches.* New York: State University of New York Press.

Collections

Applegate, Celia. 2004. "A Europe of Regions: Reflections on the Historiography of Sub-National Places in Modern Times". In: *Regions and Regionalism in Europe*, edited by Michael Keating, 128–153. Cheltenham: Edward Elgar. Reprint of: Applegate, Celia. 1999. "A Europe of Regions: Reflections on the Historiography of Sub-National Places in Modern Times". *American Historical Review*, 104, no. 4: 1157-82.

Bahlcke, Joachim. 2011. "Górny Śląsk – studium przypadku powstawania: regionów historycznych, wyobrażeń o obszarach kulturowych, historiograficznych koncepcji przestrzeni". In: *Historia Górnego Śląska*, edited by Joachim Bahlcke, Dan Gwarecki, and Ryszard Kaczmarek, 17–38. Opole-Gliwice: Dom Współpracy Polsko-Niemieckiej.

Beuchler, Steven M. 2008. "Teorie nowych ruchów społecznych". In: *Dynamika życia społecznego. Współczesne koncepcje ruchów społecznych*, edited by Krzysztof Gorlach, and Patrick H. Mooney, 161–190. Warszawa: Wydawnictwo Naukowe Scholar.

Collins, Randall. 2001. "Social Movements and the Focus of Emotional Attention." In: *Passionate Politics: Emotions and Social Movements*, edited by Jeff Goodwin, James M. Jasper, and Francesca Polletta, 27–44. Chicago: University of Chicago Press.

Cordell, Karl, and Stefan Wolff. 2010. "The study of ethnic conflict: An introduction". In: *Ethnic Conflict: Causes, Consequences, Responses*, edited by Karl Cordell, and Stefan Wolff, 1–12. London-New York: Routledge.

Czapliński, Marek. 2002. "Dzieje Śląska od 1806 do 1945 roku". In: *Historia Śląska*, edited by Marek Czapliński, 250–425. Wrocław: Wydawnictwo Uniwersytetu Wrocławskiego.

Czapliński, Marek. 2006. "Pamięć historyczna a tożsamość śląska". In: *Dynamika śląskiej tożsamości*, edited by Marek S. Szczepański, Janusz Janeczek, 56–67. Katowice: Wydawnictwo Uniwersytetu Śląskiego.

Dalton, Russell J., and Hans-Dieter Klingeman. 2010. "Obywatele a zachowania polityczne". In: *Zachowania polityczne*. Vol. 1, edited by Russell J. Dalton, and

Hans-Dieter Klingeman, 33–58. Translated by Andrzej Brzóska, Tomasz Płudowski. Warszawa: Wydawnictwo PWN.

Dziuba, Adam. 2014. "Województwo katowickie w Polsce Ludowej". In: *Encyklopedia Województwa Śląskiego*. Vol. 1, edited by Ryszard Kaczmarek, Anna Kubica, Mirosława Kowalska, and Michał Garbacz. Accessed: 10.09.2020. http://ibrbs.pl/mediawiki/index.php/Wojew%C3%B3dztwo_katowickie_w_Polsce_Ludowej.

Dziurok, Adam, and Bernard Linek. 2011. "W Polsce Ludowej (1945–1989)". In: *Historia Górnego Śląska*, edited by Joachim Bahlcke, Dan Gwarecki, and Ryszard Kaczmarek, 267–286. Opole-Gliwice: Dom Współpracy Polsko-Niemieckiej.

Dziurok, Adam. 2015. "Górny Śląsk w 1945 roku". In: *Tragedia w cieniu wyzwolenia Górnego Śląska w 1945 roku. Materiały edukacyjne*, edited by Daria Nielser, 6–11. Katowice: IPN.

Fearon, James D. 2006. "Ethnic mobilization and ethnic violence". In: *Oxford Handbook of Political Economy*, edited by Barry R Weingast, and Donald Wittman, 852–868. Oxford: Oxford University Press.

Gehrke, Roland. 2011. "Od Wiosny Ludów do I wojny światowej". In: *Historia Górnego Śląska*, edited by Joachim Bahlcke, Dan Gwarecki, and Ryszard Kaczmarek, 193–218. Opole-Gliwice: Dom Współpracy Polsko-Niemieckiej.

Geis, Anna. 2018. "The Ethics of Recognition in International Political Theory". In: *The Oxford Handbook of International Political Theory*, edited by Chris Brown, and Robyn Eckersley. Oxford: Oxford University Press.

Gerlich, Marian G. 2004. "Co Górnoślązacy myślą o swoim narodzie? (Czyli w kręgu potoczności i lapidarnej werbalizacji)". In: *Nadciągają Ślązacy. Czy istnieje narodowość śląska?*, edited by Lech M. Nijakowski, 165–186. Warszawa: Wydawnictwo Naukowe Scholar.

Greiner, Piotr. 2011. "Historia gospodarcza Górnego Śląska (XVI-XX wiek)." In: *Historia Górnego Śląska*, edited by Joachim Bahlcke, Dan Gwarecki, and Ryszard Kaczmarek, 309–339. Opole-Gliwice: Dom Wspołpracy Polsko-Niemieckiej.

Gudaszewski, Grzegorz. 2015. "Identyfikacje etniczne w Narodowym Spisie Powszechnym Ludności i Mieszkań z 2011 roku". In: *Mniejszości narodowe i etniczne w świetle Spisu Powszechnego*, edited by Sławomir Łodziński, Katarzyna Warmińska, and Grzegorz Gudaszewski, 56–120. Warszawa: Wydawnictwo Naukowe SCHOLAR.

Gurr, Ted R. 2000. "The Ethnic Basis of Political Action in the 1980s and 1990". In: *People versus State. Minorities at Risk in the New Century*, Ted R. Gurr, 3–20. Washington D.C.: US Institute for Peace.

Gwarecki, Dan. 2011. "O poszukiwaniu górnośląskich tożsamości". In: *Historia Górnego Śląska*, edited by Joachim Bahlcke, Dan Gwarecki, and Ryszard Kaczmarek, 57–74. Opole-Gliwice: Dom Współpracy Polsko-Niemieckiej.

REFERENCES

Hajduk-Nijakowska, Janina. 2010. "Deficyty w zakresie badań współczesnego folkloru". In: *Deficyty badań śląskoznawczych*, edited by Marek S. Szczepański, Tomasz Nawrocki, and Andrzej Niesporek, 67–84. Katowice: Wydawnictwo Uniwersytetu Śląskiego.

Hannan, Kevin. 2005. "Naród i język śląski w perspektywie etnolingwistycznej". In: *Górny Śląsk wyobrażony: wokół mitów, symboli i bohaterów dyskursów narodowych = Imaginiertes Oberschlesien: Mythen, Symbole und Helden in den nationalen Diskursen*, edited by Juliane Haubold-Stolle, and Bernard Linek, 138–156. Marburg: Verlag Herder-Institut.

Heinisch, Reinhard, Emanuele Massetti, and Oscar Mazzoleni. 2019. "Populism and Ethno-Territorial Politics – Conclusions". In: *The People and the Nation: Populism and Ethno-Territorial Politics in Europe*, edited by Reinhard Heinisch, Reinhard, Emanuele Massetti, and Oscar Mazzoleni, Emanuele Massetti, and Oscar Mazzoleni, 279–290. London-New York: Routledge.

Hroch, Miroslav. 2009. "Regional Memory: the Role of History in (Re)constructing Regional Identity". In: *Frontiers, Regions and Identities in Europe*, edited by Steven G. Ellis et al., 1–15. Pisa: Pisa University Press.

Janusz, Grzegorz. 2018. "Południowoszlezwickie Zrzeszenie Wyborców jako regionalna partia mniejszości narodowej". In: *Europejskie i polskie doświadczenia z etnicznością i migracjami w XXI wieku*, edited by Anita Adamczyk, Andrzej Sakson, and Cezary Trosiak, 15–28. Poznań: Wydawnictwo Naukowe WNPiD UAM.

Jones, Roger, and Wyn R. Sully. 2010. "Introduction". In: *Europe, Regions and European Regionalism*, edited by Roger Jones, and Wyn R. Sully, 1–15. London: Palgrave.

Kaczmarek, Ryszard. 2011. "II Wojna Światowa (1939–1945)". In: *Historia Górnego Śląska*, edited by Joachim Bahlcke, Dan Gwarecki, and Ryszard Kaczmarek, 255–265. Opole-Gliwice: Dom Współpracy Polsko-Niemieckiej.

Kaczmarek, Ryszard. 2015. "Górny Śląsk". In: *Encyklopedia Województwa Śląskiego*. Vol. 1, edited by Ryszard Kaczmarek, Anna Kubica, Mirosława Kowalska, and Michał Garbacz. Accessed: 10.09.2020. http://ibrbs.pl/mediawiki/index.php/Narodowo%C5%9B%C4%87_%C5%9Bl%C4%85ska.

Kasprowicz, Dominika. 2016. "Mieszane schematy badawcze". In: *Metodologia badań politologicznych*, edited by Roman Baecker et al., 97–113. Warszawa: Polskie Towarzystwo Nauk Politologicznych.

Kornacka, Monika. 2013. „Górny Śląsk – dom „ukrytej opcji niemieckiej"?" In: *Vademecum Śląsk: badania śląskoznawcze*, edited by Katarzyna Stelmach, Joanna Podgórska-Rykała, Jarosław Wichura. Katowice: Towarzystwo Inicjatyw Naukowych.

Kranz, Jerzy. 2010. "Jak rozumieć suwerenność? Próba opisu". In: *Suwerenność państwa i jej granice*, edited by Sławomir Sowiński, and Janusz Węgrzecki, 15–46. Warszawa: Wydawnictwo UKSW.

Kulik, Grzegorz. 2014. "Narodowość śląska". In: *Encyklopedia Województwa Śląskiego*. Vol. 1, edited by Ryszard Kaczmarek, Anna Kubica, Mirosława Kowalska, and

Michał Garbacz. Accessed: 10.09.2020. http://ibrbs.pl/mediawiki/index.php/Narodowo%C5%9B%C4%87_%C5%9Bl%C4%85ska.

Kuzio-Podrucki, Arkadiusz. 2014. "Bytomskie Państwo Stanowe". In: *Encyklopedia Województwa Śląskiego*. Vol. 1, edited by Ryszard Kaczmarek, Anna Kubica, Mirosława Kowalska, and Michał Garbacz. Accessed: 10.09.2020. http://ibrbs.pl/mediawiki/index.php/Bytomskie_Pa%C5%84stwo_Stanowe.

Kwaśniewski, Krzysztof. 2004. "Jeszcze o narodowości śląskiej". In: *Nadciągają Ślązacy. Czy istnieje narodowość śląska?*, edited by Lech M. Nijakowski, 69–89. Warszawa: Wydawnictwo Naukowe Scholar.

Lipset, Seymour M., and Stein Rokkan. 1967. "Cleavage Structures, Party Systems, and Voters Alignments: An Introduction". In: *Party Systems and Voter Alignments: Cross-National Perspectives*, edited by Seymour M. Lipset, and Stein Rokkan, 1–63. New York: Free Press.

Lubina, Michał. 2009. "W stronę społeczeństwa obywatelskiego." In: *Związek Górnośląski 1989-2009: księga pamiątkowa*, edited by Andrzej Czajkowski et al., 62-72. Katowice: Drukarnia i Wydawnictwo Kaga-Druk.

Madajczyk, Piotr. 2005. "Obcość jako wyznacznik powstawania i funkcjonowania granic etniczno-narodowych na Górnym Śląsku". In: *Górny Śląsk wyobrażony: wokół mitów, symboli i bohaterów dyskursów narodowych = Imaginiertes Oberschlesien: Mythen, Symbole und Helden in den nationalen Diskursen*, edited by Juliane Haubold-Stolle, and Bernard Linek, 109–122. Marburg: Verlag Herder-Institut.

Masnyk, Marek. 2011. "Prowincja górnośląska (1919–1922)". In: *Historia Górnego Śląska*, edited by Joachim Bahlcke, Dan Gwarecki, and Ryszard Kaczmarek, 219–238. Opole-Gliwice: Dom Współpracy Polsko-Niemieckiej.

Mazzoleni, Oscar, and Sean Müller. 2016. "Introduction: Explaining the policy success of regionalist parties in Western Europe". In: *Regionalist parties in Western Europe. Dimensions of success*, edited by Oscar Mazzoleni, and Sean Müller, 1–21. London-New York: Routledge.

McAdam, Doug. 2008. "Model procesu politycznego". In: *Dynamika życia społecznego. Współczesne koncepcje ruchów społecznych*, edited by Krzysztof Gorlach, and Patrick H. Mooney, 19–42. Warszawa: Wydawnictwo Naukowe Scholar.

Möckl, Karl. 1978. "Der Regionalismus und seine geschichtlichen Grundlagen". In: *Regionalismus Phänomen Planungsmittel Herausforderung für Europa*, edited by Fried Esterbauer, 17–27. Münch: Bayerische Landeszentrale für Politische Bildungsarbeit.

Mommsen, Hans. 1984. "Die Nation ist tot. Es lebe die Region". In: *Nation Deutschland?*, edited by: Guido Knopp, Siegfried Quandt, and Herbert Scheffler. Münch: Ferdinand Schöningh Paderborn.

Montello, Daniel R. 2003. "Regions in geography: Process and content". In: *Foundations of Geographic Information Science*, edited by Matt Duckham, Michael F. Goodchild, and Michael F. Worboys, 173–189. New York: CRC Press.

REFERENCES

Montello, Daniel R. 2008. "Geographic regions as brute facts, social facts, and institutional facts". In: *The mystery of capital and the construction of social reality*, edited by Barry Smith, David M. Mark, and Isaac Ehrlich, 305–316. Illinois: Open Court.

Mucha, Janusz. 1999. "Badania stosunków kulturowych z perspektywy mniejszości". In: *Kultura dominująca jako kultura obca*, edited by Janusz Mucha, 11–25. Warszawa: Oficyna Naukowa.

Müller-Rommel, Ferdinand. 1998. "Ethnoregionalist parties in Western Europe: theoretical considerations and framework of analysis". In: *Regionalist Parties in Western Europe*, edited by Lieven de Winter, and Huri Türsan, 17–27. London-New York: Routledge.

Muś, Anna. 2017a. "Ruch śląski – wskaźniki mobilizacji etnicznej i regionalnej". In: *Miedzy tolerancją a niechęcią. Polityka współczesnych państw europejskich wobec migrantów i mniejszości*, edited by Anita Adamczyk, Andrzej Sakson, and Cezary Trosiak, 369–380. Poznań: Wydawnictwo Naukowe WNPiD UAM.

Nijakowski, Lech M. 2004. "O procesach narodowotwórczych na Śląsku". In: *Nadciągają Ślązacy. Czy istnieje narodowość śląska?*, edited by Lech M. Nijakowski, 132–156. Warszawa: Wydawnictwo Naukowe Scholar.

Nowak, Krzysztof. 2011a. "Śląsk czechosłowacki 1918-1920 – 1989-1939." In: *Historia Górnego Śląska*, edited by Joachim Bahlcke, Dan Gwarecki, and Ryszard Kaczmarek, 248–254. Opole-Gliwice: Dom Wspołpracy Polsko-Niemieckiej.

Nowak, Krzysztof. 2011b. "Śląsk czechosłowacki po 1945 roku." In: *Historia Górnego Śląska*, edited by Joachim Bahlcke, Dan Gwarecki, and Ryszard Kaczmarek, 287–294. Opole-Gliwice: Dom Wspołpracy Polsko-Niemieckiej.

Ollson, Anna. 2009. "Theorizing Regional Minority Nationalism". In: *Multiplicity of Nationalism in Contemporary Europe*, edited by Ireneusz P. Karolewski, and Andrzej M. Suszycki, 107–132. Plymouth: Lexington Books.

Pasquier, Romain. 2016. „Regional and Local Government: interpreting territorial politics." In: *The Oxford Handbook of French Politics*, edited by Robert Elgie, Emiliano Grossman, and Amy G. Mazur. Oxford: Oxford University Press.

Polak, Jerzy. 2014. Pszczyńskie Państwo Stanowe. In: *Encyklopedia Województwa Śląskiego*. Vol. 1, edited by Ryszard Kaczmarek, Anna Kubica, Mirosława Kowalska, and Michał Garbacz. Accessed: 10.09.2020. http://ibrbs.pl/mediawiki/index.php/ Pszczy%C5%84skie_Wolne_Pa%C5%84stwo_Stanowe.

Rostropowicz, Joanna. 2009. "Związek Górnośląski?" In: *Związek Górnośląski 1989-2009: księga pamiątkowa*, edited by Andrzej Czajkowski et al., 33-37. Katowice: Drukarnia i Wydawnictwo Kaga-Druk.

Seiler, Daniel-Luis. 2005. "Défendre la périphérie". In: *Les partis régionalistes en Europe. Des acteurs en développement?*, edited by Delwit Pascal, 21–50. Bruxelles: Université Libre de Bruxelles.

Smolińska, Teresa. 2006. "W poszukiwaniu symboliki śląskiej tożsamości". In: *Dynamika śląskiej tożsamości*, edited by Marek S. Szczepański, Janusz Janeczek, 113–130. Katowice: Wydawnictwo Uniwersytetu Śląskiego.

Söderbaum, Fredrik. 2003. "Introduction: Theories of New Regionalism". In: *Theories of New Regionalism*, edited by Fredrik Söderbaum, and Timothy M. Shaw, 1–21. Basingstoke-New York: Palgrave Macmillan.

Spyra, Janusz. 2012. "Dzieje polityczne." In: *Dzieje Śląska Cieszyńskiego od zarania do czasów współczesnych*, edited by Idzi Panic. Volume IV. Cieszyn: Starostwo Powiatowe w Cieszynie.

Stomper, Michael. 1995. "The Resurgence of Regional Economies, Ten Years Later: The Region as a Nexus of Untraded Interdependencies". In: *Regions and Regionalism in Europe*, edited by Michael Keating, 158–188. Cheltenham: Edward Elgar.

Swan, Coree Brown. 2020. „The Independence Question." In: *The Oxford Handbook of Scottish Politics*, edited by Michael Keating. Oxford: Oxford University Press.

Szczepański, Marek S. 2004. "Regionalizm górnośląski: los czy wybór?" In: *Nadciągają Ślązacy. Czy istnieje narodowość śląska?*, edited by Lech M. Nijakowski, 90–115. Warszawa: Wydawnictwo Naukowe Scholar.

Szul, Roman. 2012. "Regionalizm. Refleksje na temat ewolucji idei i praktyki regionalizmu w Europie". In: *Region i regionalizm w socjologii i politologii*, edited by Agnieszka Pawłowska, and Zbigniew Rykiel, 31–46. Rzeszów: Wydawnictwo Uniwersytetu Rzeszowskiego.

Tambor, Jolanta. 2008. "Etnolekt śląski jako język regionalny. Uzasadnienie stanowiska". In: *Śląsko godka*, edited by Jolanta Tambor, 115–120. Katowice: Narodowa Oficyna Śląska.

Ther, Philipp. 2003. "Einleitung". In: *Regionale Bewegungen und Regionalismen in europäischen Zwischenräumen seit der Mitte des 19. Jahrhunderts*, edited by Philipp Ther, and Holm Sundhaussen, IX–XXIX. Marburg: Verlag Herder Institut.

Von Schoultz, Åsa. 2017. "Party Systems and Voter Alignments". In: *Sage Handbook of Electoral Behaviour*, edited by Kai Arzheimer, Jocelyn Evans, and Michael S. Lewis-Beck. London: Sage.

Wanatowicz, Maria W. 2011. "Województwo Śląskie (1922–1939)". In: *Historia Górnego Śląska*, edited by Joachim Bahlcke, Dan Gwarecki, and Ryszard Kaczmarek, 238–248. Opole-Gliwice: Dom Współpracy Polsko-Niemieckiej.

Wieviorka, Michael. 2018. "Cultural insecurity in a world of violence, fear and risk". In: *Handbook of cultural security*, edited by Yasushi Watanabe. Cheltenham: Edward Elgar Publishing.

Winter, Lieven de. 1998. "Conclusion: a comparative analysis of the electoral, office and policy success of ethoregionalist parties". In: *Regionalist Parties in Western Europe*, edited by Lieven de Winter, and Huri Türsan, 204–240. London-New York: Routledge.

Wódz, Jacek, and Kazimiera Wódz. 2004. "Czy nadciągają Ślązacy". In: *Nadciągają Ślązacy. Czy istnieje narodowość śląska?*, edited by Lech M. Nijakowski, 116–131. Warszawa: Wydawnictwo Naukowe Scholar.

Wódz, Jacek. 2012. "Pożytki z refleksji z zakresu socjologii i antropologii polityki – zamiast wstępu". In: *O pożytkach z badań z dziedziny socjologii i antropologii polityki. Próby refleksji*, edited by Jacek Wódz, 7–17. Katowice: Wydawnictwo Uniwersytetu Śląskiego.

Wódz, Jacek. 2015. "Niedokończone tożsamości polityczne. Kilka słów o polskiej niedokończonej tożsamości narodowej". In: *Niedokończone tożsamości społeczne – szkice socjologiczne*, edited by Jacek Wódz, and Grzegorz Libor, 11–34. Katowice: Wydawnictwo Uniwersytetu Śląskiego.

Wróblewski, Piotr. 2015. "Narodowy Spis Powszechny z 2011 roku a legitymacja uniwersum symbolicznego narodowości śląskiej". In: *Mniejszości narodowe i etniczne w świetle Spisu Powszechnego*, edited by Sławomir Łodziński, Katarzyna Warmińska, and Grzegorz Gudaszewski, 215–237. Warszawa: Wydawnictwo Naukowe SCHOLAR.

Zarycki, Tomasz. 2007. "W poszukiwaniu peryferii. Teoria podziałów politycznych Lipseta-Rokkana w kontekście polskim". In: *Oblicze polityczne regionów polski*, edited by Małgorzata Dajnowicz, 13–34. Białystok: Wydawnictwo Wyższej Szkoły Finansów i Zarządzania w Białymstoku.

Zygmunt, Agata. 2015. "Dylematy tożsamości w społeczeństwie sieciowym. Szkic socjologiczny". In: *Niedokończone tożsamości społeczne – szkice socjologiczne*, edited by Jacek Wódz, and Grzegorz Libor, 113–132. Katowice: Wydawnictwo Uniwersytetu Śląskiego.

Articles

Aha, Katherine. 2019. „Resilient incumbents: Ethnic minority political parties and voter accountability". *Party Politics*. https://doi.org/10.1177/1354068819881125.

Barten, Ulrike. 2015. "What's In a Name? Peoples, Minorities, Indigenous People, Tribal Groups and Nations". *Journal on Ethnopolitics and Minority Issues in Europe* 14, no. 1: 1–25.

Bértoa, Fernando. 2013. "Party systems and cleavage structures revisited: A sociological explanation of party system institutionalization in East Central Europe". *Party Politics* 20, no. 1: 16–36.

Birnir, Johanna K., Jonathan Wilkenfeld, James D. Fearon, David Laitin, Ted R. Gurr, Dawn Brancati, and Stephen Saideman, et al. 2015. "Socially Relevant Ethnic Groups, Ethnic Structure and AMAR". *Journal of Peace Research* 52, no. 1: 110–115.

Blackwood, Robert J. 2011. "The linguistic landscape of Brittany and Corsica: A comparative study of the presence of France's regional languages in the public space." *French Language Studies* 21: 111–130.

Bortliczek, Małgorzata. 2019. „Śląsk Cieszyński w refleksjach humanistów – poszukiwanie klucza do zrozumienia narracji o przygranicznym mikroświecie". *Poznańskie Studia Polonistyczne. Seria Językoznawcza* 26, no. 2: 41–60.

Bracanti, Dawn. 2005. "Pawns Take Queen: The Destabilizing Effects of Regional Parties in Europe". *Constitutional Political Economy* 16: 143–159.

Burszta, Wojciech J. 2015. "The frontiers of identity and the identity of frontiers". *Sprawy Narodowościowe* 47: 2–14.

Chandra, Kanchan. 2005. "Ethnic Parties and Democratic Stability". *Perspectives on Politics* 3, no. 2: 235–252.

Chandra, Kanchan. 2011. "What is ethnic party?" *Party Politics* 17, no. 2: 151–169.

Chandra, Kanchan and Steven Wilkinson. 2008. "Measuring the Effect of Ethnicity". *Comparative Political Studies* 41, no. 4/5: 515–563.

Copik, Ilona. 2014. "Górny Śląsk – opowieść niewysłowiona". *Anthropos?* 22: 34–44.

Cybula, Adrian, and Tatiana Majcherkiewicz. 2005. "Wielokulturowość regionu środkowoeuropejskiego a narody i państwa narodowe. Przykład Górnego Śląska". *Sprawy Narodowościowe* 26: 135–158.

Dandoy, Régis. 2010. "Ethno-regionalist parties in Europe: a typology". *Perspectives on Federalism* 2, no. 2: 194–220.

Dziki, Tomasz. 2013. "Podział administracyjny Polski w latach 1944–1999. Z badań na ustrojem ziem polskich w XIX i XX wieku". *Studia Gdańskie* 10: 433–450.

Eisenstadt, Shmuel, and Bernhard Giesen. 1995. "The construction of collective identity". *European Journal of Sociology* 36, no. 1: 72–102.

Elias, Anwen. 2008. "Introduction: Whatever Happend to the Europe of the Regions? Revisiting the Regional Dimension of European Politics". *Regional & Federal Studies* 18, no. 5: 483–492.

Gerlich, Marian G. 1992. "Współczesne podziały górnośląskiej zbiorowości regionalnej jako problem etnograficzny". *Etnografia polska* XXXVI, no. 1: 35–63.

Gerlich, Marian G. 1994. " Śląska krzywda" – przejaw zbiorowego poczucia poniżenia wśród górnośląskiej rodzimej ludności (okres międzywojnia)". *Etnografia polska* XXXVIII, no. 1–2: 5–25.

Gurr, Ted R. 1993. "Why Minorities Rebel: A Global Analysis of Communal Mobilization and Conflict Since 1945". *International Political Science Review/ Revue internationale de science politique* 14, no. 2: 161–201.

Hamlin, Alan, and Colin Jennings. 2011. "Expressive Political Behaviour: Foundations, Scope and Implications". *British Journal of Political Science* 41, no. 3: 645–670.

Héraud, Guy. 1970. "Les principes du fédéralisme et la fédération européenne". *Revue internationale de droit comparé* 22, no. 3: 602–604.

REFERENCES 255

Hołomek, Małgorzata. 2014. "Ruch separatystyczny, nacjonalizm czy naród?" *Górnośląskie Studia Socjologiczne. Seria Nowa* 5: 152–171.

Horowitz, Donald. 2014. "Ethnic Power Sharing: Three Big Problems". *Journal of Democracy* 25, no. 2: 5–20.

Huysseune, Michel, and Theo Jans. 2008. "Brussels as the capital of a Europe of the regions? Regional offices as European policy actors". *Brussels studies* 16: 1–12.

Jarzyńska, Irena. 2010. "Edukacja regionalna dzieci w procesie kształcenia zintegrowanego". *Edukacja elementarna w teorii i praktyce: kwartalnik dla nauczycieli* 1–2: 79–91.

Jaskułowski, Krzysztof, and Piotr Majewski. 2017. "Politics of memory in Upper Silesian schools. Between Polish homogeneous nationalism and its Silesian discontents". *Memory Studies* 13, no. 1: 60–73.

Józefowicz, Anna. 2013. "Region oraz edukacja regionalna w podstawach programowych wychowania przedszkolnego i szkoły podstawowej". *Ars inter Culturas* 2: 105–117.

Kamusella, Tomasz. 2004. "Standaryzacja języka górnośląskiego i jej implikacje społeczno-polityczne (ze szczególnym uwzględnieniem Śląska Opolskiego)". *Sprawy Narodowościowe* 24–25: 113–132.

Kansteiner, Wulf. 2002. "Finding Meaning in Memory: A Methodological Critique of Collective Memory Studies". *History and Theory* 41, no. 2: 179–197.

Keating, Michael, and Alex Wilson. 2014. "Regions with regionalism? The rescaling of interest groups in six European states". *European Journal of Political Research* 53, no. 4: 840–857.

Keating, Michael. 2004. "European Integration and Nationalities Question". *Politics & Society* 32, no. 3: 367–388.

Kijonka, Justyna. 2004. "Spory o narodowość śląską w kontekście członkostwa Polski w Unii Europejskiej". *Pisma Humanistyczne* 6: 37–53.

Kisielewicz, Danuta. 2015. "Historyczne uwarunkowania odrębności regionu Śląska Opolskiego". *Pogranicze. Polish Borderlands Studies* 3, no. 1: 7–18.

Kitschelt, Herbert. 1995. "Formation of Party Cleavages in Post-Communist Democracies". *Party Politics* 1, no. 4: 447–472.

Kitschelt, Herbert. 2000. "Citizens, politicians, and party cartellization: Political representation and state failure in post-industrial democracies". *European Journal of Political Research* 37, no. 2: 149–179.

Kitschelt, Herbert. 2015. "Analyzing the Dynamics of Post-Communist Party Systems: Some "Final Thoughts" on the EEPS Special Section". *East European Politics and Societies* 29, no. 1: 81–91.

Kociński, Cezary. 2007. "Normy domniemania w prawie samorządu terytorialnego cz. II". *Samorząd Terytorialny* 5: 9–24.

Kopka, Aleksander. 2014. "Język, tożsamość, pamięć – myślenie Śląska jako dekonstrukcja". *Anthropos?* 22: 45–55.

Lake, David A., and Donald Rothchild. 1996. "Containing Fear: The Origins and Management of Ethnic Conflict". *International Security* 21, no. 2: 41–75.

Langholm, Silvert. 1971. "On the Concepts of Centre and Periphery". *Journal of Peace Research* 8, no. 3–4: 273–278.

Lucardie, Paul. 2002. "Prophets, Purifiers and Prolocutors. Towards a Theory on the Emergence of New Parties". *Party Politics* 6, no. 2: 175–185.

Łodziński, Sławomir, Maria Szmeja, and Katarzyna Warmińska. 2014. "Wprowadzenie: mniejszości narodowe i etniczne w badaniach socjologicznych po 1989". *Studia Humanistyczne AGH: półrocznik Akademii Górniczo-Hutniczej im. Stanisława Staszica* 13, no. 3: 9–29.

Michna, Ewa. 2014. "Odrębność językowa małych grup etnicznych i jej rola w procesach walki o uznanie oraz polityce tożsamości: analiza porównawcza sytuacji Rusinów Karpackich i Ślązaków". *Studia Humanistyczne AGH: półrocznik Akademii Górniczo-Hutniczej im. Stanisława Staszica* 13, no. 3: 115–130.

Mieczkowski, Janusz. 2014. "Mniejszości narodowe w Polsce a partie etniczne – możliwości i bariery". *Uniwesytet Szczeciński. Zeszyty Naukowe – Acta Politica* 815: 179–190.

Muś, Anna. 2016. "Ideologia euroregionalizmu". *Racjonalia* 6: 85–110.

Muś, Anna. 2017b. "Zjednoczeni dla Śląska" – Upper-Silesians Support for Regional Initiative". *Political Preferences* 14: 157–174.

Muś, Anna. 2019. "Politicisation of Ethnicity. The Moravian-Silesian movement in the Czech Republic and the Silesian movement in Poland – A Comparative Approach." *Nationalities Papers. The Journal of Nationalism and Ethnicity* 47, no. 6: 1048–1066.

Muś, Anna. 2020. "Regional Politics and Ethnic Identity: How Silesian Identity Has Become Politicisied". *Nationalities Papers. The Journal of Nationalism and Ethnicity.* DOI: https://doi.org/10.1017/nps.2020.48.

Myśliwiec, Małgorzata. 2013. "Ślōnskŏ godka – prašny folklor, czy język regionalny?" *Przegląd Prawa Konstytucyjnego* 15: 99–120.

Myśliwiec, Małgorzata. 2019. "The Results of Elections for the Śląskie Voivodeship Assembly in 2018 in the Reality of Territorial Heteronomy". *Political Preferences* 23: 2336.

Nawrot, Dariusz. 2017. "Rogawscy z Mijaczowa i powstanie na Nowym Śląsku w 1806 i 1807 roku". *Zeszyty Myszkowskie* 4: 29–47.

Orlewski, Patryk. 2019. "Identity and Distribution of the Silesian Minority in Poland". *Miscellanea Geographica – Regional Studies on Development* 23, no. 2: 76–84.

Penrose, Jan. 2002. "Nations, States and Homelands: Territory and Territoriality in Nationalist Thought". *Nations and Nationalism* 8, no. 3: 277–297.

Peszyński, Wojciech. 2011. "Kandydat czy partia? W poszukiwaniu determinant zachowań wyborczych elektoratu". *Preferencje polityczne* 2: 227–248.

Plis, Jan 2014. "Wprowadzenie do problematyki koncepcji praw człowieka trzeciej generacji Karola Vasaka". *Ius et Administratio* 1: 42–50.

Popieliński, Paweł. 2014. "Etniczność i narodowość rdzennych mieszkańców Górnego Śląska po 1989 roku". *Poznańskie Studia Slawistyczne* 8: 137–152.

REFERENCES

Ruiz-Rufio, Ruben. 2013. "Satisfaction with Democracy in Multi-ethnic Countries: The Effect of Representative Political Institutions on Ethnic Minorities". *Political Studies* 61, no. 1: 101–118.

Saul, Matthew. 2011. "The Normative Status of Self-Determination in International Law: A Formula for Uncertainty in the Scope and Content of the Right?" *Human Rights Law Review* 11, no. 4: 609–644.

Saxton, Gregory. 2005. "Repression, Grievances, Mobilization and Rebellion: A New test of Gurr's model of ethnopolitical rebellion". *International Interactions* 31, no. 1: 87–116.

Schattkowsky, Ralph. 1994. "Separatism in the Eastern Provinces of the German Reich at the End of the First World War". *Journal of Contemporary History* 29, no. 2: 305–324.

Sitter, Nick. 2002. "Cleavages, Party Strategy and Party System Change in Europe, East and West". *Perspectives on European Politics and Society* 3, no. 3: 425–451.

Smith, Peter B., Marco Giannini, Klaus Helkama, and Sigrfied Stumpf. 2005. "Positive Auto-stereotyping and Self-construal as Predictors of National Identification". *Revue internationale de psychologie sociale* 18, no. 1: 65–90.

Storm, Eric. 2003. "Regionalism in history 1890–1945: The cultural approach". *European History Quarterly* 33. no. 2: 251–266.

Strijbis, Oliver, and Michał Kotnarowski. 2015. "Measuring the electoral mobilization of ethnic parties: Towards comparable indicators". *Party Politics* 21, no. 3: 456–469.

Strimska, Maximillian. 2002. "A Study on Conceptualisation of (Ethno)regional Parties". *Central European Political Studies Review* 4, no. 2–3.

Surażska, Wisła. 1995. "Central Europe in Rokkanian Perspective". *Historical Social Research / Historische Sozialforschung* 20, no. 2: 226–243.

Szczepankiewicz-Battek, Joanna. 2017. „The geographical coverage of Sorbian languages." *Region and Regionalism* 13, no. 1: 239–255.

Szmeja, Maria. 2014. "Pamięć o przeszłości w kulturze śląskiej". *Studia Humanistyczne AGH: półrocznik Akademii Górniczo-Hutniczej im. Stanisława Staszica; Kraków: Wydawnictwa AGH* 13, no. 3: 219–234.

Ther, Philipp. 2003. "Einleitung". In: Regionale Bewegungen und Regionalismen in europaischen Zwischenraumen seit der Mitte des 19. Jahrhunderts, edited by Philipp Ther, and Holm Sundhaussen, IX-XXIX. Marburg: Verlag Herder Institut.

Toole, James. 2007. "The Historical Foundations of Party Politics in Post-Communist East Central Europe". *Europe-Asia Studies* 59, no. 4: 541–566.

van der Zwet, Arno. 2015. "Operationalising national identity: the cases of the Scottish National Party and Frisian National Party." *Nation and Nationalism* 21, no. 1: 62–85.

Van Morgan, Sydney. 2006. "Language politics and regional nationalist mobilisation in Galicia and Wales". *Ethnicities* 6, no. 4: 451–475.

Wimmer, Andreas, Lars-Erik Cederman, and Brian Min. 2009. "Ethnic Politics and Armed Conflict: A Configurational Analysis of a New Global Data Set". *American Sociological Review* 74, no. 2: 316–337.

Wimmer, Andreas. 2017. "Power and Pride. National Identity and Ethnopolitical Inequality around the World". *World Politics* 69, no. 4: 605–639.

Wódz, Jacek. 2010. "Górny Śląsk jako problem polityczny – spojrzenie socjologiczne". *Górnośląskie Studia Socjologiczne. Seria Nowa* 1: 34–51.

Wódz, Jacek. 2012. "Pomiędzy ruchem społecznym w regionie a protopartią i partią regionalną. Kilka refleksji na tle zmiany reprezentacji politycznej w regionach". *Górnośląskie Studia Socjologiczne. Seria Nowa* 3: 28–46.

Wróblewski, Piotr. 1998. "Regionalny nacjonalizm. Śląska ideologia narodowa/The Regional Nationalism. The Silesian National Ideology". *Borussia. Kultura-Historia-Literatura* 16: 97–105.

Zamfira, Andreea. 2015. "Methodological Limitations in Studying the Effect of (Inter) ethnicity on Voting Behaviour, with examples form Bulgaria, Romania and Slovakia". *Erdkunde* 69, no. 2: 161–173.

Zuckerman, Alan. 1975. "Political Cleavage: A Conceptual and Theoretical Analysis". *British Journal of Political Science* 5, no. 2: 231–248.

Working Papers and Others

Birnir, Johanna K., David Laitin, Jonathan Wilkenfeld, Agatha S. Hultquist, David Waguespack, and Ted R. Gurr. 2016. "Socially Relevant Identity: Addressing Selection Bias Issues and Introducing the AMAR (All Minorities at Risk) Data". *CIDCM Working Paper*, CIDCM: Maryland.

Library of Congress. n.d. "Treaty of Peace between the Allied and Associated Powers and Germany". Accessed 29.06.2020. https://www.loc.gov/law/help/us-treaties/bevans/m-ust000002-0043.pdf.

Lynch, Peter. 2007. "Organising for a Europe of the Regions: The European Free Alliance-DPPE and Political Representation in the European Union". *European Union Studies Association conference*. Montreal 17th to 19th May 2007 (unpublished).

Łodziński, Sławomir. 2005. "Wyrównanie czy uprzywilejowanie? Spory dotyczące projektu ustawy o ochronie mniejszości narodowych (1989–2005)". *Biuro Studiów i Ekspertyz*. Raport no. 232.

Młodzi 2011. 2011. Warszawa: Kancelaria Prezesa Rady Ministrów.

Platform EDUŚ. n.d. "Homepage". Accessed 01.08.2020. http://edus.ibrbs.pl/.

Szczepański, Marek S., Anna Śliz. 2010. "Dylematy regionalnej tożsamości. Przypadek Górnego Śląska".

REFERENCES 259

Tambor, Jolanta. 2010. "Kulturowe wyznaczniki tożsamości: Tożsamość mieszkańców województwa śląskiego". Paper at Śląski Kongres Kultury 23–25 September 2010.

Vermeersch, Peter. 2011. "Theories of ethnic mobilisation: overview and recent trends". Leuven: *CRPD Working Paper* No 3.

Articles in Newspapers

"Jaskółka Śląska" No. 9 September 2006.

"Jaskółka Śląska" No. 9/10 2002.

Bartkiewicz, Artur. 2018. *Wojna polsko-polska, defilada i hipokryzja.* "Rzeczpospolita". Accessed 15.08.2020. https://www.rp.pl/Komentarze/180819545-Wojna-polsko -polska-defilada-i-hipokryzja.html.

Bieniasz, Stanisław. 1990. *O autonomię Górnego Śląska.* "Kultura". Website of Kultura Paryska. Accessed 21.08.2020. http://static.kulturaparyska.com/attachments/1e/66/ 776fd2ca1071043e46667a479f97de2e8c2261df.pdf#page=6.

Jaskółka Śląska. n.d. *Homepage.* Accessed 15.06.2020. http://www.jaskolkaslaska.eu/.

Klasik, Andrzej. 1988. *Tożsamość Górnego Śląska*, "Gość niedzielny". Website SBC. Accessed 21.08.2020. http://www.sbc.org.pl/dlibra/applet?mimetype=image/ x.djvu&sec=false&handler=djvu&content_url=/Content/66542/_index.djvu.

Kositz, Antoni. 1991. *Autonomia – jedynym wyjściem.* "Jaskółka Śląska" no 1.

Portal Samorządowy. 2016. *Śląsk – nowy przedmiot edukacja regionalna.* Accessed 15.08.2020. http://www.portalsamorzadowy.pl/edukacja/slask-nowy-przedmiot -edukacja-regionalna-takze-w-innych-szkolach-prowadza-rozmowy-w-tej -sprawie,78564.html.

Przybytek, Justyna. 2016. *Niemy protest Ślązaków na placu Szewczyka w Katowicach.* "Dziennik Zachodni". Accessed 21.08.2020. http://www.dziennikzachodni.pl/wiado- mosci/katowice/a/niemy-protest-slazakow-na-placu-szewczyka-w-katowicach -zdjecia-wideo-infografika,10793006/.

Redakcja DZ. 2013. *Spowiedź wielkanocna Ślązaków. Dupowatość, nietolerancja ... Oto nasze grzechy.* "Dziennik Zachodni". Accessed 20.08.2020. https://dziennikzachodni .pl/spowiedz-wielkanocna-slazakow-dupowatosc-nietolerancja-oto-nasze-grzechy -czytaj-i-komentuj/ar/793490.

Redakcja DZ. 2018. *Wybory samorządowe 2018: Sondaż DZ: Katowice, Sosnowiec, Rybnik, Bytom, Zabrze, Częstochowa, Bielsko-Biała. Kto wygra wybory?* "Dziennik Zachodni". Accessed 15.08.2020. https://dziennikzachodni.pl/wybory-samorzadowe-2018 -sondaz-dz-katowice-sosnowiec-rybnik-bytom-zabrze-czestochowa-bielskobiala -kto-wygra-wybory/ar/13530608.

Redakcja Katowice. Nasze miasto. 2018. *Marsza Autonomii Śląska przeszedł przez Katowice.* "Katowice. Nasze miasto". Accessed 21.08.2020. http://katowice.naszemiasto.pl/artykul/marsz-autonomii-slaska-2018-przeszedl-przez-katowice,4725955,artgal,t,id,tm.html.

Redakcja Polska the Times. 2011. *Kaczyński: Zakamuflowaną opcją niemiecką jest śląskość w wydaniu RAŚ.* "Polska the Times". Accessed 21.08.2020. http://www.polskatimes.pl/artykul/389276,kaczynski-zakamuflowana-opcja-niemiecka-jest-slaskosc-w-wydaniu-ras,2,id,t,sa.html.

Redakcja TVN 24. 2017. *Marsz Autonomii przeszedł ulicami Katowic.* "TVN 24". Accessed 21.08.2020. http://www.tvn24.pl/wiadomosci-z-kraju,3/zwolennicy-autonomii-slaska-mamy-konkretny-pomysl-na-samorzadnosc,757234.html.

Semik, Teresa. 2016. *Raś i SLD przed Telewizją Katowice.* "Dziennik Zachodni". Accessed 21.08.2020. http://www.dziennikzachodni.pl/wiadomosci/katowice/a/protest-ras-i-sld-przed-telewizja-katowice,9999414/.

Treter-Sierpińska, Katarzyna. n.d. *Ukryta opcja niemiecka szczerzy kły: RAŚ oskarża Polskę o etnobójstwo Ślązaków,* "wPrawo.pl". Accessed 21.08.2020. http://wprawo.pl/2018/01/07/ukryta-opcja-niemiecka-szczerzy-kly-ruch-autonomii-slaska-oskarza-polske-o-etnobojstwo-slazakow/?publisher-theme-comment-inserted=1#comment-77443.

Twaróg, Marek. 2014. *Nasza śląska krzywda.* "Dziennik Zachodni". Accessed 21.08.2020. http://www.dziennikzachodni.pl/artykul/3406645,twarog-na-wielki-piatek-nasza-slaska-krzywda,id,t.html.

Internet Resources

Ethnologue. n.d. "Silesian". Languages of the World. Accessed 13.06.2020. http://www.ethnologue.com/language/szl.

Lexico Oxford Dictionary. n.d. "Potential". Accessed 26.07.2021. https://www.lexico.com/en/definition/potential.

MSWiA (Ministerstwo Spraw Wewnętrznych i Administracji). n.d. "Charakterystyka mniejszości narodowych i etnicznych w Polsce". Official Website. Accessed 10.06.2020. http://mniejszosci.narodowe.mswia.gov.pl/mne/mniejszosci/charakterystyka-mniejs/6480,Charakterystyka-mniejszosci-narodowych-i-etnicznych-w-Polsce.html.

Silling. n.d. "Korpus". Accessed 21.07.2021. https://silling.org/kontext/first_form.

Index

auto-identification   35, 61, 90, 91, 139, 140, 142, 189, 191, 192, 193, 194, 195, 196, 197, 199, 200, 201, 216, 225, 226, 230, 232

autonomy   1, 6, 17, 25, 34, 57, 59, 72, 77, 79, 81, 82, 83, 85, 100, 101, 111, 116, 130, 131, 158, 170, 171, 172, 173, 175, 179, 187, 204, 228, 230

centre-periphery opposition   3, 4, 8, 9, 44, 87, 88, 89, 187, 212, 228, 230, 231

Cieszyn Silesia   46, 47, 48, 49, 53, 55, 58, 77, 78, 124, 125

Demokratyczna Unia Regionalistów Śląskich   74, 109, 114, 133, 136, 166

ethnic conflict   3, 15, 16, 17, 18, 20, 34, 43

ethnic mobilisation   3, 15, 18, 19, 20

ethnicity   1, 6, 15, 16, 17, 18, 19, 20, 24, 25, 28, 30, 31, 35, 43, 44, 75, 85, 90, 109, 128, 140, 149, 159, 181, 182, 185, 186, 187, 189, 191, 193, 199, 209, 214, 215, 220

ethnoregionalist parties   22, 23, 25, 26, 27, 125, 127, 207, 209, 210, 211, 212, 214, 215, 216, 217

ethnoregionalist party   3, 23, 76, 206, 211, 227, 230, 231

Fundacja "Silesia"   73, 93, 96, 98, 99, 136

Hulčin   46, 47, 48, 53

Initiative der kulturelle Autonomie Schlesiens   74, 95, 136

Katowice Silesia   46, 47, 49, 50, 51, 52, 53

Lipset-Rokkan theory   4, 5, 6, 8, 26, 87, 213, 228, 231

minority   8, 9, 17, 18, 19, 20, 29, 34, 35, 36, 38, 39, 40, 41, 42, 46

Mniejszość na Śląsku   117, 118, 137, 207, 217, 218, 219, 226

Moravskoslezký Kraj   45, 47

nationalism   12, 23, 28, 74, 85, 108, 175, 185

non-dominant culture   1, 7, 8, 9, 21, 27, 43, 38, 187

Opava Silesia   46, 47, 48, 53

Opole Silesia   46, 47, 50, 51, 52, 144

Opolskie Voivodeship   45, 46, 47, 56, 57, 64, 65, 66, 68, 78, 87, 174, 204

political behaviour   1, 3, 5, 10, 19, 44, 71, 87, 88, 90, 91, 92, 94, 189, 192, 205, 216, 217, 218, 219, 220, 221, 223, 224, 230

Political Behaviours Index   218, 219, 221

politicisation   1, 16, 18, 20, 23, 85, 91, 96, 137

Pro Loquela Silesiana   73, 93, 95, 97, 98, 99, 104, 114, 136, 168, 169

Rada Górnośląska   2, 91, 93, 95, 96, 98, 104, 105, 106, 108, 110, 111, 112, 114, 168, 181, 182, 217, 218, 219

regional community   36, 37, 38, 40, 57, 59, 62, 84, 85, 102, 123, 145, 190

regional education   74, 95, 96, 101, 105, 109, 110, 114, 115, 116, 119, 128, 132, 133, 136, 164, 165, 166, 167, 169, 180, 185, 202, 203

regionalism   11, 14, 15, 29, 79, 84, 85, 96, 98, 100, 103, 105, 106, 108, 109, 110, 112, 113, 176, 179, 214

Ruch Autonomii Śląska   2, 72, 73, 81, 82, 92, 93, 95, 98, 100, 102, 105, 112, 114, 117, 120, 128, 130, 131, 132, 134, 136, 158, 172, 175, 182, 207, 217, 218, 219, 226, 235

Silesian Autonomous Voivodeship   52, 56, 57, 174

Silesian language   49, 53, 56, 61, 67, 68, 69, 82, 95, 96, 97, 98, 99, 101, 102, 104, 109, 110, 111, 114, 116, 118, 132, 136, 145, 146, 161, 165, 167, 168, 169, 170, 199, 200, 201, 202, 203, 229, 232

Silesianism   75, 142, 144, 148, 191, 192, 196, 228, 231

Silesians   1, 40, 46, 47, 48, 51, 52, 53, 55, 56, 57, 58, 60, 61, 62, 66, 67, 68, 69, 70, 71, 72, 73, 74, 75, 77, 78, 79, 80, 81, 83, 96, 98,

Silesians (*cont.*)
100, 103, 104, 105, 106, 107, 108, 109, 110,
112, 113, 114, 115, 116, 119, 120, 130, 132, 133,
134, 140, 141, 143, 144, 147, 148, 149, 151,
154, 155, 156, 157, 158, 159, 160, 161, 162,
163, 164, 166, 167, 177, 185, 186, 189, 190,
192, 193, 194, 195, 196, 199, 201, 202, 209,
210, 214, 215, 220, 221, 225, 226, 228, 229,
231, 233, 235
Stereotypes 89, 195, 196
Stowarzyszenie "Nasz Wspólny Śląski
Dom" 74, 95, 110
Stowarzyszenie "Przymierze Śląskie" 73
Stowarzyszenie Osób Narodowości
Śląskiej 74, 95, 103, 110, 136
Śląska Partia Ludowa 58, 77
Śląska Partia Regionalna 2, 74, 98, 101, 105,
106, 109, 114, 116, 124, 126, 129, 137, 177,
182, 183, 205, 206, 208, 210, 212, 215,
219, 226
Śląskie Voivodeship 2, 13, 45, 46, 47, 55, 56,
57, 58, 59, 62, 63, 64, 65, 68, 71, 72, 73, 78,
87, 92, 100, 102, 108, 111, 117, 118, 119, 121,
122, 123, 124, 125, 128, 131, 132, 133, 134,
136, 165, 174, 189, 190, 203, 202, 205, 208,
210, 212, 214, 228, 231
Ślōnskŏ Ferajna 73, 93, 95, 104, 105, 114, 137
Ślonzoki Razem 74, 96, 111, 115, 116, 120, 125,
127, 137, 182, 205, 206, 207, 208, 210, 215,
217, 219, 226

the right of the people to
self-determination 55
Towarzystwo Społeczno-Kulturalne
Niemców 72, 76, 11, 119, 132, 136

Upper Silesia 1, 2, 3, 6, 27, 45, 46, 47, 50, 51,
54, 55, 56, 57, 58, 60, 61, 62, 63, 65, 66,
68, 69, 70, 72, 78, 79, 80, 81, 83, 85, 87,
88, 89, 91, 92, 94, 95, 96, 97, 99, 100, 101,
102, 107, 108, 109, 112, 119, 120, 125, 130,
131, 136, 144, 145, 147, 149, 153, 155, 156,
164, 167, 170, 174, 175, 177, 181, 183, 184,
189, 189, 193, 197, 201, 204, 205, 206, 210,
211, 212, 214, 220, 221, 223, 224, 228, 229,
231, 232, 233
Upper Silesian ethnoregionalist
movement 1, 3, 53, 82, 83, 85, 87, 88,
90, 133, 137, 139, 170, 176, 180, 182, 183,
187, 189, 201, 206, 226, 232

Zjednoczeni dla Śląska 2, 11, 112, 116, 119, 126,
137, 177, 207, 217, 219, 226
Związek Górnośląski 72, 73, 80, 93, 95, 100,
106, 107, 108, 114, 127, 128, 131, 136
Związek Górnoślązaków 58, 78
Związek Ludności Narodowości Śląskiej 2,
73, 112, 116, 118, 120, 129, 136
Związek Obrony Górnoślązaków 78
Związek Ślązaków 73, 95, 114, 136